Manners and Murders
in the World of Louis-Napoleon

Manners and Murders in the World of Louis-Napoleon

By Roger L. Williams

University of Washington Press
Seattle and London

Copyright © 1975 by the University of Washington Press
Printed in the United States of America

Library of Congress Cataloging in Publication Data

Williams, Roger Lawrence, 1923–
    Manners and murders in the world of Louis-Napoleon.

    Bibliography: p.
    Includes index.
    1. Political crimes and offenses—France—History.
2. France—Social conditions.   3. Murder—France—
History.   I. Title.
HV6295.F8W54   345'.44'02523   75-15938
ISBN 0-295-95431-0

To Leonard and Ann Marsak

Death seems to provide the minds of the Anglo-Saxon race with a greater fund of innocent amusement than any other single subject. . . . The tale must be about dead bodies or very wicked people, preferably both, before the Tired Business Man can feel really happy.

Dorothy Sayers
1935

Preface

As THE title of this volume may suggest, I have returned to the format of my first book, *Gaslight and Shadow: The World of Napoleon III*, which was originally published in 1957. Again we have a series of vignettes, and again they amount in sum to a commentary on the social history of the Second Empire. Each chapter or subchapter is concerned with a single crime and its trial; all are criminal cases except for the final one, which involves a civil suit. Even in the instance of this civil suit, one might argue that the case involved the murder of the regime, justifiable or otherwise.

Several of the cases are familiar to French historians. The specialist knows that Jules Favre was Orsini's defender and that the defense led to Favre's political career. I use the trial to illustrate anew the mysterious ways in which Napoleon III promoted his policies—not to speak of the ambiguities in Favre's personal life and career. The specialist also knows of Louis-Napoleon's descent upon Boulogne in search of the crown and of his consequent incarceration at Ham; but he will find here new evidence of political and social associations both before and after the trial. Some of the cases, notably the Verger, Jud, Troppmann, and Trochu trials, are virtually unknown even to specialists. The cases are presented in chronological order for the reason that a number of the personages appear in more than one of the trials—lawyers, for instance—and because some of the information provided during the earlier trials contributes useful background for the later trials—notably, for the final one.

The vignettes were chosen for reasons beyond the interest inherent in each trial. That of Prince Louis-Napoleon before the Chamber of Peers in 1840 (Chaper I) introduces us to the close association between French political life in the nineteenth century and the method of conducting a trial; by this I mean not simply the lines taken by the prosecution and the defense, but also the behavior and testimony of witnesses. Issues that might seem to be peripheral are continually introduced in these chapters as necessary context for the trials, and the reader will be assisted if he anticipates these asides. In the first chapter, for instance, matters such as the financing of the Boulogne expedition, Miss Howard's alleged role, the question of betrayal, and the post-trial careers of those involved in the attempt, the prosecution, and the defense are considered in some detail.

One cannot understand the Verger case (Chapter II) without tackling the true meaning as well as popular misconceptions of the dogma of the Immaculate Conception, not to speak of such subjects as Liberal Catholicism, Gallicanism, and Ultramontanism, which are so confusing to American students of France. Evidence of a clerical underground will be found here, too, polemical in spirit and often bizarre in psychology. The Orsini case (Chapter III) exposes the ambiguities in Napoleonic government and the dictatorship, not the least of which surrounded the General Security Law of 1858 that was enacted in the aftermath of the assassination attempt. This chapter is also concerned with the career and personal life of Orsini's attorney, Jules Favre, whose political prominence was greatly enhanced by his performance during the trial. Several cases, especially those of Jud and Troppmann, but including that of Prince Pierre Bonaparte (Chapter IV) suggest the political capital to be made from exploiting public hysteria. Several of the careers touched on in the book, those of the attorney Berryer and General Trochu, should help us to understand the wellsprings of legitimacy in the nineteenth century and why legitimacy was so little comprehended even then.

Each chapter, in its own way, is something of an introduction to the fifth and last chapter, which is a civil case and seemingly different from the rest. While the last chapter might well stand alone, the debate over a variety of events relating to the military defeat of 1870–71 benefits from an examination of the character of people and events during the years that preceded the disaster; in the course of this examination the historian will find that the book challenges a fair number of what Flaubert called *idées reçues*, which date from that period. In particular, the last chapter probes the traditional hostility to General Trochu, shows that a court of law found him innocent of charges historians continue to make, and implies that a full-scale biography of him ought now to be written.

The format of the book was chosen partly to attract general readers; but I also hope that the format will remind historians and graduate students of rich source materials for social history that are often overlooked. This is not intended to be legal history or the history of jurisprudence. Instead, it focuses on courts of law as places where valuable evidence was accumulated, examined, and debated by skillful advocates, and recorded for posterity. Historians have never doubted the importance of a sensational case like the Dreyfus Affair for political or constitutional history; but even long-forgotten trials can reveal the manners and mores, the style and tone, the issues and passions of bygone times. Legal cases, moreover, encompass the lives of the great *and* the small, widening our historical lenses to include people either traditionally ignored or considered only in groups, partly because so little concrete evidence of petty lives remains.

Social history this, but not a comprehensive or systematic social history. Nor is it the conventional monograph favored by historians to present a thesis or to cope with specialized materials. Though each vignette might well stand alone as a self-contained story, their assemblage is meant to illustrate several general points about French judicial life in the nineteenth century. It may well be, for instance, that judicial procedure and custom— revering eloquence and providing lengthy opportunity for speechifying —contributed a milieu favorable to polemics. In the second place, the fuel for polemics was readily available in the continuing search for a political consensus after 1789 and burned hottest under regimes which stifled free discussion in parliament and in the press. The court of law became the safest arena from which to express opposition to an established regime, and we must deduce from circumstantial evidence that lawyers, especially defense attorneys, were attracted to cases offering a political forum, or were engaged by clients eager to obscure their crimes by converting a judicial process into a political quarrel. Aside from being a relatively safe medium for political opposition, the courtroom offered far greater publicity than did the salon, that other arena of opposition where one's finest words, quips, and innuendoes reached only the happy few. The courtroom was blessed not only by newspaper coverage, but, best of all, by a gallery of gossips who could spread the word to the four corners of Paris with a speed rivaling that of light. In sum, this volume, beyond being social history, addresses itself to the political uses and misuses of the law.

Finally, the book may be seen as an exercise in *petite histoire*, not to be understood as "the small change of history," as a condescending and ignorant reviewer once put it, but as *real* history unguided by grand intellectual designs.

I am greatly indebted to the American Philosophical Society of Philadelphia for a grant-in-aid, which enabled me to complete my research for this book in Paris. Only the Bibliothèque Nationale contains some of the obscure pamphlets, periodicals, and books which the reader will find cited in the footnotes; and though the *Gazette des Tribunaux* is now being microfilmed, a complete run of this journal has not been made available in the United States. An unofficial daily founded in 1826, the *Gazette des Tribun-*

aux contains day-by-day accounts of the most interesting or important cases in Paris and the provinces, as well as the texts of new laws. Its tone is quite professional. I found the Archives de la Préfecture de Police to be valuable, especially for the Jud case, despite the fact that these archives are not rich for the Second Empire. Finally, I acknowledge with warm thanks the highly professional comments of my colleague, Professor Richard I. Harper, who read this manuscript in first draft.

Contents

Illustrations

Manners and Murders
in the World of Louis-Napoleon

Introduction

*T*HE preface claims that the search for a political consensus after 1789 provided fuel for political debate in the nineteenth century—a statement the professional historian will understand, because he is aware of the rapid succession of regimes after the beginning of the French Revolution. Among specialists, some debate remains as to the actual number of *new* constitutions the French have had since 1789, but no one doubts that there have been many. Moreover, we suspect that inordinate preoccupation with political form deflected public attention from social and economic problems for nearly a hundred years after 1789—an era of rapid economic and social transformation. The following outline will reveal briefly the changes in regime.

1789: Overthrow of *absolutism*

1789–92: Constitutional or *limited* Bourbon monarchy

1792–1804: The First Republic

1804–14: The First Empire

1814–15: Restoration of the limited Bourbon monarchy

1815: Restoration of Empire (the Hundred Days)

1815–30: Second restoration of the limited Bourbon monarchy, defined as the *legitimate* House of France

1830: Overthrow of legitimate monarchy and establishment of a new constitutional or *liberal* monarchy under the House of Orleans

1830–48: The July Monarchy

1848–52: The Second Republic

1852–70: The Second Empire

1870–1940: The Third Republic

This simple outline does not tell the whole truth about the complexities of French political life, for none of the above regimes was consistent in spirit or principle throughout its reign. Yet, for the purposes of this book, it will suffice to know that a Legitimist backed the traditional royal family, the Bourbons; whereas an Orleanist espoused liberal, parliamentary monarchy. Republicans could all agree as to the abolition of monarchy, but argued about whether a Republic ought to be liberal, conservative, democratic, or socialist. Not even Bonapartism was a unified movement. Some Bonapartists stressed their liberal antecedents in the First Republic; others, the authoritarian heritage of the First Empire.

Under these circumstances, the two-party system as we know it could not develop. More to the point, parties or factions out of power could not constitute a true loyal opposition, as they were dedicated to ousting the incumbent regime in order to write a new constitution. Change in regime, therefore, was never orderly, as in true party government, but had to be precipitated either by revolution or *coup d'état*. Conversely, incumbent regimes were disinclined to allow their opponents much liberty, not simply because opponents were seen as disloyal, but because liberties were employed toward subversive ends, whether in parliament or in the press. As a consequence, political life not only had much excitement and invective, but also gave the appearance of an elaborate game of musical chairs. It was a Frenchman, quite appropriately, who observed that *plus ça change, plus c'est la même chose* (the more the change, the more it's the same thing).

For All Readers

Since all the crimes and legal cases described in this volume occurred between 1840 and 1872, and involved people and events of the Second Empire, a brief introduction to the legal system of that day is a prerequisite to the cases themselves. The organization and the procedures of the French legal system have been quite different from the English system familiar to us; and the French conception of the judiciary as an instrument of executive authority, rather than a separate authority, has been the fundamental difference between the two systems in recent centuries.

The French police system, as we know it in the nineteenth century, was a creation of Bonaparte in 1800. If modified in detail after that date, the initial conception of a highly centralized police organization, ultimately responsible to the chief-of-state, remained the model. The fact of centralization, however, did not prevent the development of a variety of police forces, each one charged with special duties and responsible to a different ministry. In theory the system was perfectly rational. In practice, however, these various branches of the police could reflect the rivalries or the conflicting interests within the chief-of-state's cabinet or the ministries, which meant that cooperation between the branches was often less than enthusiastic or efficient.

Bonaparte placed the most general police powers in the Ministry of the Interior, which then delegated them to the departmental prefects. The one exception was the Department of the Seine (meaning Paris), whose prefect lacked police power. A special office of Prefect of Police was created to exercise the prefectural police powers, but was also responsible to the minister of the interior. The minister of war was required to station troops in each department to assist the local prefect and the rural authorities in maintaining order. Such troops were known as the Gendarmerie, generally under the command of an army colonel and organized as a legion. The prefects could also call upon the *commissaires de police*, special police agents responsible to the Ministry of Justice. While judicial officers in name, these *commissaires* were actually the most political of all French police. Gathering information for the government, they kept track of printed material published in France and imported from abroad. One sometimes found them on the railroads where they ostensibly protected passengers, but actually used the opportunity for political surveillance.[1]

When we think of a Paris policeman in the nineteenth century, therefore, we must keep in mind that he was not a local official, but rather a representative of some branch of the national police. And the Prefecture of Police in Paris, because of its proximity to the central government, always loomed large in police affairs. By the time of the Second Empire, we can find within the Prefecture of Police three principal services, each of which had its own chief. Most obvious to the public were the Municipal Police, the policemen stationed about the city for the maintenance of order.

Another service was called the Division, occupied solely with administrative matters. Employees of the Division kept the records, including the dossiers, licenses, and passports; took charge of abandoned or lost articles; and had the responsibility for sifting through the vast number of letters written to the police by the public. Those in the Division assigned to the latter task sorted out useful information from that written by cranks, and were known as *écosseurs*, literally, "the shellers of peas or beans." Much of the correspondence was unsigned, and a bit of it came from people genuinely eager to do something useful for society. The bulk of it came from people with idle hands or heads, eager to do something to render themselves important. Two of the cases included in this volume, those of Charles Jud and Jean-Baptiste Troppmann, produced an avalanche of letters from titillated busybodies, which did nothing to expedite the investigation of the two crimes.[2]

1. Howard C. Payne, *The Police State of Louis Napoleon Bonaparte 1851–1860*, pp. 18–21.
2. Maxine Du Camp, *Paris: Ses organes, ses fonctions et sa vie dans la seconde moitié du xixè siècle*, 3:102–3, 113.

Any useful information distilled by the *écosseurs* was passed on to the "active service" of the Prefecture of Police, known as the *Sûreté*, which was dedicated to the investigation and the arrest of those who committed offenses. The Prefecture of Police could do little more than investigate criminals until this special service was created. The *Sûreté* began operation in 1811, a modest force of four men under François-Eugène Vidocq; but not until 1817, when Vidocq was given a dozen men, did the *Sûreté* become in any way effective.[3] Criminals had long been employed by the French state to hunt down their own kind, as it was generally believed that one could understand criminals only if one had been a criminal. Vidocq himself not only brought to his task this necessary background, but also hired ex-convicts as his agents. Paid by their success in making arrests, such agents only too easily became *provocateurs*, and their appearance in court as witnesses for the prosecution often offended jurors.

Consequently, the *Sûreté* was reformed under the July Monarchy. A new prefect of police, Henri-Joseph Gisquet, was appointed toward the end of 1831. Gisquet named Pierre Allard to be chief of the *Sûreté* and eliminated from the service anyone who had suffered a conviction. Henceforth, the *Sûreté* began to enjoy a reputation for integrity, and the removal of ex-convicts opened the way for a professionalism especially notable after 1852 during the Second Empire. Even an enemy of that regime could report that the police in general had become a more civil, more suitable group of men than they had been under the Restoration or the July Monarchy.[4] The number of men available to the prefect of police under the Second Empire seems modest for a city the size of Paris. The chief of municipal police generally employed between 3,800 and 4,000 uniformed policemen, known as *sergents de ville*; while the chief of the *Sûreté* presided over 4 chief inspectors, 6 police sergeants (brigadiers), and 117 inspectors (all plainclothesmen).[5]

A thirty-man unit on detached service from the Prefecture of Police, officially known as the Commissariat of the Imperial Residences, was the secret service which guarded the emperor. Its chief was Louis-Alphonse Hyrvoix, celebrated for his devotion to His Majesty. An ardent Bonapartist to the end, Hyrvoix died en route to a commemorative mass for Napoleon III in 1890.[6]

Perhaps the most mysterious police official of the Second Empire was Clément Fabre de Lagrange, who reputedly presided over an immense apparatus of political surveillance and repression. The Republicans who took

3. Philip John Stead, *Vidocq, A Biography*, pp. 56–57.
4. Auguste-Jean-Marie Vermorel, *La Police contemporaine*, p. 305.
5. Du Camp, *Paris*, 3:68–87.
6. Payne, *The Police State*, p. 261.

power on 4 September 1870, were eager to examine his files with the expectation of finding evidence embarrassing to the fallen regime. Comte Emile de Kératry, the incoming prefect of police, recommended the publication of incriminating documents; and an employee of the National Archives, Félix Rocquain, was assigned the task of uncovering them.

Rocquain found that Lagrange had indeed been appointed a *commissaire spécial* after the *coup d'état* of 1851 and had occupied an office in the Prefecture of Police. On the basis of testimony from employees in the prefecture, he learned that it had been the practice of the prefect of police to draw up a report for the emperor every day, based partly on information supplied by Lagrange and partly on information supplied by his own informants. The rough drafts as well as the final reports were burned periodically as an established procedure. Moreover, prefects leaving office customarily destroyed papers likely to be compromising—a common practice in French officialdom.

Rocquain was told that Lagrange had burned documents in his office almost continually for the two weeks preceding 4 September 1870, and that possibly he had removed papers upon making his exit. Even so, the files contained much paper, enabling Rocquain to make some reasonable deductions. Lagrange had evidently maintained a private operation, responsible to the emperor alone, to whom he was absolutely loyal; and his activity seems to have been limited to the surveillance of notable people known to be hostile to the regime. For Republican purposes, if Rocquain's discoveries were somewhat disappointing, they were not entirely sterile, as he found reports from informers signed with code names or code initials, along with one master list of informers (under their code names) showing their locations in France and abroad. Their salaries, varying according to the importance of their posts, ranged from 120 to 1,000 francs a month; and since the budget for their services came to 20,000 francs a month, the evidence suggested that Lagrange drew his secret information from a corps numbering between sixty and seventy at any given time.

Rocquain also learned that the prefect of police had had his *own* informers, often drawn from the respectable ranks of society, some serving without pay out of loyalty to the regime. But Rocquain knew that such methods of obtaining information were hardly different from those of most regimes, even democratic ones. He could presume, for the satisfaction of his employers, that police informers had been sometimes used as *agents provocateurs*, assisting the political opposition in making trouble while at the same time alerting the police to take appropriate counteraction. But he had the decency to add that, *if* such tactics had been used by Lagrange, it seemed likely that neither the emperor nor his ministers were aware of the impropriety.[7] Whatever the case, Rocquain found little incriminating evidence; and since most of the police records remaining from the Second Empire and previous regimes were later lost in the fires of the Commune, both at the Prefecture of Police and at the Ministry of the Interior, the evidence he sifted through is long since gone.

In those days, the Prefecture of Police fronted on the rue de Jérusalem (now the rue de Harlay), immediately west of the Palais de Justice, occupying space that is now included within the Palais de Justice. The Second Empire knew only three prefects: Pierre-Marie Piétri, already appointed to office as of 27 January 1852, and who resigned in the aftermath of the Orsini affair on 16 March 1858; Symphorien-Casimir-Joseph Boitelle, who served until 21 February 1866; and finally, Joachim Piétri, who fell with the regime on 4 September 1870.[8] In the same period, there were four chiefs of the *Sûreté*, the fourth of whom, the so-called Monsieur Claude, achieved an international reputation as a suave detective. Appointed to the *Sûreté* on 1 June 1859, Antoine-François Claude proved himself a true professional, so clearly nonpolitical that he was retained in his post by Kératry after 4 September and by Adolphe Thiers after the Commune.[9]

Monsieur Claude was a short, thick-set man, quiet and unassuming, somewhat cold and reserved in the style of the French magistracy, with sharp blue eyes and a carefully shaved face. His appearance virtually concealed his passionate energy and extraordinary sense of duty, which was exposed in particular when he questioned a criminal, if one considered carefully the nuances of his questions. Criminals respected him for his probity and correctness. Promises made to them were honored without exception, for which Monsieur Claude was often rewarded with unexpected bits of information. Except for a brief period in 1871 when he was jailed by the Commune because of his service under the Empire, he remained chief of the *Sûreté* until mid–1875, retiring then to the town of Vincennes where he died in 1880. He left neither the *Mémoires* nor the *Notes de police* often attributed to him, about which more later.[10]

Today, as in the nineteenth century, the French police and the judiciary are less rigidly separated than they are in Anglo-American legal procedure. Once the French police have a suspect liable to prosecution (called the *inculpé*), he is taken before a *juge d'instruction* who proceeds with the investigation. This *instruction* is not simply an interrogation. All the facts in the case are reviewed, all exhibits having to do with the case are presented, and

7. Félix Rocquain, *Notes et fragments d'histoire*, pp. 258–78.
8. Marcel Le Clère, *Histoire de la police*, pp. 87–89; and *Vingt ans de police, souvenirs et anecdotes d'un ancien officier de paix*, p. 307.
9. Gustave Macé, *La Police parisienne*, p. 142.
10. Ibid., p. 348; and Du Camp, *Paris*, 3:101–2.

Joachim Piétri, Prefect of Police, "The Fly" (tricks, spying).
From *La Ménagerie impériale*

the witnesses are heard—all in the presence of the suspect or his lawyer. In a murder case during the Second Empire, the *juge d'instruction* often ordered a confrontation between the suspect and his alleged victim so that the suspect's reaction might be observed. The suspect would be taken to the Morgue by the police in the presence of the *juge* and asked if he recognized the corpse. Very often the suspect would admit that he did.[11] If further police inquiries were necessary, they were carried on under the supervision of the *juge d'instruction*, until such time as he decided that the case ought to be dismissed or that an indictment was warranted.

In the Second Empire, when the *juge d'instruction* recommended an indictment, the case was forwarded to a *chambre des mises en accusation*,

11. Du Camp, *Paris*, 3:163–64.

where the procedures were reviewed. If found to be entirely proper, an indictment would be issued. The *inculpé* then became the *prévenu*, meaning "the indicted," and was bound over for trial before a *cour d'assises*, where he would be tried as the *accusé*, meaning "the accused" or the defendant. It seems likely that this complicated procedure with its changes in terminology account for the Anglo-American notion that a French defendant is guilty until proven innocent, for the preliminary hearings would seem to have established guilt before the actual trial. This time-honored assumption is unmerited. During the preliminary hearings, no guilt is determined. The system does establish that the prosecution has a legitimate case ready to be taken to court, and the suspect has the advantage of legal representation throughout that process. The guilt must be proven in the *assises* and to the satisfaction of a jury.

All preliminary hearings during the Second Empire were conducted in private. Only when the case reached the *assises* did the process become public, and sensational cases could jam the public sections of the courtroom. With some distress, reporters and jurists of the nineteenth century noted that women were apt to dominate the audiences—women from all classes and walks of life. They were displeasing to see because the presumed sensibility of womankind, upon which rested certain clichés about the social order, was unmasked by the obvious relish that women took in the sordid details of a case. They customarily wore black for such occasions, which, considering their true motives for being present, added an aura of hypocrisy to their distasteful zeal. At the opening of one trial during the Second Empire, the president of the court, dismayed at the number of women in the audience, announced: "The case we are now taking up involves unseemly details, so that I urge all respectable women present to retire." No one budged. The judge then added, "Bailiff, now that the respectable women have departed, will you clear the court of those who remain!" [12] The audiences for the Troppmann trial in 1870 achieved a high point of indecent curiosity.

If contrary to the popular view of womankind, these scenes squared with a view of women common in police circles during the nineteenth century, namely, that the worst criminals are likely to be women. A woman is rarely wicked, goes the Italian proverb, but when she is so, she is worse than the man. Women were believed in general to have a weaker moral sense than men, to become more easily the victim of their passions, and to be more difficult to reform once they had strayed from the straight and narrow path. [13]

Seemingly unscrupulous tactics by defense lawyers also distressed some tender souls of that era, largely because the professional ethics of the French

12. Ibid., 3:172.
13. Major Arthur Griffiths, *Mysteries of Police and Crime*, 1:282.

courtroom were little understood. In a civil case, when he knew he was defending a weak cause, a defense attorney was not expected to resort to dubious means, but rather to cooperate with the attorneys for the plaintiff and the state in reaching a just verdict and settlement. In a criminal case that scrupulosity did not apply. The defense attorney was obliged to use every possible device to save his client, and the law held that no man might be executed until he had been defended. As we shall see, in assuming the defense of the odious Troppmann, Lachaud well understood his duty.[14] Why men *became* defense attorneys is quite another matter.

The Morgue was a necessary link in the judicial chain, the word *morgue* having been used originally to designate a room in which newly arrested prisoners were closely inspected. (*Morguer* means "to look closely" or "to browbeat.") A special building where corpses could be viewed came into use only in 1804. During the Second Empire, the Morgue was situated on an islet called the Motte aux Papelards, at the southeast corner of the Ile de la Cité, since connected to the main island. All unidentified bodies were undressed and washed before exposure, then laid out under a constant stream of cold water to retard decomposition. The exposition room was fitted with a large glass to permit public viewing. Bodies were generally on display for three days, during which time officials recorded detailed observations for later identification. The chief clerk could then apply for a court order permitting burial, which was routinely granted unless there were some legal reason to postpone burial. The Morgue always attracted a crowd of the curious, notably the neighborhood brats, in whose lingo the bodies were *les artistes.* When no bodies were present, they would say "No performance today." [15]

Paris contained eight prisons during the Second Empire, including the jail at the Prefecture of Police which was intended only for temporary detention after arrest. Each prison was meant to serve a distinct function, the most obvious being Saint-Lazare for convicted women and the Petite-Roquette for juveniles. No doubt the best known prison was also the oldest, the Conciergerie, commonly called the *maison de justice* because of its proximity to the Palais de Justice. Here the accused were held immediately before and during their trials before the *assises.* On occasion, a prisoner would remain there pending the outcome of an appeal. But the Conciergerie contained only seventy-six cells during the Second Empire and was not intended for lengthy detention. It was a mark of exceptional favor to permit a condemned man to serve his sentence there, and the privilege was never granted unless the penalty was slight.

Except in the cases of people awaiting trial, cellular detention had been

14. Félix Platel, *Portraits d'Ignotus*, p. 29.
15. Du Camp, *Paris*, 1:332–38.

unknown in France before 1848. Short-term prisoners had generally been kept in Paris in central prisons where all the convicts lived and worked together in total absence of privacy. During the Second Empire, Sainte-Pélagie was such a prison. Completed in 1665, it had been used for other purposes before becoming a prison. A special wing was added after 1848 to house political prisoners, keeping them separate from common criminals. Napoleon III, remembering his own unpleasant past at Ham, was particularly eager to avoid the mistreatment of political prisoners and was very sensitive to the complaints they habitually wrote to their party newspapers. His efforts on their behalf, however, were usually ignored by prison officials.[16] Sainte-Pélagie was located in the rue de la Clef, just west of the Jardin des Plantes in the Fifth Arrondissement.

Mazas was the first Parisian prison specifically designed to house both suspects and convicts in cells. The assumption was that suspects should be isolated from convicts; moreover, the likelihood of future offenses could be greatly diminished by keeping convicts separated during their confinement. Considered a model prison for its day, Mazas nevertheless had a formidably grim appearance and atmosphere that reeked not of reform but of punishment. It stood in the boulevard Mazas (today the boulevard Diderot) in the Twelfth Arrondissement, across the street from the Gare de Lyon. Completed late in 1849, Mazas accepted its first guests in May of 1850. The Santé prison, at the corner of the rue de la Santé and the boulevard Arago in the Fourteenth Arrondissement, was opened in August of 1867, and was somewhat experimental in that its space was half cellular, half common-detention. Each half accommodated five hundred inmates.

Long-term prisoners, traditionally not kept in these Parisian central prisons, had been sent to the so-called *bagnes*, the convict prisons at the coastal arsenals of Rochefort, Brest, and Toulon. What constituted short-term or long-term confinement changed with regimes. During the Second Empire, those detained in either Sainte-Pélagie, Mazas, or la Santé were individuals whose terms were less than one year. For longer sentences, convicts could be shipped to any of the twenty-six state prisons in the provinces. Those sentenced to transportation to penal colonies overseas, a practice that began in 1851, were destined for either Cayenne or New Caledonia. En route, they were housed temporarily in the Grande-Roquette, the prison also infamous as the antechamber to the guillotine, located in the Eleventh Arrondissement in the neighborhood of Père Lachaise.

Prison reform was becoming a social issue in that day, but the process proved to be slow. State commissions, appointed first in 1869 and again in 1871, finally recommended in 1874 that cellular confinement become the

16. Constant Lefébure, *Souvenirs d'un ancien directeur des prisons de Paris*, p. 29.

rule when more modern buildings could be constructed. Mazas, Saint-Pélagie, and the Grande-Roquette were demolished in 1898 when modernization began.[17]

Contrary to popular notion, the guillotine (or an instrument similar in construction) had been known in Europe long before the French Revolution gave it lurid notoriety. Ancient tradition attributed such a device to the Persians—a story very likely invented and cherished by the Greeks. In fact, the guillotine was one more modern institution that rested on firm medieval foundations, for it had been widely used in medieval Germany. In the early modern period, the guillotine came into use in parts of England, Italy, and southern France, and was known as "the maiden" in Scotland. By 1789, however, it had fallen into disuse everywhere for at least a century and had faded from popular memory. Decapitation, on the other hand, had not gone out of fashion, as death by that means was a treasured aristocratic prerogative or privilege.

Accordingly, Dr. Joseph-Ignace Guillotin, a delegate to the Estates-General from Paris in 1789, moved that decapitation for *anyone* sentenced to death be adopted as an egalitarian measure; and his proposal came to be embodied in the revolutionary penal code of 6 October 1791. Most of those who voted for decapitation evidently presumed that it would be by sword, the custom in aristocratic executions; but the headsman of Paris, Charles-Henri Sanson, who well knew the liabilities of using the sword, favored a return to a decapitational machine. He convinced the politicians that the hacking and chopping which had so often marred an aristocratic execution would be unsuitable if decapitation were to become the general practice, and he had the greatest misgivings about the practicality of executing the lower classes with a sword—a form of execution requiring a modicum of cooperation by the victim. Every proper aristocrat knew he must face death with dignity—with a smile, a gracious gesture to the mob, and, if at all possible, a witticism appropriate to the occasion. But what could a headsman anticipate from those classes unprepared for such conduct, and especially from a generation convinced of its rights to life, liberty, and the pursuit of happiness? So a machine it had to be—one devised to help immobilize the subject as well as terminate his life.

Dr. Antoine Louis was charged with testing and recommending improvements in the device that came to be named for Dr. Guillotin, much to his embarrassment. (He died a natural death in 1814, contrary to the engaging myth that he fell victim to his own suggestion.) The testees were corpses supplied by the Bicêtre Hospital; and the contract to supply guillotines to each French department (according to Dr. Louis' specifications) went to

17. Du Camp, *Paris,* 3:187–88, 211–13, 226–27, 244–45.

Tobias Schmidt, a German pianomaker. The first live performance took place on 25 April 1792, when Sanson beheaded a highwayman named Nicolas-Jacques Pelletier to general satisfaction.[18]

By the time of the Second Empire, the guillotine was lighter and more manageable than the model perfected by Dr. Louis, though the critical mechanism and its form were virtually unchanged. The platform, roughly four meters square, was surrounded by a low railing and stood two meters above the ground supported by four legs. It required ten steps to mount the platform. The blade was held between two posts which rose four meters above the platform, a triangular steel blade encrusted with three leaden bolts to give it considerable weight—approximately sixty kilograms. As the blade fell over two meters, it attained an approximate weight of 168 kilograms upon impact. The headsman had to be both skillful and strong, for he needed one hand to activate the mechanism, one hand to help hold his victims on the block. As Sanson had foreseen, they often struggled; and the headsman's assistants were present, not to help him with the actual execution, but to tidy up thereafter. As we shall see, the Troppmann execution was a ferocious affair, with Troppmann sinking his teeth into the headsman's thumb at the last instant, thus confirming Sanson's worst fears about the future of French society.[19]

Until the nineteenth century, no place in Paris was exclusively designated for capital punishment. Under the Consulate, this honor fell to the place de Grève (at the Hôtel de Ville), the spot where Pelletier had been dispatched. In 1832, the July Monarchy transferred executions to the place de la Barrière Saint-Jacques in the Fourteenth Arrondissement, which saw service until 1851 when the facilities at the Grande-Roquette were completed. Executions henceforth were held in the *rond-point* ("circle" or "circus") of La Roquette. Meanwhile, official attitudes about the popular benefits of executions were changing. Until 1832, they had been held at four in the afternoon to obtain the greatest possible publicity, the theory being that the sight of crime punished was a deterrent to evil, which sent the citizenry scurrying after heavenly pursuits. The wonder is that judicial authorities, aware of the bestial temper released by executions, took so many centuries to arrive at a contrary conclusion. When the executions were removed to the Saint-Jacques location in 1832, it became customary to carry them out at daybreak. Discretion had at last become the rule.

In the time of the Second Empire, the process of French justice was regarded as painstaking and slow. Once a sentence of death had been pronounced, however, the pace was deliberately accelerated for humane reasons. The three weeks that transpired between Troppmann's condemnation

18. Alister Kershaw, A *History of the Guillotine*, pp. 5, 30–33, 64.
19. Du Camp, *Paris*, 3:257–59, 269–70, 278–81.

and execution was not only a typical period of delay, but ample time for processing an appeal. For the highest court, the *Cour de cassation*, was primarily concerned in such a situation to review the mechanics of the case, and to ascertain that the lawful procedures had been properly obeyed throughout the investigation and trial. A case was never retried. In the meantime, the condemned man remained unaware of the date set for his execution, but would be awakened early some morning by a committee at his door announcing that his time had come.

The disclosure that the guillotine was used in France after the revolution, indeed that it is still used, often causes surprise. Every form of execution has its social or political implications; and evidently no regime since 1789 has wished to risk abandoning the guillotine for another means, as that would be to challenge the *Egalité* in the revolutionary slogan and would hasten that awful day when every man is not Monsieur nor every woman Madame.

CHAPTER ONE

The Descent upon Boulogne:
The Strange Case of the Dramatis Personae

History is particularly difficult
when it becomes a matter of a
conspiracy, whose entirety necessarily remains—to a certain
degree, mysterious.
ANDRÉ LEBEY

RINCE Louis-Napoleon Bonaparte made two attempts to topple
the throne of King Louis-Philippe: the first at Strassburg in 1836,
and the second at Boulogne in 1840. Each was quickly quashed
by local authorities so as to make Louis-Napoleon appear a spectacularly
inept pretender. Neither his successful candidacy for the presidency of the
Second Republic in 1848, nor even his becoming Napoleon III in 1852,
ever removed the taint of ridicule from his early abortive attempts. The
Boulogne affair was by far a more complicated conspiracy than the Strassburg affair; and for those involved, both in the actual descent upon Boulogne and in its judicial aftermath, the ramifications were more extensive
than has been generally noted by historians. Not only was a network of
obligations spun at Boulogne; but in the subsequent trial judicial tactics and
political themes were also employed by the defense that would reemerge in
the Second Republic and the Second Empire—and in a manner too consistent to have been coincidental. In particular, the long and equivocal association of Louis-Napoleon and Jules Favre began at the trial, a fact one will
not find in the standard biographies of Louis-Napoleon or in descriptions of
the Boulogne affair.

As the story has often been related, a brief review of the attempt will suffice. Louis-Napoleon's timing of his second attempt upon the July Monarchy coincided with the obvious intention of that regime to exploit Bonapartist sentiment in France. Two great monuments commenced by
Napoleon I, the Vendôme Column and the Arc de Triomphe, had just

[17]

been completed by the government, which now proposed (with British compliance) to fetch the remains of Napoleon I for burial in Paris. A ship had been dispatched to St. Helena, and Louis-Napoleon, in exile in England, quite understood the political advantage of being on hand when the ship returned with its illustrious cargo. He had, moreover, been foundering in the courtship of his cousin Mathilde and knew that she would be lost to him if he did not soon acquire money and position. News of her engagement to another man also spurred him to action.[1]

Boulogne was chosen as the landing place, because a detachment of the Forty-second Infantry was posted there. The second-in-command, Lieutenant Jean-Baptiste-Charles Aladenize, was a known Bonapartist and was willing to cooperate. This meant that Louis-Napoleon must pick a day when the local commander, a loyal Orleanist, would be absent. Having obtained the support of the Forty-second Infantry, Louis-Napoleon meant to move upon Paris, having painstakingly identified all the regiments and their commanders he might encounter between Boulogne and the capital. For the channel crossing, he engaged a paddle-steamer, the *Edinburgh Castle*, ostensibly for a pleasure cruise.

The ship left London Bridge on 4 August 1840, burdened with nine horses, two carriages, a supply of French flags and uniforms, the necessary proclamations to the French, plus a quantity of food and spirits needed to guarantee the enthusiasm of the fifty-six accomplices he had recruited, who were picked up in small groups as the ship floated down the Thames. Louis-Napoleon himself embarked at Gravesend, a point not everyone might have chosen as the beginning of a new career, but only after a delay of twelve hours during which he had endeavored to shake off French agents who were shadowing him. Their persistence ought to have warned him that all was not well. As a result of the delay, the ship missed the tide, and the party could not reach its disembarkation point as scheduled at dawn on 5 August. By the time they landed early on the sixth, the loyal Orleanist commander had returned to his post in Boulogne. It would seem, indeed, that only Louis-Napoleon's supreme confidence could have justified landing at that moment.

In fact, from then on the expedition dissolved into a comedy of errors, some of which derived from the prince's commendable instructions to avoid violence. His party initially encountered customs officials, who, faithful to the habits of their breed, failed to be impressed by the statements of those

---

1. Comte E. C. Corti, "Correspondance du roi Louis et de Louis-Napoléon interceptée par la police de Metternich, 1833–1840, (première partie) Louis-Napoléon et son projet de mariage avec la princesse Mathilde," *Revue des études napoléoniennes* 26 (January–June 1926):173–76; and (deuxième partie) "Les Complots de Louis-Napoléon et l'état d'âme de son père," ibid., 248.

debarking and refused to rally to the cause. Unable to spare men to guard such dissidents, the invaders left them free to cry the alarm. The party found Lieutenant Aladenize and approached the Boulogne barracks, where the garrison of nearly four hundred seemed friendly enough but confused. Their commander rose from his bed to order his troops to muster, and they obeyed him. Louis-Napoleon and his band had to retreat, but were soon captured. An utter fiasco, the invasion was contained by eight-thirty on the morning it began.[2]

After the Strassburg attempt in 1836, the government had chosen to be lenient. After Boulogne, though official pronouncements praised the loyalty of the local population and garrison and emphasized the ludicrous in Louis-Napoleon's venture, the government acted in ways which suggested that it no longer took the pretender lightly. It seems clear that, despite the floral testimony to local loyalties, the government was keenly aware that had its commander in Boulogne been absent, or had he been seized as might be expected in an armed attempt, Louis-Napoleon's advance upon Paris might have become the sort of triumphal progress enjoyed by Napoleon I in 1815.[3]

But the July Monarchy, possessing evidence that Louis-Napoleon had received assurances of support from key military figures, had even greater cause for alarm. Indeed, that the government had been aware of a plot afoot soon led to speculation that Louis-Napoleon's plans had been betrayed to the French government, which had taken what steps it could to blunt the threat.[4] Having succeeded in arresting the pretender and his accomplices, the state meant to make an example of them through an ostentatious trial before the Chamber of Peers.

The evidence for betrayal in the affair has remained entirely circumstantial, but none the less compelling. In the first place, the French government took precautionary measures before Louis-Napoleon's expedition embarked, suggesting that it had confidential information unlikely to come from French police spies in London. In the second place, those official measures inadvertently served as a warning to certain of the French military who were disposed to cooperate with Louis-Napoleon, causing them to withhold their promised support after his landing at Boulogne. They could not know how much the government knew, and we must surmise that they would have prudently waited for news of a successful landing before revealing their hands. Louis-Napoleon, meanwhile, confident of military assistance, had minimized those initial mishaps that in retrospect seemed so fatal to his cause.

Charles, comte de Rémusat, was then minister of the interior in the

2. F. A. Simpson, *The Rise of Louis Napoleon*, pp. 173–84.
3. T. A. B. Corley, *Democratic Despot: A Life of Napoleon III*, pp. 40–41.
4. Edmond de Lignères, comte d'Alton-Shée, *Mes mémoires*, 2:66.

Thiers ministry. Rémusat evidently knew that an invasion was coming (something anyone in Louis-Napoleon's inner circle would have known); but Rémusat lacked precise details, which suggests that either Louis-Napoleon kept his exact plans fairly secret from his collaborators or that Rémusat's informant was playing a double game. Consequently, Rémusat had to alert all civil and military officials in the north and east to the expected invasion.

When the conspirators were put on trial before the peers, General Bernard-Pierre Magnan, commanding French forces in the north, would testify that he had on two occasions been approached by one of Louis-Napoleon's agents, Séverin-Louis, le duff de Mésonan, whom he had rebuffed, reporting the incidents to the government. That much was true and can account for why Rémusat took steps to obtain information in London where Louis-Napoleon's group conspired. On the other hand, General Magnan made no move to arrest Mésonan, who, after all, was proposing treason; this entitles us to believe that he had made secret commitments to assist the conspirators. Then, when Rémusat issued his alert, Magnan had opted for a prudent course.[5]

A look at Magnan's entire professional career, moreover, adds evidence of his likely sympathy for the conspirators of 1840. The July Monarchy had put him on inactive service in 1831, alleging that his measures against the insurgents in Lyon had not been sufficiently vigorous. He had then entered Belgian service until he was permitted to return to active French duty in 1839. Later, in 1851, President Bonaparte would give Magnan command of the army of Paris; in that capacity Magnan would take an active part in the *coup d'état* of 2 December, and he would be rewarded for this with a marshalcy and a Senate seat in 1852. It seems likely, therefore, that he had dickered for a marshalcy as early as 1840.[6]

But whom within Louis-Napoleon's entourage did Rémusat reach with a bribe sufficient to obtain information about the proposed attempt? Quite properly neither Thiers nor Rémusat ever revealed the name of their informant. A distinguished magistrate who participated in the *instruction*, baron Joseph Zangiacomi, privately concluded that the betrayer had been General Charles-Tristan Montholon, the comte de Lée. Not wishing to expose the regime's source at the time of the trial, Zangiacomi simply recorded his observations and deposited them with Maxime DuCamp for later reference.[7] If Zangiacomi's actions seem curious or ambiguous, we might recall that

5. Adrien Dansette, *Louis-Napoléon à la conquête du pouvoir*, pp. 169–72; and Simpson, *The Rise of Louis-Napoleon*, p. 193.

6. Marcel Rousselet, *Les Souverains devant la justice, de Louis XVI à Napoléon III*, pp. 204–5.

7. Dansette, *Louis-Napoléon à la conquête du pouvoir*, p. 173.

though he had taken a seat in the Chamber of Peers in 1832, his title dated from the First Empire, so that his loyalties may well have been shared by the two dynasties in conflict in 1840. Though the betrayal question has been proposed by historians aware of the post-trial gossip and the Zangiacomi speculation, their confidence in Montholon's guilt could have been greater had they themselves read his *instruction*.

In preparation for the trial before the peers, General Montholon was interrogated three times. Read out of context, his testimony seems evasive and self-serving. Read in context, his testimony rings of truth, albeit not the whole truth. He explained, for instance, that he had been living in London since the previous April "for personal reasons," and that he had begun to see Louis-Napoleon almost daily. Their friendship was entirely explicable considering that he, Montholon, had been part of the faithful retinue on St. Helena, one of the three French generals in that tiny and fretful band. Despite this claim upon Louis-Napoleon's confidence, Montholon avowed that the prince had never communicated the specific details of the Boulogne landing to him. Moreover, when he had argued against trying a *coup*, he had only deepened the prince's secrecy.

Montholon further confessed that when he embarked upon the *Edinburgh Castle*, however reluctantly, he had been perfectly aware that he had become a participant in an attempt upon the July Monarchy. He had surmised that the ship was bound for Ostend, after which the party would cross the frontier into France from either Belgian or German territory. When he learned that the attempt would be made at once upon Boulogne, he had put on his uniform, allegedly to protect the prince and to prevent bloodshed if possible.[8]

Louis-Napoleon, giving his own testimony during the *instruction*, said that he had not given the precise details of the expedition to Montholon, because he had been unsure whether Montholon was more loyal to the government in Paris or to his memories of the Empire. The usual assumption, both then and after, was that Louis-Napoleon's testimony was contrived to take the full responsibility upon himself and to spare his companions.[9] In fact, his secrecy in the affair was entirely characteristic. Moreover, if General Montholon had believed Ostend to be their destination, one can understand Rémusat's warning to French authorities in the north and east; the invasion would have come by land, as in 1836, rather than from the channel.

But why Montholon, the very symbol of Napoleonic fidelity? Napoleon I had appointed Montholon to be one of the three executors of his will and left Montholon two million francs "as proof of my satisfaction for his filial

---

8. *Attentat du mois d'août 1840, Cour des pairs* pp. 31–35, 58–61. This volume contains not only the formal indictment, but the *instructions* of all the defendants.

9. Ibid., pp. 1–3.

attentions, and to compensate him for the losses that his presence on St. Helena produced." [10] The executors of the will, however, had been deliberately frustrated after Napoleon's death by the Bourbon regime and by the banker Jacques Lafitte, who was anxious to appease the Bourbons after his long association with Bonaparte. Only after many legal difficulties and court actions did the legatees receive their funds in 1826, the sums as a result being lower than the will had provided. Montholon, the largest beneficiary, realized 1,331,000 francs. [11]

Unfortunately, Montholon lacked the sophistication to survive fame and fortune. He lived foolishly and lavishly thereafter, bled by those leeches invariably drawn to wealth or talent (in this case, to wealth alone), and was induced to invest in dubious enterprises, until the money was gone. Ruined, he found himself liable for corporational losses. For a time he endeavored to meet obligations by selling the mementoes he had from Napoleon, and at length fled to London to escape going to prison for debt. The death of his stepfather, the marquis de Sémonville, in 1839, produced an inheritance that somewhat relieved his poverty. [12]

When the July Monarchy made its decision to bring back the remains of Napoleon, a commission to go to St. Helena was appointed under the chairmanship of the Prince de Joinville, Louis-Philippe's third son. Of the three generals who had lived with Napoleon on the island, only Bertrand and Gourgaud were invited to participate. The government knew by then that Montholon had been frequently seeing Louis-Napoleon, just as it knew that Montholon risked arrest if he returned to France—hardly an ornament for a great occasion. [13] On the other hand, Montholon's financial embarrassment did make him an obvious target for a bribe, though he had apparently tried to quiet his conscience by arguing against an attempt upon the July Monarchy, and to redeem his honor by accompanying the prince after failing to dissuade him.

By 15 December 1840, the day set for Napoleon's funeral procession in Paris, the Boulogne attempt had long since failed. From prison Montholon would apply for a pass that he might take his rightful place in the cortege, promising to return to prison after he had performed his "filial" duties. His request would be denied. [14] Yet, he had been allowed to receive a mistress almost at once upon entering prison, even before Louis-Napoleon was ac-

10. Edme-Théodore Bourg, *Procès du prince Napoléon-Louis et de ses coaccusés devant la cour des pairs*, pt. 1, p. 91.

11. Rousselet, *Les Souverains*, pp. 183–87.

12. Bourg, *Procès du prince Napoléon-Louis*, pp. 92–97; and Rousselet, *Les Souverains*, p. 208.

13. Albéric Cahuet, *Napoléon délivré: Le coup de théâtre de 1840*, p. 112.

14. Ibid., p. 209.

corded that privilege, which suggests that Montholon enjoyed some official favor.

When Louis-Napoleon made plans to escape from that prison in 1846, he would keep them secret from Montholon, but not from his other intimates. Did he still wonder where Montholon's loyalties lay? Soon after his election to the presidency in 1848, Louis-Napoleon would examine the official papers relating to the Boulogne affair, but would keep his discoveries to himself and have the documents destroyed.[15] It would have been awkward to disavow Montholon, a link in the Napoleonic legend; and by then Louis-Napoleon had learned something of the art of politics. With the Empire restored in 1852, the new emperor would give Montholon 50,000 francs and an annual pension of 6,000 francs—the pension being paid to the widow of Montholon beginning in 1853. What price glory!

How had, in fact, the Boulogne attempt been financed? The facts are few, and much of what has been written about the financing has been erroneous. From his mother, Queen Hortense, he had inherited an annual income of roughly 100,000 francs in 1837.[16] Never a shrewd manager of money, he risked much of his own capital in the venture of 1840. During the several years he lived in London between the Strasburg and Boulogne attempts, Louis-Napoleon was regularly received at Gore House, home of the talented and notorious Marguerite, Countess of Blessington, and her charming lover, Alfred, comte d'Orsay. This exquisite pair, drifting toward bankruptcy and unable to contribute funds to Louis-Napoleon's cause, did introduce him to society and to businessmen who were in a position to lend him money, notably the banker Benjamin Oliveria.[17]

Tradition has it, too, that Lady Blessington introduced him to the beguiling Miss Howard, who became his mistress and advanced him money, even offering to sell her diamonds for the Boulogne enterprise. We are even given a picture of her wishing him success and kissing him goodbye as he boarded the *Edinburgh Castle*.[18] Since it is indisputable that Miss Howard did become Louis-Napoleon's mistress, and since it seems probable that the two did first meet at Lady Blessington's, most of us have accepted this version of Miss Howard's financial sacrifice, along with the story that she visited her lover in prison after the attempt to seize the throne failed.[19] One regrets to relate that this enchanting legend of love and sacrifice could not have been.

15. Dansette, *Louis-Napoléon à la conquête du pouvoir*, p. 173.

16. Simpson, *The Rise of Louis-Napoleon*, p. 159.

17. Maurice Lecomte, *Le Prince des dandys: Le Comte d'Orsay, 1801–1852*, p. 188.

18. Edouard-Ferdinand, vicomte de Beaumont-Vassy, *Mémoires secrets du dix-neuvième siècle*, pp. 327–32; and André Lebey, *Les Trois coups d'état de Louis-Napoléon Bonaparte*, vol. I, *Strasbourg et Boulogne*, p. 327.

19. Lebey, *Les Trois coups d'état*, p. 416.

In 1838, when the two are alleged to have met, Miss Howard was still Elizabeth Ann Haryett, who, to the despair of her family, aspired to a theatrical career. She broke with her family in the name of high art sometime in 1839, dropping the name Haryett. We soon find her living with a well-known jockey, Jem Mason, who served as a prop while she was getting her start on the stage. In 1841 she transferred her affections to a wealthy man, Major Mountjoy Martyn, entirely bored with his wife, and who put her up in handsome style. The child born to them the following year, being illegitimate, had to be given her maiden name: Martin Constantine Haryett, and was later falsely attributed to Louis-Napoleon as the consequence of a prison visit. Aware that he could have no children by his wife, Major Martyn was inordinately delighted to have this bastard son; and he bestowed considerable money, mostly in real estate, upon Miss Howard as a way of supporting the child whom he could not legally recognize. She engaged Nathaniel W. J. Strode, financier and landowner, to manage her business affairs. This was the same Strode who owned Camden House in Chislehurst which the exiled Bonaparte family would rent in 1871.

Thus, Miss Howard had become a rich woman by the time she in fact met Louis-Napoleon at Gore House in June of 1846, shortly after his escape from prison.[20] She fell in love with this taciturn prince and abandoned Major Martyn, luckily for Louis-Napoleon whose personal funds had been nearly exhausted by the expenses of his expedition and his purchases while in prison. It is true that Louis-Napoleon inherited a second fortune upon the death of his father, King Louis, in 1847;[21] but Miss Howard's new association with Louis-Napoleon provided her the possibility of a far greater role in Paris—a far cry from Brighton, dear place of her nativity—than the theater had ever offered and she believed the part to be worth serious financial investment.

With some insight she regarded herself as unready to become empress of the French and so engaged tutors to fill her educational chasm. The most notable of these was Alexander Kinglake, the historian. A bachelor by choice, because he had noted early in life that women seem to prefer other men to their own husbands,[22] Kinglake soon had a light in his lecherous eye. But Miss Howard resisted the invitation to become his mistress, remaining loyal to Louis-Napoleon; and when Lord Ragland later commissioned Kinglake to do his history of the Crimean War, Kinglake would tailor his interpretations to gain revenge.[23] How much Miss Howard ultimately

20. Simone André Maurois, *Miss Howard and the Emperor*, pp. 19–30; and Charles Nauroy, *Les Secrets des Bonaparte*, p. 38.
21. Simpson, *The Rise of Louis-Napoleon*, p. 259.
22. Reverend William Tuckwell, *A. W. Kinglake: A Biographical and Literary Study*, p. 38.
23. F. A. Simpson, *Louis Napoleon and the Recovery of France*, p. 382.

invested to advance Louis-Napoleon's executive career remains unclear. When she signed a legal settlement in 1853, paving the way for his marriage to Eugénie de Montijo, she accepted an arrangement that brought her five and one-half million francs from Louis-Napoleon by 1855, although she had pressed unsuccessfully for more. Created comtesse de Beauregard by him as further compensation, she became by marriage Mrs. Clarence Trelawny, retiring from the limelight to enjoy her final role, that of Virtue Wronged.[24]

THE TRIAL

The trial of Louis-Napoleon Bonaparte and his accomplices before the Chamber of Peers in 1840 brought together a remarkable cast of characters under one roof. As soon as the news of the arrest in Boulogne reached Paris,[25] the government moved to convoke the peers for a judicial session. In response to a Royal Ordinance, the chancellor summoned the peers for Tuesday, 18 August, so that the machinery for a High Court could be established, which would include the appointment of a commission for the *instruction*.[26] After the charges were read to the peers that day, they were asked to vote on whether to hear the case. That there were no negative votes hardly tells the story. While the sources available differ somewhat in recording the membership of the chamber, we are roughly correct in citing the total membership on that date as 313. Twenty-six members did not attend the session; 156 members attended but abstained from voting; and only 131 members voted to hear the case.[27] That in itself should have encouraged the defendants.

What is more, the membership of the Chamber of Peers reflected the social and political structure of the July Monarchy. That regime, born of the Revolution of 1830 which had turned out the Bourbons for the second time, was indeed officially liberal; but it is no longer acceptable to consider the July Revolution as the displacement of the landed interests by businessmen. In 1830 men returned to public office who had seen service during the First Empire, but who had been out of office under the Restoration—from which circumstance derived the liberalism. At the time of the trial in 1840, the Chamber of Peers contained 192 men, out of a membership of 313, who in some way had been favored by the First Empire. Among them were four ministers, six marshals, fourteen councillors of state, fifty-six generals, nine-

---

24. *Papiers secrets et correspondance du second empire* pp. 99–100; and Maurois, *Miss Howard and the Emperor*, pp. 76, 93, 99, 123.

25. *Gazette des Tribunaux*, 8 August 1840.

26. Albert Ferme, *Les Grands procès politiques: Boulogne d'après les documents authentiques*, pp. 23–31.

27. *Gazette des Tribunaux*, 19 August 1840; and Bourg, *Procès du prince Napoleon-Louis*, pp. 22–23; Fermé, *Les Grands procès politiques*, p. 31; Lebey, *Les Trois coups d'états*, p. 398.

teen prefects, seven ambassadors, and twenty-one chamberlains whose titles or offices dated from the Empire. No fewer than thirty-eight former senators, who had recognized Napoleon II following the second abdication, can be detected within the membership. Of the 192 identified in some way with the First Empire, only 68 voted to hear the trial. Though there was no Bonapartist party as such in 1840, the Chamber of Peers was essentially Bonapartist in experience and background, and the defendants would soon reveal that they were aware of this.[28]

Baron Pasquier, the chancellor of France who presided over the peers, included himself on the *instruction* commission he had appointed. Etienne-Denis, baron Pasquier (later duc), had begun his public legal career under Napoleon I and had been prefect of police from 1810 to 1814. He had adhered to the Restoration and had served it during its liberal period, being raised to the peerage in 1821; but he had combatted the reactionary drift thereafter. Louis-Philippe called him to the presidency of the peers in 1830 and gave him the title Chancellor of France in 1837.

The remaining members of the *instruction* commission were the duc Decazes, comte Portalis, maréchal comte Gérard, baron Girod de l'Ain, and the attorney Persil. A brief sketch of each will suffice to show their predispositions. Elie, duc Decazes, was a lawyer who had seen service under the First Empire, most notably as a councillor in King Louis Bonaparte's cabinet in 1807. The high point in his career had come, however, as a chief minister under Louis XVIII, from whom he received his title. Decazes fell from favor during the reactionary period after 1820.

Joseph-Marie, comte Portalis, had also been a lawyer and an official during both the Empire and the Restoration. Though named to the peerage during the Restoration, he had rallied to the July Monarchy and had been rewarded with the vice-presidency of the Chamber of Peers.

Etienne-Maurice, maréchal comte Gérard, had reached the rank of brigadier-general in 1806. He adhered to Louis XVIII in 1814, then rallied to Napoleon during the Hundred Days, at which time he became a peer. Fleeing from France after Waterloo, he returned in 1817 to represent Paris in the Chamber of Deputies as a liberal. He had then supported Louis-Philippe, who gave him the marshalcy. Gérard was the only marshal of the six in the Chamber of Peers who voted to hear Louis-Napoleon's trial, which probably accounted for his presence on the *instruction* commission.

Louis-Gaspard-Amédée, baron Girod de l'Ain, was another lawyer and legal official whose employment dated from the First Empire. In 1827 he was elected as an opposition deputy from Indre-et-Loire and became one of

28. Bourg, *Procès du prince Napoléon-Louis*, pp. 5–14; and David H. Pinkney, "The Myth of the French Revolution of 1830," David H. Pinkney and Theodore Rapp, eds., *A Festschrift for Frederick B. Artz*, pp. 65–66.

the revolutionaries of 1830. He was president of the Chamber of Deputies in 1831 when Louis-Philippe raised him to the peerage; and he was several times a minister.

Finally, Jean-Charles Persil, by profession a lawyer, had been elected as deputy from Condom in 1830. For a time he was *procureur-général* to the Cour Royale of Paris. Raised to the peerage only in 1840, it fell to him to draw up the *instruction* report.

The peers reconvened on 15 September to hear the reading of the *instruction* report, which required two days; [29] at the end of which the peers had heard all the details of the Boulogne attempt. One of the startling facts to emerge was that Louis-Napoleon, in his decree proclaiming the overthrow of the July Monarchy, had indicated his intention to retain Louis-Philippe's own chief minister, Adolphe Thiers, in that office. [30] The 134 peers present by the end of the reading accepted the recommendations of the *instruction* commission: they voted to drop all charges against thirty-five of the minor figures in the conspiracy, but bound over for trial the nineteen major participants as well as two men who had never been captured (Henri-Richard Siegfroi de Querelles and Flandin Vourlat). Declaring themselves competent to hear the case, the peers set the trial for 28 September. [31]

In the meantime, Louis-Napoleon had been held incommunicado at the Conciergerie until 4 September, when he had been allowed to select attorneys for his defense. His choices were Pierre-Antoine Berryer, a Catholic Legitimist, to be assisted by Pierre-Thomas-Alexandre-Amable Marie de Saint-Georges (called Marie), a Republican, and by Ferdinand Barrot, brother of Odilon Barrot, the well-known constitutional monarchist. [32] When the chancellor opened the first session of the trial on 28 September, he asked the "first defendant" to rise and give his name, age, and profession. Louis-Napoleon answered the chancellor, saying, "a French prince in exile." He immediately asked to make an opening statement before the examination should begin, which the chancellor allowed.

"For the first time in my life," Louis-Napoleon read from a prepared text, "I am permitted to make myself heard in France and to speak freely to Frenchmen . . . finding myself within the Senate, among you, gentlemen, whom I know. . . . If I refer to the prerogatives imposed upon my family by the nation, I do so only to remind you of the duties which those prerogatives imposed upon us all.

"Do not believe that I have endeavored to restore the Empire against the

---

29. *Attentat du mois d'août 1840*, p. 1; and Blanchard Jerrold, *The Life of Napoleon III*, 2:151.
30. *Gazette des Tribunaux*, 16 September 1840.
31. Ibid., 17 September 1840; and Fermé, *Les Grands procès politiques*, pp. 38, 57.
32. Jerrold, *Life of Napoleon III*, 2:152–53.

national will for personal ambition. I have been better taught than that and have been inspired by nobler examples. I am the son of a King who gave up his [Dutch] throne with no regrets when he recognized that he could no longer reconcile the interests of France with those of the people he had been called upon to govern. My uncle, the Emperor, preferred to abdicate rather than accept [the loss of territory through treaty]. For not a single day have I forgotten such lessons. The cruel and unmerited act of proscription that has brought me in twenty-five years from the steps of the throne to the dungeon from which I have just emerged has failed to make me lose heart, nor has it estranged me from the glory, the rights, and the interests of France. . . .

"In 1830, when the nation recovered her sovereignty, I anticipated that the outcome would be as proper as the recovery itself; . . . but the country has since experienced ten unhappy years. Under such circumstances, I concluded that the votes of four million citizens, which had raised my family to supreme power, imposed upon me the duty of making an appeal to the nation and to consult the popular will. I would have convened a national congress [where] I would have had the right to remind the nation of the glorious past, to speak about the Emperor's elder brother [Joseph, the direct heir], and to contrast [the weakened and ignored France of today] with the France of that day—strong and respected at home and abroad. The nation could then have chosen: Republic or Monarchy; Empire or Kingdom. . . . As for my enterprise, I repeat that I had no accomplices. The plans were mine alone. . . . I hope that [my friends] will not accuse me of having trifled with their devotion and courage, and that they will understand the motives of honor and prudence that prevent me from divulging—even to them—how great were my reasons for anticipating success.

"A last word, gentlemen. I represent here a principle, a cause, and a defeat. The principle is the sovereignty of the people; the cause is that of the Empire; the defeat, Waterloo. The principle—*you* have accepted it; the cause—*you* have served it; the defeat—*you* would avenge it. No, there is no difference between you and me, and I cannot believe that I shall be made to bear the penalty for the defection of others. . . ." [33]

Was this skillful speech, so cleverly devised for its audience, really the work of Louis-Napoleon? Apparently, when the prince chose his defense attorneys from a variety of political loyalties not his own, he assured them that he would refrain from saying anything in court that would offend their political principles. He prepared a draft of his opening speech; and three days before the trial opened, he gave it to Marie along with an alternative speech written by Berryer, asking Marie to reconcile the two in a form that would be congenial to all three parties. What Marie did was to write a third speech

33. *The Political and Historical Works of Louis Napoleon Bonaparte*, 1:50–52.

which eliminated any pretence to imperial legitimacy, to the Napoleonic heritage, or to Louis-Napoleon's rights as a pretender. Obviously, Louis-Napoleon did not deliver that incarnation of the speech on 28 September, and Marie was both astonished and infuriated as he listened to the Bonapartist creed that day.

The speech as delivered was largely Louis-Napoleon's inspiration, including the assertion that he represented a principle and a cause: the sovereignty of the people and the Empire. Such views he had published only the year before in a well-known pamphlet, which revealed, incidentally, that he had studied Adolphe Thiers' *History of the Revolution* in developing his Napoleonic ideas.[34] Berryer not only approved of the line taken, but contributed the phrase about Louis-Napoleon also representing a defeat—Waterloo. As we shall see, Berryer the Legitimist hardly intended to ignore the issue of legitimacy in the defense. Marie, on the other hand, thereafter refused to take the floor on Louis-Napoleon's behalf, leaving the oratory to Berryer, but remained a member of the defense team to avoid compromising the defense.[35]

Antoine Berryer, fifty years of age by 1840, had for twenty-five years been gaining a reputation as a first-rate defense attorney, and it was recognized that he had a penchant for defending lost political causes. He had, for instance, represented Ney, Cambronne, and Lamennais, whom he held to be victims of the reaction after 1815. Yet, he was a Catholic Legitimist loyal to the restored Bourbons and had taken his seat in the Chamber of Deputies in 1830 just before the revolution, representing Puy (Haute-Loire). He had been the only Legitimist not to resign his seat after the July Revolution.[36]

Berryer opened his speech for the defense by noting that he had previously defended men loyal to the Empire—and for the reason that in a country which had had such a succession of regimes after 1789, it seemed evident that the most energetic and dedicated men, those most faithful to principle and to their word, would become the men most vulnerable to the charge of being "bad or factious" citizens as regime succeeded regime. Justice, in consequence, had been under considerable strain, for she had been periodically called upon to condemn as criminal what she had formerly been enjoined to impose as law. What Berryer sought to show was the difficulty of loyal opposition after 1789, though he did not use that term. Opposition had come to smack of treason, and political differences put men's lives in jeopardy. So, Berryer explained, he began to take such cases in complete indifference to his clients' politics, interested solely in seeing justice done.

34. "Des Idées napoléoniennes," *Oeuvres de Napoléon* III, 1:37, 46.

35. Elias Regnault, *L'Histoire de huit ans 1840–1848*, 1:308–9; and Mme. Alix (Choiseul-Gouffier) de Janzé, *Berryer, souvenirs intimes*, pp. 68–69.

36. Janzé, *Berryer*, p. 59.

Having thus taken the oath of impartiality, the intensely partisan Berryer proceeded to an assault upon the House of Orleans under the guise of defending Louis-Napoleon: this Bonaparte prince had not simply invaded France; he had come to contest the sovereignty of the House of Orleans in the name of the sovereign rights of his own family! "He did this by the same title and in virtue of the same political principle as that on which you have founded the present monarchy. . . . He invokes your own principles." Berryer could not, as he maliciously pointed out, raise the question of true legitimacy in the trial (since in his mind both regimes in the contest were illegitimate). On the other hand, as the July Monarchy insisted after 1830 that it rested upon national sovereignty, the peers must recognize that the national will had been consulted in 1804, *but not in 1830*. The voters in 1804 conferred hereditary right upon the imperial family, and Berryer cited this to suggest that the Bonapartes at least possessed a bastard legitimacy which the Orleans lacked.

Berryer then drove his argument straight at the peers. They must determine in their own minds whether their mission was simply to defend the established regime—in which case the trial was political; or whether they were there to see justice done—in which case they had no right to condemn. Ignoring, for the moment, the law, the feeble attempt upon the crown, and the constitution, could the peers in clear conscience avow that had Louis-Napoleon succeeded in his attempt they would have declared him a usurper? Would they have refused to participate in his government? Would they have turned their backs upon him? "*If* he had succeeded, and you would still have denied his right, then I could accept you as his judge."

Finally, Berryer turned to the death penalty, which was applicable in such a case. "Is it possible," he asked, "for you to put the name [Napoleon] on a magnificent tomb and at the same time vote to send another [Napoleon] to the scaffold? Not at all! Your sentence will not be death. . . . Counts, barons, you who were ministers, generals, senators, marshals, to whom do you owe your honors? To your evident merits, no doubt. But you are no less indebted to the munificence of the Empire for your presence here and for your place in the judgment seat. . . . A condemnation to an infamous punishment is surely not possible." [37]

The defense was aware that the peers had been touched. Attorneys for the remaining defendants conducted routine defenses, except for young Jules Favre—only thirty-one at the time—who created something of a sensation with his speech for Lieutenant Aladenize, the betrayer of his regiment in Boulogne. Favre portrayed Aladenize as a passionate patriot and liberal. He had supported the Revolution of 1830 and the July Monarchy in the expec-

37. Jerrold, *Life of Napoleon III*, 2:164–75.

tation that they would lead to liberty and national greatness, and had seen his hopes dashed by the incumbent regime. Thus, his decision to aid Louis-Napoleon at Boulogne derived not from any particular loyalty to Louis-Napoleon or his ambitions, but from a desire to secure a government for his beloved country that could make France respected and great. How could this be treason!

Favre, a Republican, was certainly aware of the Bonapartist temper of his audience. He reminded his hearers of Bonaparte in Egypt in 1799—aware of the weakness of his home government and of the peril that such weakness might bring to France. Bonaparte's decision to abandon his command illegally and to return home in order to alter the regime in the direction of national revival could hardly be condemned by the peers. They must recognize that political action by a soldier might well be the highest form of patriotism. Emerging from this sophistry, Favre finished by reminding the court of an actual fact. At a critical moment within the Boulogne garrison, when an armed clash had seemed likely, Aladenize had acted to prevent bloodshed. He had not meant to risk the lives of his military comrades.[38]

It will later become obvious that Favre's attempt to excuse Lieutenant Aladenize as a passionate patriot and liberal would find fuller expression in his defense of Orsini in 1858. But Favre's other argument for Aladenize became in essense that of Louis-Napoleon in 1851 as a justification for his *coup d'état*: he had broken the law (and violated his oath) to do what was right for France. After 1851, of course, the argument lost its allure for Jules Favre and his Republican colleagues. But he, at least, should have refrained from pointing at the *coup d'état* with such moral outrage.

The arguments for the defense in 1840 also illustrate the struggle in nineteenth-century France to find a satisfactory form of government, after the French Revolution had destroyed legitimate monarchy. Each party or faction sought to establish its own legitimacy, and thus, Berryer's defense of Louis-Napoleon was sounder than Favre's defense of Aladenize, for Berryer went directly to the matter of legitimacy, albeit for reasons of party interest. He showed that, by standing on popular sovereignty as expressed through plebiscites, the Bonapartes were on firmer ground than was the July Monarchy; Louis-Napoleon would take that same route in 1850 when the Republic of 1848 began moving away from political democracy. He would remain the champion of universal suffrage.

However uneasy Berryer's and Favre's arguments may have made the

---

38. Bourg, *Procès du prince Napoléon-Louis*, pt. 3, pp. 231–35. The reference to Egypt was the more pointed in that the Thiers ministry, in its support of Mohammed Ali's claim to Syrian territory, had led France into European isolation and diplomatic disaster in the late summer of 1840. Britain, Austria, Russia, and Prussia had stood by Turkey; and Louis-Philippe necessarily backed away from war.

peers (and those arguments may well have erased any possibility of the death penalty), no amount of gilded rhetoric could eliminate the fact of an armed attempt to overthrow the government. The defendants had been arrested in the act, Louis-Napoleon had freely admitted his intentions in the *instruction* and in his opening statement to the court, and he took upon himself all responsibility for the attempt and refused to incriminate others. This left no great problem for the *procureur-général* (the state's prosecuting attorney), France-Paul-François-Emile Carré, known as Franck-Carré. He ridiculed not the Napoleonic tradition, but the man who claimed to be its heir—the petty plotter who had arrived in France surrounded by domestics in masquerade! Could *he* be competent to wield the sword of Austerlitz? The true upholders of the Napoleonic tradition, Franck-Carré concluded, were the distinguished captains serving the Orleans dynasty.[39]

The sixth and final session of the trial took place on 6 October, when the verdicts were rendered. Alton-Shée, the youngest of the peers, was asked to vote first, and he voted the death penalty for Louis-Napoleon. No other peer followed his example.[40] Consequently, Louis-Napoleon was sentenced to perpetual imprisonment within France, Aladenize to transportation for life. Of the remaining seventeen brought to trial, four were acquitted because of insufficient evidence of willful attempt to overthrow the government, and thirteen were sentenced to prison for terms ranging from five to twenty years, about which more later.

The prisoners awaited the verdicts in the Conciergerie. Warned of his probable sentence, Louis-Napoleon remarked: "How long does perpetuity last in France?" When the court official actually read the sentence, he replied: "At least, Monsieur, I shall die in France." [41] The verdict had been signed by 152 peers, not even half the membership of the House.[42] The July Monarchy may have accomplished its mission, but if the trial had not been overshadowed in the press by the concurrent trial of Madame Lafarge, accused of poisoning her late husband, the regime might well have regretted the publicity it had furnished to Bonapartism.

THE AFTERMATH: DEFENDERS AND PROSECUTORS

Louis-Napoleon was transferred to the fortress of Ham in the Somme to begin his life sentence (from which he would escape in 1846). General Montholon, wishing to repeat history, was allowed to serve his twenty-year sentence at Ham (from which he would be released in 1847). Louis-

39. Jerrold, *Life of Napoleon III*, 2:163–64.
40. Alton-Shée, *Mes mémoires*, 2:68–69.
41. Lebey, *Les Trois coups d'état*, p. 395; and Jerrold, *Life of Napoleon III*, 2:180–81.
42. *Gazette des Tribunaux*, 7 October 1840; Fermé, *Les Grands procès politiques*, p. 209; and Lebey, *Les Trois coups d'état*, p. 398.

Napoleon sent Berryer a letter expressing his great satisfaction with Berryer's effort, enclosing a check for 25,000 francs, but Berryer refused the fee. Wrote Louis-Napoleon again: "You are right [to refuse]. Our relations are not those of client and attorney. We are equals. If I be a prince by birth, you are in mind and talent." [43] In Louis-Napoleon's mind, perhaps, this was true but probably not in Berryer's. His line of defense may have credited the Bonapartes with a hereditary right to the crown according to the plebiscite of 1804; but that did not mean Berryer accepted that foundation for legitimacy as superior to the old foundation, and he was consistent in his beliefs thereafter.

Following the February Revolution in 1848, Berryer took a seat in the new National Assembly as a Legitimist representing Marseille (Bouches-du-Rhône). That France again had a Republic based upon popular sovereignty convinced some Legitimists that monarchy had no future in France unless it

"Come come, Champagne . . . you are making your Republic so thin . . . that nothing will be left of it. . . ." Cartoon from *La Semaine,* September 1850

43. Janzé, *Berryer,* p. 72.

The Temptation of Saint Anthony. Cartoon from *La Semaine,* June 1850

could be sanctioned by national vote. Berryer disagreed and led a faction of
hardliners who believed that such a procedure would violate the true foundation of Legitimacy—Divine Right. In a letter dated from Wiesbaden, 30
August 1850, the Bourbon pretender, the comte de Chambord "formally
and absolutely condemned this system of appeal to the people, which implies the negation of the great national principle of hereditary monarchy,"
thus siding with Berryer.[44]

Monarchists planning the demise of the Second Republic were anticipated by Louis-Napoleon with his *coup d'état* of 1851, by which he established a veritable dictatorship, though by consent of the governed.
Berryer not merely disapproved of the presidential decree dissolving the Assembly, but was one of the deputies who gathered at the *mairie* of the Tenth
Arrondissement to protest against the *coup.* He wanted the deputies to de-
pose Louis-Napoleon as president, proposing that General Magnan should
be ordered to put his troops under the authority of the Assembly. This activity won Berryer temporary incarceration in Vincennes. He declined thereaf-

44. Claude-Noël Desjoyeaux, *La Fusion monarchique, 1848–1873,* pp. 13–14.

ter to stand for election and did not accept a seat again from Marseille until 1863, a seat he held until his death in 1868.[45]

Meanwhile, he had been honored by election to the *Académie française*, on 22 February 1855, for the *Académie* made it a practice to elect Louis-Napoleon's enemies. The famed orator's maiden speech at the *Académie* was eagerly awaited by the intelligentsia. For some reason, perhaps because he was not in a familiar courtroom, his performance was unimpressive and disappointing. On the other hand, he made his mark by asking to be spared the customary call upon the chief-of-state. Louis-Napoleon, now Napoleon III, gave him permission to do as he wished, though regretting that the motives of the politician had transcended the duties of the academician. As for Berryer personally, Napoleon let it be known that he would remember Berryer, not as the adversary of the moment, but as the defender of yesterday.[46]

Marie, the sullen defense attorney in 1840, represented Paris in the Chamber of Deputies from 1842 until 1848, then became minister of public works in the provisional government after the February Revolution and minister of justice under Cavaignac. Inevitably Marie opposed the election of Louis-Napoleon to the presidency and found himself defeated for reelection to the Assembly in 1849. Like Berryer, he was absent from active political life until 1863, when he won a seat in the lower house as a Republican.

Ferdinand Barrot, the constitutional monarchist, was the only one of the three defense attorneys to rally to Louis-Napoleon, serving him briefly as a secretary in 1848. He was then for a time minister to Sardinia-Piedmont and was rewarded, after 1851, with a Senate seat.

The most durable and equivocal connection to emerge from the trial of 1840 was that of Louis-Napoleon and Jules Favre. Political opponents from beginning to end, Favre and Louis-Napoleon both had dabbled in utopian socialism in their youth, both retained a genuine sympathy for the suffering of the masses throughout their careers, and they found each other personally likable. Though both Berryer and Favre carried on implacable war against the Second Empire, of the two Louis-Napoleon clearly preferred Favre and was careful of his person. Despite their differences, an "affinité de rêveries" united them.[47]

Equivocation, moreover, was a pronounced feature of Jules Favre's career, and came to a head in 1848 with the Republicans ostensibly in power. In elections held on 23 April for the new National Assembly, three members of the Bonaparte family had been returned and were allowed to

45. Georges Le Bail, *Grands avocats politiques XIXe siécle*, pp. 4–5.

46. Janzé, *Berryer*, p. 117; and R. L. Williams, *Gaslight and Shadow: The World of Napoleon III*, pp. 82–83.

47. Pierre Jacomet, *Avocats républicains du second empire: Jules Favre—Léon Gambetta*, p. 45.

take their seats: Prince Jerome-Napoleon, Prince Pierre, and Napoleon Murat. This implied that the law of 10 April 1832, banishing the family, had become a dead letter. Therefore, Pierre Piétri, a deputy from Corsica (who would later be a prefect of police), moved that the law be abrogated, a maneuver to prepare the way for Louis-Napoleon to run in the by-election of 4 June. A parliamentary committee, which included Jules Favre, was appointed to examine Piétri's proposal.

Meanwhile, Favre, who held the post of secretary-general in the Ministry of the Interior as well as his seat in the Assembly, had been involved in a political scheme to indict the radical Louis Blanc for allegedly inciting a mob to riot on 15 May. The investigating committee's report, read to the Assembly by Favre, recommended indictment, but was defeated by thirty-two votes. After this Favre was forced by the Executive Commission to resign his position in the Ministry of the Interior. Consequently, he had earned the wrath of left-wing Republicans and was an embittered man when he approached the question raised by Piétri.

Piétri's proposal was considered in committee on 2 June, two days before the critical by-election. It may come as no surprise to veterans of committee meetings that a decision had not been reached by election day, thus enabling Louis-Napoleon to press his candidacy. He won in four of the twenty-three departments participating in the by-election, opting for Charente-Inférieure. When the committee resumed its deliberation on the eighth, Jules Favre was among those who argued that the popular will had to be respected. Despite the anxiety of the Executive Commission, the committee resolved that since Louis-Napoleon had entered the country legally, and that since his candidacy had been tolerated, he must be regarded as legally elected. Favre tried to sweeten the situation for his fellow Republicans with assurances that Louis-Napoleon would be no threat to the Republic—that he was a pigmy—but the suspicion remained (and remains) that Favre had deliberately maneuvered in committee to take revenge against his enemies on the Left.[48]

Louis-Napoleon attempted to resolve the issue in a letter written from London on 11 June, in which he said he would resign the seat because he was the cause of so much uneasiness. Once again, however, he acknowledged popular sovereignty: "If the people impose responsibilities upon me, I shall know how to fulfill them. But I disavow those who attribute to me ambitions I do not have. My name is a symbol of order, the nation, and of glory, and I would be most unhappy to see it used to increase the troubles and the disunity of the fatherland. To avoid such a misfortune I should prefer to remain in exile. I am ready to make any sacrifice for the welfare of

---

48. Dansette, *Louis-Napoléon à la conquête du pouvoir*, pp. 221–25; and Jerrold, *Life of Napoleon III*, 2:397–407.

France." It was quite properly noted that the letter contained no reference to the word *republic*, though his formal letter of resignation the following day claimed that the resignation was dedicated to the preservation of the Republic.[49]

Favre emerged from the midsummer crises with a reputation for treachery within his party. He made matters worse in December by voing for Louis-Napoleon for the presidency, later explaining his vote by saying "I thought the prestige and popularity of [his] great name would serve marvelously in consolidating the Republic by the reconciliation of parties"[50]—rather a large task for a pigmy. Favre seemed to be Louis-Napoleon's most likely collaborator during the presidential years. Yet, by 1851, he had not rallied to the president and had begun to denounce the evident preparations for a *coup d'état*. Like Berryer, Favre openly opposed the *coup* when it came on 2 December, but was omitted from the list of opponents to be jailed during the crisis. Subsequently, when Louis-Napoleon decreed the confiscation of approximately two-thirds of the Orleans properties in France, he based his action upon a proposal Jules Favre had recommended to the Assembly in July of 1848, but which had been successfully fought by Berryer at that time.[51]

We shall return to Monsieur Favre as the defender of Louis-Napoleon's would-be assassin in 1858. Meanwhile, what of those men who officially participated in Louis-Napoleon's condemnation and imprisonment in 1840? Duc Pasquier, who had presided over the trial and chaired the *instruction* commission, retired from active political life upon his election to the *Académie française* in 1842 at the age of seventy-five. He plunged into the composition of his memoirs, was eighty-five at the commencement of the Second Empire, and died at ninety-five in 1862. At that time, Napoleon III aspired to fill the vacant seat in the *Académie*, in recognition of his own work on Julius Caesar, but was snubbed.

As for the other members of the *instruction* commission, duc Decazes retired from politics after the February Revolution at the age of sixty-eight, while baron Girod de l'Ain was called unto his fathers in 1847. But J.-C. Persil, who had put together the report of the *instruction* commission, was named a councilor-of-state by Louis-Napoleon in 1852 and promoted to the Senate in 1864, where he remained until 1870. Both comte Portalis and maréchal comte Gérard were appointed to the Senate by their ex-enemy in 1852.

49. Charles-Hippolyte Castille, *Histoire de la seconde république française*, 3:26, 54–55, 60–66.

50. Theodore Zeldin, *Emile Ollivier and the Liberal Empire of Napoleon III*, pp. 52–53.

51. Dansette, *Louis-Napoléon à la conquête*, p. 260; Jacomet, *Avocats républicains du second empire*, p. 45; and Jerrold, *Life of Napoleon III*, 3:357.

Franck-Carré, the prosecuting attorney in 1840, who had specialized in prosecuting radical opponents of the July Monarchy, had been rewarded in 1841 with the presidency of the Court of Rouen. When President Bonaparte visited Rouen in 1849, he was welcomed and congratulated rather too effusively by Franck-Carré, who at least retained the dignity of office and was reappointed by Napoleon III after the proclamation of the Second Empire.[52] A despot he may have been at that point in his career, but could hardly be called cruel and revengeful. Even Alton-Shée, who had thirsted for the death penalty in 1840, devoted himself to business affairs during the Second Empire without fear that he might be the victim of reprisal.

THE AFTERMATH: LOUIS-NAPOLEON'S ACCOMPLICES

Franck-Carré had ridiculed Louis-Napoleon's henchmen at the trial before the peers as domestics in disguise. His charge was almost exactly a half-truth. Of the fifty-six participants, twenty-nine were found to be servants: some actually in Louis-Napoleon's London household, some employed by his more important collaborators, and some simply unemployed and looking for work. Nine of the twenty-nine were not even French: one was Italian; one, Belgian; three, Polish; and four, Swiss. Only one of the domestics even stood trial, and most of them vanished thereafter from the historical scene, their one encounter with great events a disappointment.

Three of the domestics, however, found lucrative careers at Boulogne. Pierre-Paul-Frédéric Bachon, equerry to Louis-Napoleon in 1840, became equerry to the prince imperial during the Second Empire at a salary of 6,000 francs; and he received a gift of 162,000 francs from the emperor that was paid to him in installments over a period of twenty-seven months. Léon Cuxac, having been a cook in Louis-Napoleon's household in London, became the first valet de chambre during the Empire, in which position he took on the airs of the first councilor of the realm. Aside from a salary, the emperor gave him several houses in London and money to furnish them. The third was Charles Thélin, originally in Queen Hortense's service as valet to Louis-Napoleon. He received official permission to reside in prison with his master, though he himself was not sentenced, and was thus free to leave Ham after Louis-Napoleon's escape. Under the Empire, when Bure became treasurer-general of the crown, Thélin took over as the emperor's private bursar.

That position had originally been held by Pierre-Jean-François Bure who had been a member of the Boulogne team, but his association with Louis-Napoleon went back to their first years. Born to Colette Bure in 1807, who was Louis-Napoleon's wet nurse in 1808, Bure was always called the

52. Gabriel Perreux, *Les Conspirations de Louis-Napoléon Bonaparte*, p. 87.

prince's *frère de lait*, or foster-brother. At the time of Boulogne, Bure had been a traveling salesman, often in London, and he served as paymaster for those recruited to overthrow the July Monarchy. Under the Second Republic, he became the president's bursar at a salary of 6,000 francs; as treasurer-general of the crown beginning in 1853, he received a salary of 30,000 francs with an annual expense allowance of 11,000 francs, earning in his service a reputation for the scrupulosity of his accounts.

But the imperial service had its dubious side for Bure. As is well-known, Louis-Napoleon, while in prison, had two sons by his local laundress, Alexandrine-Eléonore Vergeot. For a time, these boys were reared by Colette Bure, who received a pension from Louis-Napoleon; they then lived briefly with Miss Howard, who adored them. Ultimately, in 1858, Louis-Napoleon arranged the marriage of Vergeot and Bure, so that the two boys came to bear his name—though Bure remained indifferent to his ready-made sons. Both were ennobled by imperial decree in 1870.[53]

Seven of the minor accomplices at Boulogne had had some military experience but were not on active service at that time. Charges were dismissed against four of them. Of the remaining three, Henri-Richard Siegfroi de Querelles was never arrested for trial; and Mathieu Galvani, and Prosper Alexandre (called Desjardins) were acquitted. Querelles, who had also participated in the Strassburg attempt, died in 1847, but Napoleon III later remembered his son with an occasional gift, ultimately amounting to 4,400 francs. The records also show that Querelles's sister was given 2,400 francs. Galvani also died too soon to benefit personally, but his widow was awarded a pension from the civil list, 1,200 francs beginning in 1853. Desjardins received a pension of 2,400 francs from the same source. Another minor accomplice who never stood trial, Pierre-Joseph-Léon Gillemand, had given Louis-Napoleon and Persigny fencing lessons in 1840. He was remembered with a pension of 1,200 francs beginning in 1853, in spite of the fact that the skills he had taught had not been utilized.

Lieutenant Charles Aladenize, the one royal officer on active duty implicated in the plot, had been sentenced to transportation for life. He might well have been sentenced to death had it not been shown during the *instruction* that he had prevented Persigny from killing the garrison commander and had threatened to turn against the invaders should there be bloodshed. He had, thus, contributed to the failure of the *coup* at a critical moment, though his action was consistent with Louis-Napoleon's orders.

Aladenize was blessed with a pardon during the first year of Louis-Napoleon's presidency, along with a gift of 600 francs. He enjoyed a monthly pension of 500 francs beginning in 1850, which was doubled in

---

53. Roger L. Williams, *The Mortal Napoleon III*, p. 50; and Simpson, *The Rise of Louis Napoleon*, p. 259.

1853, the year his daughter was given a 100,000-franc dowry by the emperor. Unfortunately for His Majesty, Aladenize was perennially in financial difficulty through failures in business; and the records show repeated gifts from the imperial coffers to keep him afloat. Even after his death in 1865, his estate received 5,000 francs a month from the emperor. All told, Aladenize cost Napoleon III nearly 400,000 francs during the Second Empire for no services rendered, explicable only as blind loyalty to old friends.

Indeed, how else to account for his charitable treatment of General Montholon, who, as noted above, was well paid before his death in 1853. It remains however, to account for the other major accomplices who received sentences in 1840. Three of them predeceased the Second Empire and were unable to benefit from their investment: Jean-Baptiste Voisin, a retired cavalry colonel from Tarbes, who had been sentenced to ten years detention; Séverin-Louis, le duff de Mésonan, a retired naval officer from Quimper, sentenced to fifteen years detention; and Denis-Charles Parquin, a former officer in the municipal guard of Paris, who had been given a term of twenty years.

Hippolyte-François-Athale-Sébastien Bouffet de Montauban was sentenced to five years detention, during which time he lost his soap factory and was ruined. Louis-Napoleon gave him 25,000 francs in 1849 and had him appointed as a tax-collection official. Bouffet, irritated at not being entrusted with a more responsible position than Pierre Bure obtained in the plot for the *coup d'état* in 1851, resigned his office in a huff and retired to London.

The aged Etienne Laborde, a retired lieutenant-colonel who had served Napoleon I on Elba, had been sentenced to five years of imprisonment. Napoleon III named him to be governor of the Luxembourg Palace, a post he held until his death in 1865 at an annual salary of 3,000 francs. Laborde also received gifts from the emperor relative to the position at the Luxembourg that totalled 60,000 francs.

Jules-Barthelemy Lombard, a one-time military surgeon from Strassburg, who had been implicated in the Strassburg attempt in 1836, had been a Bonapartist publicist and was regarded as a major accomplice in 1840, thus receiving a twenty-year sentence. The gossip of that day claimed that he had sold information to the Thiers regime, which may account for why he received no employment under the Second Empire, but Napoleon III did give him 20,000 francs in 1853.

The Florentine businessman and banker, Guiseppe Orsi, had served the Bonaparte family as a banker in Italy and in London. Participating willingly in the expedition, he was sentenced to five years detention. Napoleon III gave him two gifts, 5,000 francs in 1851 and 50,000 in 1854. Thereafter, he was on retainer at 5,000 a month, reduced to 1,000 a month in 1858.

Napoleon Ornano, an ex-cavalry lieutenant from Ajaccio, also had a family association with the Bonapartes and was given a ten-year term. Under the Second Empire, he became an inspector of imperial buildings at a salary of 6,000 francs, and early in that period Napoleon III paid off his debts to the tune of 52,850 francs.

Jean-Baptiste-Théodore Forestier, having been an active Bonapartist publicist, was given a ten-year sentence. During the presidency, Louis-Napoleon gave him a salary of 6,000 francs a year as a paymaster and a gift of 12,500 francs. Under the Empire he received several gifts for a total of 35,000 francs, and Napoleon III furnished him 100,000 francs to acquire a commercial concession in Algeria.

Martial-Eugène Bataille, a civil engineer, was given a five-year term for his participation. He ran as an official candidate for the *Corps législatif* in 1851 and, failing election, requested official appointment and pension. In 1854 he was appointed to the Council of State, for which he touched

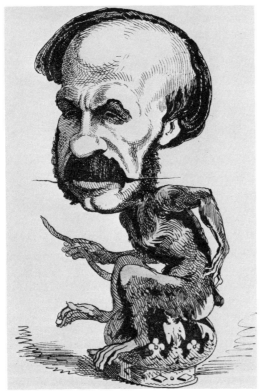

The duc de Persigny, "The Monkey" (servile imitation). From *La Ménagerie impériale*

Dr. Henri Conneau, "The Leech" (attachment, voracity).
From *La Ménagerie impériale*

10,000 a month, and the records show a gift of 54,000 francs. The budget was relieved by his death in 1864.

Louis-Napoleon's best known co-conspirators were Persigny and Dr. Conneau. Jean-Gilbert-Victor Fialin de Persigny, self-appointed to the aristocracy (until Napoleon III made him a duc in 1863), was a devoted Bonapartist and had attempted to kill the commander of the Boulogne garrison, for which he received a sentence of twenty years. Persigny held public office under the Second Republic and the Second Empire in a manner that became a model for bureaucratic ineptitude, and Napoleon's kindness was never better illustrated than in his toleration of this troublesome friend. In addition to his salary as minister to Prussia, ambassador to Britain, minister of the interior, and member of the Privy Council, the gifts Persigny received between 1849 and 1870 amounted to 446,500 francs. This pompous ass (regrettably missed by Daumier), who was less appropriately caricatured after 1870 as a monkey,[54] believed himself to have been insufficiently regarded.

Dr. Henri Conneau, finally, was a faithful family retainer who had been with Queen Hortense before becoming Louis-Napoleon's physician. Conneau freely admitted his participation in the Boulogne attempt, and was allowed to serve his five-year term at Ham with Louis-Napoleon. Thélin and he helped their master to arrange his escape, keeping Montholon in the dark. Conneau remained with Napoleon as chief physician from 1848 until the end. Probably his medical knowledge had become outdated, but he was the emperor's closest confidant during the Second Empire and was with him at his death in England in 1873. Napoleon's last mumbled words were for Conneau, recalling that they had been together, not at Boulogne, but at Sedan.[55]

The affair at Boulogne was not only unsuccessful as an attempt upon Louis-Philippe's throne, but led to a trial which condemned the pretender to prison. Yet, that trial also laid bare the illegitimacy of the Orleanist regime and offered the Bonapartists their first public occasion to state their superior claim to legitimacy. As for the large cast of characters, both great and small, who were on stage before the peers, whether as defendants, defenders, or prosecutors, the events of Boulogne lived on to affect lives and careers for the next thirty years.

54. *La Ménagerie impériale, composée des ruminants, amphibies, carnivores et autres budgétivores qui ont dévoré la France pendant 20 ans* (Paris: Rossignol, n.d.), no. 13.

55. The biographical and financial details for Louis-Napoleon's accomplices are drawn from the *instructions* in *Attentat du mois d'août 1840, Cour des pairs;* and from *Papiers secrets et correspondance du second empire,* pp. 50–54, 329–68.

CHAPTER TWO

Death Comes for the Archbishop

I shall not die of a cold,
my son. I shall die of
having lived.
WILLA CATHER

Murder most foul,
As in the best it is;
But this most foul,
Strange, and unnatural.
SHAKESPEARE

*S*ATURDAY, 3 January 1857, the festival of Saint Genevieve, patron
saint of Paris, was a chill and rainy day, which did nothing to
improve the spirits of the Archbishop of Paris, Marie-
Dominique-Auguste Sibour. Custom required him to go to the church of
Saint-Etienne-du-Mont—where rested the relics of Saint Genevieve—to be
present for the opening of the novena of Saint Genevieve; and it had been
announced he would attend.[1] But he had been ailing, feeling his sixty-four
years, and was disturbed by anonymous threatening letters that had been
coming his way. On the morning of the third, he thought to cancel his appearance. Feeling better in the afternoon, he proceeded to his duty.

First he sat through a sermon delivered by Monsignor Lacarrière, formerly bishop of Basse-Terre (Guadeloupe), then retired to the sacristy to don
his vestments. Despite the dreary day, a considerable throng of the faithful
waited to receive the archiepiscopal blessing. Four-thirty had sounded when
the clerical procession was formed. Preceded by the Abbé Dufour, vicar of
Saint-Etienne-du-Mont, Archbisiop Sibour moved into the throng. At his
sides, his grand vicar, Surat, and his secretary, Abbé Cutolli, held up his
long cope to relieve him of its weight; but they were gradually forced back-
ward by the supplicants who approached the popular archbishop until they
trailed him.

---

1. Pierre Mermet, "L'Assassinat de Mgr. Sibour, archevêque de Paris," *L'Information historique* 19(1957):197.

Suddenly a pale young man, dressed entirely in black, rose from his knees as Archbishop Sibour approached. With his left hand, he seized the archbishop's left arm, forcing him into a half-turn to the left. Almost simultaneously he delivered a knife-blow between the ribs in the direction of the heart, thereupon crying out, "No more goddesses! Away with goddesses!" All this had occurred so swiftly that none in the official procession realized what had happened. One parishioner, a Madame Mérard, had actually seen the knife. Surat, thinking Sibour had been slapped, slapped the face of the young man who kept repeating his peculiar cry. A tumult broke out, chairs were overturned, as the archbishop sank back muttering what sounded to be, "*le malheureux, le malheureux.*" Thought to be fainting, Sibour was carried into the sacristy and a doctor summoned. Only there did they discover the truth. Surat at once administered the last rites, and in a moment the archbishop passed into the next life of his faith.[2]

Meanwhile, angry parishioners had overwhelmed the assassin and were quickly aided by a policeman. In fact, the young man had made no move to flee. He was taken immediately to the *mairie* of the Twelfth Arrondissement in the place du Panthéon (now the Fifth Arrondissement). Though in mufti, the suspect identified himself as a priest, Jean-Louis Verger, born 20 August 1826, in Neuilly-sur-Seine. His overcoat pockets were found to be stuffed with brochures and tracts; and he admitted buying his weapon, a large Catalan knife, a few days earlier at a cutlery in the rue Dauphine.[3] A *juge d'instruction* was at once appointed to participate in the investigation with the police and the imperial prosecutor.

Verger was of average height, conspicuously thin and pale, but with a face of some distinction. He seemed entirely calm as the first interrogation began. When asked to explain his act, he claimed that he had not meant to strike at the person of the archbishop, but only at the dogma of the Immaculate Conception, which the archbishop personified. He explained his outcry at the moment of the fatal thrust as a "protest against the Immaculate Conception and against the Brotherhood of Genevievans." Admitting premeditation, he said that he had come to Saint-Etienne-du-Mont intending to strike for the archbishop's heart, and knew that the blow had been fatal when delivered. His calm only cracked when he was asked whether he understood the gravity of his crime. Then, in tears, he responded: "Yes, it is frightful."[4]

The late archbishop lay in state for two days at the archiepiscopal palace in the rue de Grenelle. The desecrated church of Saint-Etienne-du-Mont

---

2. Armand Fouquier, *Causes célèbres de tous les peuples,* 1:2; and Jean-Joseph-François Poujoulat, *Vie de Mgr. Sibour, archevêque de Paris,* pp. 377–80.
3. Mermet, "L'Assassinat," p. 198; and Taxile Delord, *Histoire du second empire,* 2:273–74.
4. *Gazette des Tribunaux,* 4 January 1857; and Fouquier, *Causes célèbres,* 1:2–3.

remained closed until the ceremony of expiation and purification could be held on 12 January, after which the archbishop's heart was transferred there from Notre-Dame for interment in the chapel of Saint-Genevieve.[5] Wrote Dupanloup, Bishop of Orleans, on hearing the news and recalling that Sibour's predecessor had also died violently in 1848: "Paris! Paris! in this long, unending sequence of our calamities, must the ancient seat of your pontiffs always be flooded, not only by the sweat [of their labors], but by the tears and blood they shed!"[6] Dupanloup had particular reason to be horrified, for he knew Verger to be one of his former students, in whom he had recognized "a base character," and which education had not altered. Worse, barely two months before the murder, Verger had appealed to Dupanloup for help and had been rebuffed.

It should not pass unnoticed that, in murdering Archbishop Sibour as the personification of the dogma of Immaculate Conception, Verger had chosen an unlikely target. Sibour had indeed ultimately reconciled himself to the new dogma, but he had been well-known for his initial lack of enthusiasm. One could argue, in the absence of satisfactory evidence, that a priest might be ignorant of episcopal politics and, thus, be unaware of the subtleties of Sibour's position. On the other hand, we must recognize at the outset the possibility of motives more complex in Verger's action than were expressed at his first interrogation. Had his enemy been the dogma of the Immaculate Conception alone, it seems apparent that he could have found a more vulnerable member of the hierarchy for his blade.

To the outsider, the Roman Catholic Church often gives the appearance of massive unity; but no churchman in nineteenth-century France could have entertained such an illusion. The Gallican Church housed a variety of factions after 1815 when French Catholics sought to recover from the traumatic years beginning in 1789, and the factionalism had become even more intense after Louis-Napoleon's seizure of absolute power in 1851. The quarreling encompassed both temporal and spiritual issues, giving the factionalism a complexity maddening to those alien to them.

Under the Bourbon restoration, the French hierarchy had been Legitimist and Gallican, logical only in that the state was then officially Christian. Seen in a larger historical context, however, this deliberate proximity of church and state had become a politically unsound policy. Given the gradual secularization of European society since the medieval period, the temporal had encroached upon the spiritual power; and especially after the experience with Napoleon I, no one should have argued that the Church could indefinitely prosper or be independent in close association with the

5. Fleury and Sonolet, *La Société du second empire*, 1:388.
6. François Lagrange, *Vie de Mgr. Dupanloup, évêque d'Orléans*, 2:242.

state. In the old days when religious quarrels pitted kings against popes, the independence of the Gallican hierarchy from Roman jurisdiction had been won in alliance with the French monarchy, and the so-called Gallican liberties meant independence. But the new contest was between the Revolution and the Church; and the new liberals, seeing in Gallicanism only enslavement to the state, were arguing for separation of church and state and for the revival of ultramontanism.

When legitimate monarchy was replaced by the non-Christian July Monarchy in 1830, the poverty of the Gallican position was fully exposed. On the other hand, ultramontanism was feasible for the new Liberal Catholics only so long as the Vatican was not absolutistic. It was their misfortune to have in Rome Gregory XVI, the outspoken enemy of liberalism in any form on the grounds that liberalism was the pernicious offspring of the Revolution. Consequently, neither Gallicanism nor Liberal Catholicism seemed to have any future, and one heard convincing predictions that the Church was on the brink of extinction.[7] The election of a liberal pope in 1846, Pius IX, gave momentary comfort to the ultramontanes, until his rejection of liberalism after the revolutionary events of 1848–49 restored the former impasse.

By the time Sibour became archbishop in 1848, clerical factionalism had refined itself sufficiently to make it possible for people to be in several camps at once. Gallicanism still contested with ultramontanism; there were liberals as opposed to conservatives (traditionalists); and Catholic lay journalists and intellectuals meddled in ecclesiastical affairs as never before through polemical journals, in other words the self-annointed *versus* the ordained.

Catholic liberals, having argued for religious liberty through separation of church and state, had had to reckon that liberty is a universal right. The conservatives, however, insisted that liberty is merely a privilege granted to truth alone; that no freedom may be accorded to error or evil; and that it is the obligation of the state to work with the church against error and evil (which meant, among other things, against the increasing secularization of society). What this amounted to, as the liberal Catholic layman, the comte de Montalembert, saw, was that the Church demanded liberty for itself. Yet, it was ready to abolish its opponents' liberty, or at least to demand that the state infringe upon it.

Most conservatives greeted Louis-Napoleon's *coup d'état* of 1851 with enthusiasm, but even some of the liberals accepted an authoritarian regime as necessary to save religion from radicalism after the June Days of 1848.[8] Louis-Napoleon was a nonbeliever, and his Bonapartist creed was grounded on the popular sovereignty and the anticlericalism of the Revolution. His

7. Philip Spencer, *Politics of Belief in Nineteenth Century France*, pp. 40–50, 82–87.
8. Adrien Dansette, *Religious History of Modern France*, 1:279–81.

personal indifference to religion, on the other hand, enabled him to strive for a political settlement that would permit believers and nonbelievers, liberals and conservatives, to inhabit the same society in peace.

During 1852, when he actively promoted the restoration of the Empire, he sought to define in his speeches a new association of church and state which employed neither the words *alliance* nor *separation*. The state should support religion for its own sake, not to please any party or faction nor for political advantage, but in recognition of the good that religion can do and of the truths that it teaches. Thus, both the clergy and the government should work for society and for civilization, but in their different spheres.[9] His formula made it possible to be simultaneously clerical and anticlerical (anticlerical in principle but clerical in action), and he would adhere to this formula during the first decade of his reign. Consequently, Archbishop Sibour, along with the five French cardinals in the Senate, voted to recommend the restoration of the Empire on 6 November 1852.[10]

Obviously, the proximity of the archbishop of Paris to the seat of secular power made him, whoever he was, uniquely sensitive within the hierarchy to Parisian politics. Sibour had been nominated for the see of Paris by the Cavaignac regime in 1848 after the death of Archbishop Affre during the June Days. Affre had been struck down by a stray bullet when he had sought to put an end to the fighting. Before his appointment to Paris, Sibour had been Bishop of Digne, where he had won a reputation for liberalizing the administration of his diocese. This recommended him to French Republicans, who sought for Paris a bishop of liberal bent who could cooperate with a liberal republic. The Republicans thereafter were generally pleased with Sibour's conduct, except for his ultimate support of Louis-Napoleon. They found him to be liberal, they saw no taint of ultramontanism, and noted with satisfaction that he had been an opponent of what one Republican writer called the "absurd" dogma of the Immaculate Conception.[11]

But the editor of *l'Univers religieux*, Louis Veuillot, who had turned his newspaper into an ultramontanist organ hostile to Liberal Catholicism, was soon at loggerheads with Sibour. Early in his episcopacy, Sibour had been assured by Rome that the various treatises and theological texts used in French seminaries, Gallican in spirit, ran no danger of condemnation. Veuillot was not only critical of such works, but resented the use of classics dating from antiquity in Catholic schools, a practice which both Sibour and Dupanloup had encouraged. The battle was entended in 1851 when the Abbé Jean-Joseph Gaume published a book entitled *The Cankerworm* (*Le*

9. *Oeuvres de Napoléon III*, 3:339.

10. Jean Maurain, *La Politique ecclésiastique du second empire de 1852 à 1869*, p. 41.

11. Ernest Hamel, *Histoire illustrée du second empire*, 2:211–12. Also note Delord, *Histoire du second empire*, 2:218–22.

Ver rongeur des sociétés modernes ou le paganisme dans l'éducation), aimed at liberal education that included the classics, and at the Jesuits as traditional compromisers. Both Sibour and Dupanloup saw Veuillot's hand in this quarrel, and Dupanloup raised the question of lay interference. Aware that many clergymen read *l'Univers*, he suggested that a journalist ought not to be permitted to intrude between a bishop and his priests.

Veuillot was hardly intimidated, and he scored an impressive victory on 7 December 1852 when the treatise on theology most commonly used in French seminaries was put on the Index, a direct blow at Gallicanism. In his annoyance, Sibour condemned *l'Univers* on 17 February 1853, forbidding the priests in his archdiocese to read it. He was at once challenged on the matter by the Bishop of Moulins, and the dispute was referred to Rome. Pius IX responded with the encyclical *Inter multiplices*, 21 March 1853, wherein he called upon all bishops to encourage writers inspired by good intentions to deal with them with "fatherly words and prudence" should they err. In a separate letter to Veuillot, the Pope granted him permission to continue his work, though recommending prudence, adding, "those who attack you will end by recognizing your talent and your zeal." Sibour had no choice but to withdraw his ban.[12]

By that date, the matter of the Immaculate Conception was near definition after centuries of debate. The absence of direct scriptural basis for such a dogma had been the traditional barrier. On the other hand, "the great and peculiar privileges of Mary" in the long history of the Church and the accepted evidence of her sanctity as the Mother of God made it logical to deduce that she had been conceived without sin. The belief, as it would come to be defined, was that "the Virgin Mary, at the moment of her conception (which, in itself, was a normal, human conception) was miraculously exempted from the taint of original sin."[13] Pressure for the new dogma came from conservative churchmen seeking a trump to check the growth of skepticism in the nineteenth century and was especially strong after 1830 when a novice, Catherine Labouré, reported a vision of the Virgin in the rue du Bac.

Pius IX appointed a commission of theologians to study the question on 1 June 1848; and the following February, he issued the encyclical *Ubi Primum*, asking the bishops for their prayers and advice on the matter. If the great majority were enthusiastic for a new dogma, Sibour demurred, saying that the belief was not definable. By this he probably meant, as did some bishops in countries heavily Protestant in population, that such a dogma was

12. Maurain, *La Politique*, pp. 37–49; Dansette, *Religious History* 1:281–82; and Delord, *Histoire du second empire*, 2:228–29.
13. E. E. Y. Hales, *Pio Nono: A Study of European Politics and Religion in the Nineteenth Century*, pp. 146–47.

impolitic in the nineteenth century and unlikely to impress those already skeptical about Catholic doctrine. Be that as it may, Pius IX proclaimed the dogma of the Immaculate Conception on 8 December 1854, on his own authority and without summoning a council of the bishops, an action that became a precedent for Papal Infallibility.

The French bishops in particular were more distressed by the procedure than by the dogma itself; but twenty of them, including Sibour, went to Rome for the ceremony. It is said that Sibour became reconciled to the dogma during his visit to Rome—a reconciliation sweetened by the promotion of his relative and vicar-general, Léon Sibour, to the title of Bishop *in partibus* of Tripoli, the title enabling him to become auxiliary Bishop of Paris.[14] Thereafter, it was emphasized that Sibour had not opposed the doctrine itself, but the timeliness of its definition.[15] In truth, he had opposed it to the limits of discretion.[16] When Verger brought Sibour down in January of 1857, as the presumed champion of Immaculate Conception, consciously or otherwise he confused the issues and motives in the bizarre murder.

After the initial questioning, Verger was taken to Mazas where the *instruction* proceeded. He asked for food, having fasted that day; and he talked rather freely. When asked how a priest could commit such a heinous crime, the thirty-year-old Verger laid the blame on priestly celibacy: "Why are not priests allowed to marry like other men?" As for his origins, he had come from poverty. (His father still worked as a tailor in Neuilly.) A quiet, withdrawn child, his family had assumed that he was naturally disposed to study and to piety, but there was no money to prepare him for the religious life. The situation was brought to the attention of the marquise de Rochefort, known as Sister Mélanie, Superior of the Filles de Saint-Vincent-de-Paul in Neuilly, who provided money for Louis Verger's religious education. He entered the novitiate of Saint-Nicholas-du-Chardonnet in Paris at the age of fourteen (1841), then under the direction of the Abbé Dupanloup. His behavior convinced Dupanloup that he would do the ecclesiastical calling no honor, and he was expelled in 1844 after the purchase of unauthorized books by Racine and Voltaire. He had evidently stolen sixty francs to make the purchases, but insisted that the money had been a gift. He left the novitiate with a reputation for "bad character."

The *instruction* uncovered the fact that Verger had then studied philosophy privately with the Canon Firmin Vervorst, after which he had been accepted by the seminary of Meaux (in 1846), evidently upon Vervorst's warm recommendation. Verger remained there four years, where he was described as taciturn and withdrawn, but not eccentric. He performed well, if without

14. Maurain, *La Politique*, pp. 95–96.
15. Poujoulat, *Vie de Mgr. Sibour*, pp. 341–42.
16. Spencer, *Politics of Belief*, p. 152.

distinction. On a rating scale from three to six, he generally got fours and fives in his studies; and fives for conduct, which included piety, regularity, character, and devotion to work. During his final year, he became exercised about an inheritance he thought was due him and seemed peculiarly embittered by its loss, at least for someone presumably dedicated to the life of poverty.[17] But here no one seems to have suspected him of bad character.

As a seminarian, Verger was assigned teaching and supervisory duties at the local novitiate. The details of his failure are slim; either he had no talent for the tasks, or the students were incorrigible. Verger exposed a short temper and soon had to be sent "to take the country air," while some of the pupils were returned to their families. For a brief period thereafter, he assisted the Abbé Réaume, curé of Mitry-Mory, who was writing his *Guide du jeune prêtre*. Réaume reported favorably on Verger to the seminary, having found him gentle, shy, and correct.[18]

Verger was ordained in 1850 and received his first parish, Guercheville (Seine-et-Marne) on 1 June. He soon wrote to the Abbé Renard, his former superior at Meaux, about his satisfaction with the position, but added words which suggest he had found the protected atmosphere of the seminary more than simply congenial: "I left the seminary with much regret; for a time I thought that I would be inconsolable. But I have shed my fear and am now heartily at work."[19]

At work he was, but not to universal satisfaction. He was continually embattled with his parishioners, more often than not involving money. Within his first year at Guercheville, he became engaged in such furious controversy with a creditor, to local scandal, that the Bishop of Meaux felt obliged to transfer him to nearby Jouarre on 20 October 1851. Verger, meanwhile, had lost his financial suit in court. He lasted at Jouarre only until 1 February 1852, when he was transferred to the parish of Bailly-Carrois. By that time he was appealing for assignment in Paris, but in vain since Paris was outside the diocese of Meaux.[20]

Evidently he secured once again the intervention of the marquise de Rochefort, and on 1 November 1852, he was permitted to leave his parish for Paris. The Abbé Legrand, curé of Saint-Germain-l'Auxerrois, agreed to provide for him as a *prêtre habitué*, meaning as an "unbeneficed priest." Thanks to his previous follies, Verger had by then accumulated substantial debt. Legrand advanced him eight hundred francs to clear the indebtedness

17. Fouquier, *Causes célèbres* 1:3; *La Semaine Religieuse* 7(25 January 1857): 98–101; and André Barrault, "Louis Verger (1826–1857): Assassin de Mgr. Sibour," *Bulletin de la Société d'histoire et d'art du diocèse de Meaux* 13(1962):170–71.
18. Barrault, "Louis Verger," p. 171.
19. *La Semaine Religieuse*, 25 January 1857.
20. Barrault, "Louis Verger," p. 171.

and gave him a room in his rectory. The money was to be repaid, probably Legrand's method of disciplining Verger.[21]

For employment, Verger was assigned to be a cross-bearer in the chapel at the Tuileries. Proximity to the great overwhelmed Verger with importance for a time, and he reveled in the expectation of a glittering ecclesiastical career. But as the months passed and he bore his cross more realistically, his disenchantment eroded into bitter resentment against his benefactor (and creditor). He sought Archbishop Sibour's assistance in finding a new post, telling Sibour confidentially that Legrand had been making improper advances. Sibour investigated the charge, of course, and came to the conclusion that it was groundless, which infuriated Verger. Rather understandably, Legrand decided to dismiss him from his assignment in the imperial chapel.[22]

This provoked Verger—in the summer of 1855, three and a half years after his arrival in Paris—to write a libelous letter to Legrand, sending copies of it to a number of people: "From the time I became one of the priests in your parish, I have often complained of your dealings with me. The outrageous propositions that you have made to me since the time of my arrival are at the bottom of our innumerable quarrels. Now that it has become an absolute certainty in my mind that you intend to complete my disgrace, I prefer to go into seclusion and to abstain from any further holy function." [23] Clergymen who knew Legrand called Verger's accusation odious, but that did not necessarily refute the charge. More convincing was Legrand's letter in September to the prefect of police in which he reported the nature of Verger's attack.[24]

Given Verger's penchant for quarrels, one might write off the incident as simply a new weapon in his arsenal for troublemaking were it not for his admitted hostility to clerical celibacy and the dogma of the Immaculate Conception, all of which suggests that behind this distressed personality lay a frustrated, disturbed, or confused sexuality. Although the definition of Immaculate Conception did not preclude sexual intercourse, it has been so misconstrued, more often than not. One would expect a priest to understand its true meaning, particularly one who had been in seminary when the Pope had set in motion the machinery that led to the new dogma. Yet, Verger's allusion to goddesses hardly implies clear perception, and it *may* be that he shared the vulgar notion of Immaculate Conception as a kind of spontane-

21. Alister Kershaw, *Murder in France*, p. 25.

22. René-François-Wladimir Guettée, *Souvenirs d'un prêtre romain devenu prêtre orthodoxe*, pp. 240–42.

23. Fouquier, *Causes célèbres*, 1:3: Barrault, "Louis Verger," p. 172; and Pierre Bouchardon, *L'Assassinat de l'Archevêque*, p. 40.

24. *Gazette des Tribunaux*, 19–20 January 1857.

ous combustion that could render sexual union obsolete. We know nothing, furthermore, of Verger's sexual sophistication or education, except to note that seminarial curricula were not celebrated for their incursions into that realm—beyond the prescription of cold showers.

For the remainder of 1855, Verger was officially unemployed. Unofficially, he was heavily occupied writing letters to ecclesiastical and civil authorities, especially to Archbishop Sibour and to the office of the public prosecutor, and he also expanded his literary efforts to include brochures and tracts. He even wrote to the the Abbé Legrand, threatening him with further scandal if he, Verger, were not reinstated at Saint-Germain-l'Auxerrois with a fixed income of 2,300 francs—a proposal the more striking given his avowed anger over Legrand's "outrageous propositions."

He had become a pamphleteer, a prideful man with a talent for conflict and blackmail, who found himself at war, not simply with the diocese of Paris, but with the regulations and the dogmas of Catholicism.[25] He interrupted his polemical existence for a brief period in November to go on a retreat to Montivilliers in Seine-Inférieure, where he tried to examine his conscience calmly in search of possible fault. The results of this fruitless inquiry were seen in Paris on 3 February 1856, when he appeared in the Church of the Madeleine wearing a small sign in Latin on his chest: "I am cold, and they have not clothed me. I am hungry, and they have not fed me." And then a postscript in French: "I am neither inhibited nor under ban, yet they let me die of hunger." [26]

We would recognize today hints of paranoia in Verger's behavior dating from the time he had become a parish priest and capped by this performance in the Madeleine. Freud originally proposed in 1911 that unconscious homosexual conflicts are at the root of most cases of paranoia.[27] Even though subsequent research has both confirmed and revised the exclusive etiological relation between homosexuality and paranoia,[28] Verger's projection of homosexuality on Legrand certainly suggests either repressed homosexuality or pseudohomosexual anxiety.

The police, already aware of Verger, plucked him from the Madeleine and subjected him to a lengthy medical examination to determine his sanity. He told the examining physician that the young clergy had been oppressed long enough, that it was high time they gained revenge against the

25. Bouchardon, *L'Assassinat*, p. 41.

26. *Gazette des Tribunaux*, 19–20 January 1857; and Fouquier, *Causes célèbres*, 1:4.

27. The view was also stated in his famous Viennese lectures in the winters of 1915–17. See Sigmund Freud, *A General Introduction to Psychoanalysis*, p. 317.

28. Marvin L. Aronson, "A Study of the Freudian Theory of Paranoia by Means of the Rorschach Test"; and Lionel Ovesey, "Pseudohomosexuality, the Paranoid Mechanism, and Paranoia," Reed, Alexander, and Tomkins, eds., *Psychopathology: A Source Book*, pp. 360–86, 388–403.

hierarchy. He made it quite plain that he had not become a priest in order to suffer. Dr. Lasseigne, the examining physician, reported that Verger was sane, but that he was potentially dangerous as a man who believed himself particularly marked for persecution. Consequently, Verger was released, though a policeman was assigned to keep him under surveillance for as long as the diocese deemed it wise. Unwittingly they had released a man who already meditated murder.

During those months of ecclesiastical unemployment in 1855 and 1856, Verger found refuge in the home of Martial Parent du Châtelet. Parent would go to some pains in his pamphlet to prove that Verger had arrived uninvited, had been admitted to the house by the concierge and given an attic room, all while Parent was absent from Paris.[29] If so, his concierge must have been a remarkable deviator from the practices of that suspicious species! In fact, because Parent was a well-known Jansenist, involved in the publication of the anticlerical *L'Observateur Catholique*, who frequented a variety of priests and laymen hostile to the hierarchy, it would seem altogether too remarkable a coincidence for Verger to have found his way into that circle as innocently as Parent would have us believe.[30] In other words, Verger had joined a group given to polemics and ideas of schism, though with no unanimity of opinion.

By December of 1855, aware that Verger was confining himself to his room for extended periods, Parent became alarmed for Verger's state of mind. He found Verger to be without fuel or food, and so began to have Verger fed at his own table morning and night. Parent also wrote to the vicar-general in Meaux, Josse, to inform him of Verger's plight, as it seemed evident that the diocese of Paris would not give him employment; and Verger, after all, had been ordained in Meaux. Parent, noting that Verger was not under ban, described him as an honorable man, learned, intelligent, firm of character, and (that ultimate recommendation) a good writer. All considered, it seemed to Parent that the diocese of Meaux ought to find a place for Verger; he added that if nothing could be done for him, there would be cause for regret, as Verger possessed "an imagination fortified by dire need." Something had to be done at once to prevent serious trouble.[31] At the same moment, Archbishop Sibour, weary of Verger's antics and sensitive to his association with the architects of *l'Observateur Catholique*, was also insisting that the diocese of Meaux face up to its responsibilities and take him home.[32]

29. Martial Parent du Châtelet, *Réponse à quelques malveillants et calomniateurs*, pp. 1–2.
30. Barrault, "Louis Verger," p. 172.
31. Parent, *Réponse*, pp. 2–3.
32. *L'Observateur Catholique* (revue des sciences ecclésiastiques et des faits religieux) began publication in October of 1855.

Parent's appeal to Josse was dated 31 January 1856, several days before Verger's exhibition at the Madeleine. The *instruction* would produce from Verger's papers a document with that precise date on which he had written, "I alone have premeditated, I developed the plan, I struck the blow which has just struck down the Archbishop of Paris." [33] This was approximately eleven months before the actual deed. We cannot know how much Parent knew of Verger's intentions in predicting "serious trouble," but clearly he had reason to urge the diocese of Meaux to assume responsibility for Verger. Josse promised on 5 February to look into the matter, and in March wrote a second letter to Parent assuring him that Verger would soon have a new post in the diocese of Meaux.

On 12 March 1856, Monsignor Allou of Meaux gave Verger the tiny parish of Serris in Seine-et-Marne. Within the next nine months, the period of his tenure, Verger proved to be as incorrigible as ever. No fewer than three incidents required the attention of both civil and ecclesiastical authorities, the most serious being his intervention in a murder trial in Melun. A grocer from Chaumes named Lamy was accused and convicted of poisoning his wife. Medical testimony had been given against the defendant by three local physicians, though the famous Dr. Tardieu of Paris had failed to find any trace of poison. Verger publicly attacked the verdict of the court, arguing that Lamy, well-known as a brutal husband, was convicted because of local prejudice against him. [34] Be that as it may, clerical intervention in a civil affair was a major indiscretion.

Aside from these incidents, Verger seems to have pursued two conflicting courses during his months at Serris: he continued to seek a more comfortable post within the Church, while at the same time promoting religious ideas likely to lead to interdiction. The ambiguity was a further key to his aberrance. He sought in the Church neither service to God nor to mankind, and the salvation foremost in his mind was that of this world. He sought money and position, and emancipation from the poverty of his childhood; but above all he strove to escape from the emotional insecurity or instability rooted in his background. (The *instruction* would expose the sordid suicides of his mother and brother.) [35] That Verger had failed to find solace in the Church became manifest in his radical stances.

In his first parish, he had found himself nearly "inconsolable" away from the community of the seminary. Now in Serris, he pleaded with Bishop Dupanloup of Orléans to "open his arms." "Seven years I have been a priest, and seven years I have been miserable!" He confessed of having ac-

33. Bouchardon, *L'Assassinat*, p. 44.
34. Jean-Louis Verger, *Réflexions impartiales d'un auditeur aux débats de la cour d'assises de Seine-et-Marne, séant à Melun le 15 novembre 1856*, pp. 1–7.
35. *Gazette des Tribunaux*, 5 January 1857.

cumulated a debt of 2,000 francs, and, though only thirty years of age, feared that his usefulness at Serris had come to an end and that his renewed presence in the diocese of Meaux had proved to be "unfruitful." He had detected all around him indiscreet and uncharitable people, and felt he had to get away—to new air, to solitude, to a new group of clerics. Having been Dupanloup's *"enfant à St. Nicolas,"* could he not now become his *"fils à Orléans?"* While he would accept *any* post to to get out of the diocese of Meaux, what he would most like would be to work immediately with Monsignor Dupanloup himself—not, of course, because of the honor of such a position, but because of the "fabulous works that you know how to share with those around you." Secretarial work, research assistance, anything that His Grace might need, and at any hour, day or night was acceptable. In the top margin of the document was penned Dupanloup's response: *Refusé.* [36]

A month later, 12 December 1856, the Bishop of Meaux withdrew Verger from the parish of Serris and put him under ban giving the following reasons: first, for his improper involvement in the criminal case heard in Melun; second, for his sermons against the dogma of the Immaculate Conception; and third, because of an unpublished piece of writing in his possession, his *Testament,* which contained an attack upon ecclesiastical discipline, notably upon clerical celibacy. [37] (He had already been to Belgium in search of a publisher for a brochure based upon his *Testament.*) [38] "We believe," the bishop wrote to Verger, "that you require care in a mental home." [39] Verger's response was to return to Paris.

In the three weeks that remained before Verger plunged his knife into Archbishop Sibour, he made a last grasp for all that had eluded him, through black magic. He called upon Eliphas Lévi (pseudonym of Alphonse-Louis Constant) in search of a rare handbook for magicians attributed falsely to Pope Honorius IV. The evidence for Verger's visit to Constant rests entirely upon Constant's version of it, which did not emerge until 1861; [40] but the bizarre facts of Constant's life strongly suggest that Verger would have been attracted to him. Constant, too, had attended the novitiate of Saint-Nicolas du Chardonnet, entering in 1825. He had studied philosophy in Issy for two years, beginning in 1830, and then had entered the seminary of Saint-Sulpice.

36. Bibliothèque Nationale, Nouvelles Acquisitions françaises #24714, Verger to Dupanloup, 8 November 1856.

37. Barrault, "Louis Verger," p. 172; and Paul Mélot, "L'Assassinat de Mgr. Sibour, archevêque de Paris," *Miroir de l'histoire* 93(September 1957):354.

38. *Gazette des Tribunaux,* 5 January 1857; and Fouquier, *Causes célèbres,* 1:4.

39. Canon L. Crisiani, "L'Assassinat de Mgr. Sibour," *L'Ami du Clergé* 67(5 December 1957):736.

40. In his book, *La Clef des grands mystères.* Also see Raymond Baumgarten, "La Mort de Mgr. Sibour," *La Vie judiciaire* 633(26–31 May 1958):8–9.

Though ordained in 1835, Constant soon found he had little taste for clerical austerity and aspired to be an artist; in addition, a love affair with a Swiss girl, Adèle Allenback, jeopardized his situation. He eventually joined Flora Tristan's circle where he was introduced to socialist and communist theories. In 1839, mired in his personal dilemma, he entered the Benedictine convent of Solesmes. In the library there he fell upon works on mysticism. By then the hierarchy had its eye on him, and when he returned to Paris he was granted only a mediocre teaching position. In secret he began to write a radical work, *La Bible de la liberté*, published early in 1841, which won him eight months in Sainte-Pélagie for "attacks upon private property and upon public and religious morality." During captivity he began to read Swedenborg, the eighteenth-century Swedish visionary and mystic.

By the age of thirty-six (1846), Constant had had two mistresses, one of whom, Noémi Cadiot, six months pregnant, forced him into a civil marriage. The following year his pamphleteering again earned him a brief prison term, during which his wife became known as a writer under the name Claude Vignon. In 1851, she had their marriage annulled. During the Second Empire, Constant remained a quiet socialist, devoting himself primarily to painting and to writing on mysticism. He acquired a following despite the fact that he completely opposed experiments with magic, such as the parlor tricks of Daniel Dunglas Home, and insisted that his disciples concern themselves only with the speculative aspects of occult philosophy. A few minutes with Verger convinced Constant that his interest in black magic was pernicious, and he gave Verger no help.[41]

Archbishop Sibour had been alarmed about the activities of renegade priests and undisciplined clergy in Paris from the outset of his episcopate. On 20 February 1849, he had written about the problem to the clergy within his diocese, emphasizing that he had no authority to assign duties to such priests and certainly not the financial resources to provide them with the permanent assistance for which they often applied. Since such ecclesiastics were usually in a disturbed state of mind, the inevitable poverty in Paris could only heighten their discontent and disillusionment. Henceforth, Sibour concluded, the only "foreign priests" who may reside in Paris are those authorized by their bishops to come to Paris for study and who are supported financially by their home dioceses.[42]

Unhappily for Sibour, this regulation did not wither the problem. In December of 1856, he began preparing a new circular letter on the subject for *all* French bishops, requesting their help in solving the matter. Clergy

41. Paul Chacornac, *Eliphas Lévi, rénovateur de l'occultisme en France (1810–1875)*, pp. 9–20, 31–60, 97–101, 173–75.

42. *Mandements, lettres et instructions pastorales, de Monseigneur Sibour*, 2:n.p.

without positions or livings inevitably landed in Paris, he emphasized, but were not under his supervision. Too often they behaved deplorably, exciting police attention; and in an era when the public was all too ready to believe the worst of clergy and the Church, it was simply impolitic to turn the national capital into a "receptacle" for discarded priests, or a kind of clerical penitentiary. He requested that they please, therefore, direct their problems elsewhere! [43] The circular was dated five days before the assassination.

The officials who conducted the *instruction* after 3 January 1857 had little trouble in reconstructing the crime and Verger's career. They had a confession, a document proving premeditation, the record of prior police surveillance, and considerable correspondence between Verger and his superiors. Consequently, the *instruction* was completed in five days, suggesting that the entire affair would be terminated swiftly. [44] The recommendation for indictment emerging from the *instruction* was then taken to the *Chambre des mises en accusation* on the eighth by the public prosecutor. An indictment for premeditated murder was issued on the ninth and Verger was bound over for trial before the *Cour d'assises* on the seventeenth. Since he wanted to defend himself without counsel, the court had to appoint an attorney for him, Nogent-Saint-Laurens; and Verger was transferred from Mazas to the Conciergerie in preparation for the trial. [45]

Verger was given five days to lodge an appeal against the indictment, but he waited until the last day, the fourteenth, to do so. The *Cour de cassation* reviewed the appeal on the following day and, finding that the proper procedures had been used, rejected it. Consequently, the trial opened on schedule under the presidency of Claude-Alphonse Delangle, a Bonapartist magistrate who had been appointed to the Senate soon after the *coup d'état* of 1851. Exactly two weeks had passed since the assassination. [46]

Having recognized at the outset he had committed a frightful crime, Verger had since been generating confidence until he had become arrogant and seemingly unaware of his mortal danger. He saw in the trial the opportunity to rally public opinion in his favor, seemed ready to tackle the hierarchy on any question of dogma or discipline, and was insulting to anyone who offered him disagreement. "My case shall become a *cause célèbre* and will be long remembered," he insisted, and he became furious when the authorities denied his request to be photographed for public benefit. Far from being repentant, he now regretted not having gone to Rome to strike at the Pope himself. So confident was he of the outcome of the trial that he had not intended to make any appeal against the indictment. Nogent-Saint-

43. Ibid., 2:435.
44. *Gazette des Tribunaux*, 9 January 1857.
45. Ibid., 10, 11, 15 January 1857.
46. Ibid., 16 January 1857.

Laurens had insisted on the maneuver as one means of gaining time to prepare his defense, but it had been a futile gesture.[47]

Most of the seats in the courtroom had been reserved for officials, magistrates, and embassy personnel, and no one could enter without a pass signed by President Delangle. Even so, a large crowd was on hand at the Palais de Justice as early as six o'clock, and hundreds of robed lawyers crowded the staircases in the hope of entry. Verger was brought in shortly after ten, outwardly calm, but frequently licking his lips in nervous expectation.

As soon as President Delangle and his two assistant judges were seated, the public prosecutor stood to read the indictment. It emphasized not merely the premeditation of the actual murder, for which there was documentary evidence; but that Verger had admitted during the *instruction* buying an ax, after Legrand had dismissed him from Saint-Germain-l'Auxerrois in 1855, with the idea of killing both Legrand and Sibour. Moreover, on the day he did kill Archbishop Sibour, Verger had drawn up a will making a brother sole heir, indicating not simply premeditation but recognition of the probable consequences. Verger's violent opposition to ecclesiastical authority and discipline was easily illustrated by quotations from his *Testament*, and the unpleasant details of his attacks upon the Abbé Legrand were fully reviewed. Verger's confession, finally, was cited to show that the murder had not simply been a matter of dogma, but an act of revenge, of personal vengeance against the hierarchy. By his own admission he had written the note of 31 January 1856, revealing his plans to assassinate the archbishop, when he had been "without resources" and in great difficulty.[48]

With the indictment read, the witnesses—eighteen of them—were brought into the courtroom; but before they could be heard, Verger asked for the privilege of making a statement to the jury about the manner in which the *instruction* had been conducted. Granted the floor, he began in the manner of a priest delivering a sermon: "Nineteen centuries ago, a very important message was given to humanity by a man who was more than a man, by Jesus Christ, at once man and God. The message was *pax vobis*, *pax omnibus*, peace to you, peace to mankind. In our own time, another man whom you love, whom you venerate, and whom I love and venerate as you do, has repeated the message by saying, '*l'Empire c'est la paix.*' "[49]

Here the president interrupted this rather too blatant appeal to Bonapartist

47. Fouquier, *Causes célèbres*, 1:6–7.
48. *Gazette des Tribunaux*, 18 January 1857; and Fouquier, *Causes célèbres* 1:7–8. Alister Kershaw, in his book *Murder in France*, previously cited, has a chapter on Verger that he calls "Murder on Principle." Kershaw writes: "Verger could scarcely have been anything but French. Subject to inevitable correction, there is no record of, say, an Englishman murdering for a purely philosophical motive, whereas Verger is by no means unique in France. . . . Of course, in fact Verger's crime did not spring from so rarefied a germ as all that; but he *thought* it did, and there is the significance: *ideas* are a French speciality."
49. Spoken by Louis-Napoleon in Bordeaux, 9 October 1852.

sympathies to ask Verger if he would please get to the point he had been given permission to make. Verger then began to discuss the incriminating documents brought in against him, but as he warmed up to his subject he became increasingly impassioned, seeming to address the audience rather than the court or the jury. There were *other* documents taken from his residence by the judicial authorities, documents that would prove, if they had not been deliberately concealed, that he was the victim of an "abominable intrigue" engineered by the Roman Inquisition. He demanded, therefore, that the state produce those documents that would reveal attempts to get him to renounce his faith and thus to get rid of him as a priest. Rambling on, Verger charged that he had been denied the right to call helpful witnesses, being permitted only one of the sixty he had wanted to summon for the trial. He read a copy of a letter he had just sent to the minister of justice reporting this gross miscarriage of justice, asking him to refer the letter to the emperor—a letter which added the charge that he had been denied the necessary time to prepare his defense.

Once again the president interrupted Verger, this time to explain to the jury the timing of the procedures and the scheduling of the trial, which had been properly done under the law. As for the calling of witnesses, he recommended that Verger consult his attorney about the proper procedures. Nogent-Saint-Laurens was granted several minutes by the court to explain them to his client and to advise him on courtroom behavior in his own interest. But there was no reasoning with Verger, who was determined to pose as the victim of conspiracy, until the president tried to calm his passion by reminding him of the ostensible devotion to peace in his opening statement. Finally the judges withdrew from the courtroom to reconsider all the witnesses Verger wished to call. Well aware that he wanted witnesses who would attack the French clergy rather than witnesses who had something germane to his crime to report, the court inevitably ruled that only relevant witnesses could be called. The list of appropriate witnesses had been agreed upon in advance by the prosecuting and defense attorneys in conference, as was the custom, and that list would stand. At that, Verger's fury redoubled. Screaming that he had been "dreadfully mistreated" at the time of his arrest, he turned to the audience to display two small rips in his coat, and said "I was kicked in the rear. Such an arrest was hardly *moral!*" What *was* dreadful was Verger's behavior in court. He appeared to be totally devoid of humility—an arrogant, insulting, rude, impossible man.[50]

The arresting policeman remarked that such "violence" was only too likely in the hasty attempt to seize an assassin. When the church usher was asked to describe what he had seen, Verger at once contradicted him:

50. *Gazette des Tribunaux,* 18 January 1857; and Fouquier, *Causes célèbres,* 1:8–10.

"When I struck Monseigneur, my back was turned to the altar. I faced the Archbishop, and I was *not*" (as the witness had said) "facing the Holy Virgin or Saint Genevieve. He is a false witness." When the poor woman who rented chairs in the church was called to testify, Verger responded: "Her testimony is of no value. Our Lord Jesus Christ teaches us that we may receive nothing in holy places, and I paid this woman ten centimes to enter the nave. That is simony. I hope that [she] will remember it and that her soul will profit by it."

The curé of Saint-Séverin was called to testify about an insulting letter he had received from Verger after delivering a sermon. The curé related he had inquired into the background of the letter writer and had been told that Verger was a rebel against religious institutions and fought against them, not insanely, but with an evil logic. He had also been told that Verger was—he hesitated to use the phrase—genuine *canaille*. Answered Verger: "I accept that tag until it is proved otherwise. . . . I am the sworn enemy of the present priesthood as Jesus Christ was the sworn enemy of the priests who lived around him. I hate the prelates of today as He hated the Pharisees. I am the enemy of all that is Pharisaical and all that is hypocritical." He then proposed to deliver a recitation of his religious views. When halted by the president, Verger turned again to the gallery to announce he was being denied freedom of speech.

The President: "You are not here to glory in your personal beliefs."

Verger: "I am not boasting—I am full of grief."

The President: "Let us see your grief then."

Verger: "I do reveal it, *Monsieur le Président*, through my energy, with God's strength."

The President: "No, through your humility."

Verger: "No, by my energy."

A whole series of witnesses followed to verify the sorry story of Verger's career. Abbé Millaud from the novitiate of Saint-Nicholas-du-Chardonnet described Dupanloup's early prediction that Verger would dishonor the ecclesiastical profession; a man named Legentil recalled Verger's desire to be married. Verger continually interrupted and insulted the witnesses, and the court repeatedly called him to order. During the Abbé Legrand's testimony, when letters Verger had written to him were read to the jury, Verger became so enraged and abusive that the president put on his hat and suspended the hearing, ordering Verger to be removed from the room. Verger sprang to his feet to appeal to the gallery: "People, defend me!" But many in the gallery, some of them rising, responded with shouts of *Canaille!* or *Assasin!* [51] The hearing was resumed after a fifteen-minute recess.

51. Fouquier, *Causes célèbres*, 1:10–12.

Parent du Châtelet, at whose home Verger had lived, was called simply to identify a letter in Verger's hand. The one witness to put in a good word for Verger was the Abbé Guettée, a friend of Parent. Guettée had long been a critic of the Church, beginning with its pedagogical methods, and one cannot read his memoirs without suspecting he was a professional sorehead. He had written a lengthy history of the Church in France, which was honored by being placed on the Index on 22 January 1852. In the ensuing hassle with the hierarchy, Guettée saw everywhere the evil hand of the Ultramontanes. He became part of that group of Catholics with grievances against the official Church that revolved around the Jansenist Parent du Châtelet, and he would eventually end his priestly career in the Greek Orthodox Church.[52] At Verger's trial, Guettée merely claimed to believe that Verger had been a good priest, and that he had tried in vain to persuade Sibour of that fact. When pressed by the court as to whether he had read Verger's brochure *Le Catholicisme régénéré*, Guettée would not admit having seen it.[53] What he did not tell the court was his opinion that Verger was insane.[54]

After the witnesses had been heard, custom required the public prosecutor to make his statement. He endeavored to do so, but was shouted down by Verger. The president again had to remove him from the room for the remainder of the prosecutor's speech—an action made possible under articles nine and ten of the law of 9 September 1835. Given the circumstances of the case and Verger's behavior in court, the prosecutor's task was not difficult, and he could be brief. The gist of his statement was that Verger was a perverse, ambitious, ferocious individual, vomited up from hell, whose mind had been so perverted by pride, whose existence had become so enmeshed in evil that it could only culminate in crime—a crime he had not merely committed, but had committed with premeditation. He had struck not simply at an individual, but had meant to strike at religion and even at society. "Now he dreams of being celebrated by the people as he goes to the scaffold." The proper response to that aspiration, he concluded, had already been given [by the gallery]: *Assassin!* [55]

Nogent-Saint-Laurens' turn came next. He made it clear at the outset he had undertaken Verger's defense as a professional obligation after his appointment by the court, and that he had no sympathy for his client or for his deed. Yet, the law in a civilized country requires a proper defense. Asked to account for such a dreadful crime, many might answer that such a criminal

---

52. Guettée, *Souvenirs*, pp. 27, 62–70.
53. *Gazette des Tribunaux*, 18 January 1857.
54. Guettée, *Souvenirs*, pp. 244–48.
55. Fouquier, 1:12–13.

would have to be mad; and, indeed, it would be reassuring to society to find that no reasonable man could commit such a crime. The prosecution, on the other hand, had sought to prove premeditation—that Verger had thought through his action and knew what he was doing. The defense was inclined to a third view—that Verger was subject to temporary or occasional insanity—and Nogent appealed to the deepest prejudice of the nineteenth century by asserting that the most dangerous forms of madness are likely to arise from religious passions or ideas. More to the point, he showed that there had been madness in Verger's family. His mother, in a fit of madness, had thrown herself into a well; one of her other children had also drowned by jumping into the Seine; and Dr. Tardieu had described Verger as unbalanced.

Nogent-Saint-Laurens then carefully picked his way through the testimony for hints of madness, and they were not hard to find. In summing up he claimed that if the jurors were inclined to believe there had been madness in the case, then they must conclude that there had been neither comprehension, premeditation, nor will. "Human reason was not stained by this execrable crime. Madness alone must bear the responsibility for it in the centuries to come." [56] In other words, let us not believe that sanity could produce such an act.

As the trial approached its end, President Delangle was required by law to instruct the jury. He first complimented the defense attorney for his professional skill and devotion to professional duty, adding that he agreed it would be good for public morale if this odious crime could be attributed to insanity. Turning to the jury, Delangle said that the jury must *also* consider whether the defense by Nogent-Saint-Laurens—"the only possible defense in the case"—squared with the testimony, including that given by the physician. Or, was the murder the act of a man contemptuous of justice, prideful to a fatal degree, totally lacking respect for his superiors, an enemy of the law and the established order, and a self-appointed reformer of dogma and the clergy, as the prosecutor had claimed? "If you find him mad," Delangle concluded, "then you must acquit. If you believe that he reflected, that he desired the death of the Archbishop, then you have a terrible duty to fulfill." [57] There could be little doubt about Delangle's views of the matter.

Verger awaited the verdict in his cell. The jury was out for a bare twenty minutes, returning with a verdict of guilty on the grounds of willful homicide, that it had been premeditated, and that the victim had been waylaid. Upon the recommendation of the public prosecutor, the court then sentenced Jean-Louis Verger to death and ordered that the verdict be read to

56. Ibid., 1:14–15.
57. Ibid., 1:15.

the accused in his cell. He was visibly shocked and outraged by the verdict, having become convinced that he would be justified. He screamed his hatred of the court officials and ordered them from his cell.[58]

The case had been heard and the verdict rendered within one day, 17 January 1857. After his outburst, Verger fell into deep depression; but on the eighteenth he had recovered his poise. He would not only appeal the verdict to a higher court, but also would petition the emperor for pardon.[59] In his four-page letter to Napoleon III, Verger portrayed himself as the crusader from the lower clergy who would destroy the despotism of the hierarchy—a letter which revealed his pride and his certainty of infallibility. He even recommended to the emperor that the sentence be reduced to "an honorable exile" as the most elegant solution to this miscarriage of justice.[60] And why not? As Verger saw it, the emperor and he were akin. "You wanted to save France, and I wanted to regenerate Christianity. Each of us has made his *coup d'état.*" [61]

On the nineteenth he received a visit from his father. The interview was calm, unemotional, Verger absolutely confident in the emperor's mercy.[62] Even his transfer to La Roquette later that day did not extinguish his optimism, and he insisted that the strait jacket customarily worn by the condemned be removed so he could write. Officials at La Roquette did allow his right hand to be freed, and he wrote incessantly, describing himself as someone who had acomplished a great deed, as the heroic worker who had completed his task.

The *Cour de cassation* took up his appeal on 29 January. Verger was represented by Achille Morin, who skillfully based the appeal, not upon new facts, but upon the haste with which the investigation, trial, and sentencing had been carried through. The whole process, once the *instruction* had been completed, had been accomplished between 9 and 17 January. Could anyone be absolutely certain, with such haste, that the criminal was really a murderer, or was insane? The public prosecutor's representative, however, convinced the court that, despite the short time, everything had been properly done. After a hearing of some three hours, the appeal was rejected.[63]

The emperor, meanwhile, had recognized Verger's emotional instability, yet was subject to public and political pressures to deny clemency. Sibour had been a popular prelate, widely esteemed as charitable and patriotic, and

58. Ibid., 1:15; and Mélot, p. 355.
59. *Gazette des Tribunaux*, 18 January 1857.
60. Mélot, "L'Assassinat," p. 356.
61. Céleste (Mme. Jules) Baroche, *Second Empire: Notes et souvenirs de seize années, 1855–1871*, p. 52; and *Gazette des Tribunaux*, 19–20 January 1857.
62. *Gazette des Tribunaux*, 21 January 1857.
63. Ibid., 30 January 1857.

sympathy was scarce for his assassin. Many of the more sophisticated in society, moreover, would not buy the insanity plea, seeing Verger as a vain and calculating man, eager for power, seeking notoriety, and ready to commit crime to escape from obscurity; they saw him as merely one of the hundreds of such outcasts in Paris who were rebels against all authority, who saw their superiors as tyrants and oppressors, and who were enemies of established society.[64] Even so, the emperor asked Dr. Henri Conneau, his chief physician, to consult a committee of doctors about the medical evidence in the case. The committee report, which reached the emperor on 29 January, the very day the *Cour de cassation* rejected Verger's plea, assured His Majesty that Verger had indeed enjoyed the free exercise of his reason.[65]

Since the political opposition during the Second Empire was wont to see the magistracy as the emperor's supine instrument, the emperor's doubts about the verdict in the Verger case offer evidence to the contrary. In the second place, the reader today, aware that had Verger been tried in our own time, he might have received a less drastic sentence in view of his paranoiac state, might reach the conclusion that the verdict of 1857 was so patently unjust as to be explicable only as a political act of revenge. No doubt there was ample outrage directed against a man who would seem to threaten the established order by assuming his right to assassinate Sibour; but by the legal canons of that day, Verger was sentenced appropriately.

The question of the insanity plea has troubled jurists right down to the moment. What is more, because the issue is a variation of the ancient controversy over whether man has any "free will" at all, opinions about the insanity plea reflect views of the human condition which far transcend the insanity issue alone. Modern psychology, for instance, by emphasizing environmental determinism, has tended to doubt free will. Geneticists emphasize certain inherent and immutable qualities (which the behaviorists prefer to ignore), which would also limit free will.

Jurists, on the other hand, have historically been suspicious of such concepts as condoning antisocial behavior and as being a threat to social order. Therefore, freedom of the will is, and has been, a basic concept of the law; for if moral responsibility is nonexistent, not only will the enforcement of criminal law be undermined, but the social order itself will also be threatened. At the time of Verger's conviction, it was usual for jurists to apply, as President Delangle did, rules we would call M'Naghten (dating from 1843), namely, that to establish a defense on the grounds of insanity, it must be clearly proved that the defendant labored under such a defect of reason as not to understand the nature of his act or not to understand that he was

64. Count Horace de Viel Castel, *Memoirs: A Chronicle of the Principal Events, Political and Social, during the Reign of Napoleon III from 1851 to 1864,* 2:6–7.
65. Fouquier, *Causes célèbres,* 1:16.

doing wrong.[66] Verger *knew* he was murdering Sibour, and he *knew* the likely penalty.

When all routes for appeal had been exhausted, the public prosecutor ordered the prison authorities to proceed with the execution on 30 January. During the night of the twenty-ninth, the guillotine was installed in the place de la Roquette, and the crowd began to gather. Shortly after seven on the morning of the thirtieth, one of the prison chaplains, the Abbé Hugon, whom Verger had previously refused to see, entered the cell to announce that his time had come and that he must take refuge in divine mercy. Verger scoffed. They were toying with him, he insisted, out of curiosity about his reaction; and he knew the emperor would not permit the execution. He would write again to the emperor for confirmation. Hugon gently explained that it would be useless and sought to lead him from the cell, but Verger screamed, "No priests, no relics!"

He had suddenly understood that his execution was imminent. Collapsing on his bed, he said that he would not leave the cell, that they would have to take him by force. By then, the prison officials had come into the room; and someone allowed comte Alfred-Emilien Nieuwerkerke, the Superintendent of Fine Arts, to enter. Unfortunately, Verger recognized him as a personage he had seen at the Tuileries. Nieuwerkerke had no place at La Roquette, as executions were not counted among the fine arts; but he had been curious and had exploited his rank to gain entrance. Poor Verger mistook him for the emperor's emissary and fell on his knees in supplication,[67] whereupon the prison officials fell upon Verger and tried to drag him to an outer chamber where he would be dressed for execution. Crying, shouting, swearing, and bellowing, he was more than a match for them, until they summoned the powerful headsman Heindreicht (officially known as Monsieur de Paris), who customarily awaited his victim outside the cell.

Once in the outer room, Verger calmed down, but it was seen that he had aged ten years in fifteen minutes, his eyes haggard and his features dreadfully contracted—so swift a decomposition that life seemed to abandon him even before he reached the scaffold.[68] The Abbé Hugon was at last able to confess Verger and to grant him absolution, for he now repented both his act and his errors: "I retract and I renounce all the errors, all the calumnies, that I propagated. I offer my life to God in expiation for all the evil I have done." [69] Then, supported on either side, he walked to the scaffold, bab-

66. Sheldon Glueck, *Law and Psychiatry: Cold War or Entente Cordiale*, pp. 5–11, 20.
67. Abbé Georges Moreau, *Souvenirs de la Petite et de la Grande Roquette*, 1:78–80.
68. Viel Castel, *Memoirs*, 2:11–12. and Maxime Du Camp, *Paris: Ses organes, ses fonctions et sa vie dans la second moitié du xix* siècle*, 3:303.
69. "Derniers moments de Verger," *La Semaine Religieuse* 7(8 February 1857):137–39. The full confession was noted by lay as well as by clerical officials present.

bling religious and patriotic words: "Lamb of God, have pity on me, Jesus Mary, my country, France how much I have loved you." Having mounted the stairs, he embraced his confessor as his last act before the blade fell. The scene was enjoyed by a throng of ten thousand.[70]

70. *Gazette des Tribunaux,* 31 January 1857; and Fouquier, *Causes célèbres,* 1:16.

CHAPTER THREE

Felice Orsini's Defenders

Open my heart and you will see
Graved inside of it, 'Italy'.
ROBERT BROWNING

England is not merely the con-
soler of the distressed, but
also the refuge for sinners.
LOUIS XVIII

A YEAR and ten days after the Sibour assassination, Paris was again the setting for murder, this time in the Orsini attempt upon Napoleon III. Once again the emperor would find reasons for pardoning the assassin, but would be overborne by political exigencies. Felice Orsini, born 1819 in Meldola (near Forli), son of an Italian patriot, had been for some years associated with Mazzini's Young Italy movement and was a known revolutionary. By 1856, however, he had become estranged from Mazzini, impatient to act independently, and was residing in London, writing and lecturing about his conspiratorial adventures. His lectures were reaping a substantial income, thus enabling him to finance a plot against the life of the French emperor.

In a sense the emperor was an unlikely target for an Italian nationalist. In his youth, he had enlisted in the Italian cause, participating in the abortive uprising of 1831 in the Papal States, Orsini's own native land. As emperor, he had made clear the Bonapartist sympathy for all nationalities restive to be self-governing, but as yet had done nothing to redeem the pledge to do something for Italy he had made immediately after his election to the presidency in 1848; [1] and French troops had driven the Italian nationalists from Rome in 1849, remaining there to protect Pope Pius IX. Being anticlerical in principle but clerical in practice did have its embarrassments!

The *coup d'état* in 1851 was generally seen by revolutionaries as proof

---

1. N. W. Senior, *Conversations with Distinguished Persons During the Second Empire from 1860–1863*, 2:262.

that Louis-Napoleon had betrayed his earlier sympathies, and they were un-mindful of his earlier caution to them that, as his duties to France came first, he would have to await the opportunity to serve the Italian cause. Moreover, Italian revolutionaries in particular had become aware that na-tionalist revolutions in the nineteenth century had come in the wake of up-heaval in Paris—in 1830 and in 1848. If the French emperor could be assas-sinated, the ensuing political chaos might again become the opportunity for revolutionaries elsewhere. The first attempt upon the emperor's life was made by a Roman named Giovanni Pianori, who had been in Garibaldi's Roman army in 1849. He fired two pistolshots at Napoleon III in the Champs-Elysées on 28 April 1855, for which he lost his head several weeks later.[2]

From Pianori's failure, Orsini saw the advisability of devising a more sophisticated attempt to be carried out by a team of assassins. When lectur-ing in Birmingham, he met a Tuscan named Giuseppe-Andrea Pieri, a refu-gee of some five years, who had been teaching foreign languages in Eng-land; vain, boastful, operatic, but seemingly bold and courageous, he seemed a worthy companion. He next enlisted the aid of Dr. Simon Ber-nard, a sometime French naval surgeon, originally from Carcassonne. A Republican, Dr. Bernard had published the *l'Indépendant des Pyrénées-Orientales* in Perpignan until the excitement of the February Revolution in 1848 had lured him to Paris. This rural busybody became so active in Parisian political clubs that he earned the tag "Bernard *le clubiste*," and his radicalism cost him several jail terms in 1849, after which he settled in Lon-don.[3] Orsini's third recruit was Anthony Gomez, a Neapolitan afflicted with limited intelligence; and the fourth, a Venetian of alleged noble birth, Carlo di Rudio, driven to crime by poverty.

In retrospect, the inadequacy of the team was so glaring as to cast doubt upon Orsini's capacity as a leader. Neither Gomez nor Rudio were commit-ted to the patriotic cause, but had joined Orsini out of their need for money; and neither of them were, nor could have been, entrusted with the full de-tails of the plot. Dr. Bernard, full of zeal for the death of Napoleon III, had not the slightest intention of risking his neck by reentering France, so that the team of five shrank to four upon its departure from Britain.[4] It was to be purely an Italian performance.

An Englishman named Thomas Allsop, a friend of Bernard and evidently sympathetic to any plot to assassinate Napoleon III, helped the team to procure weapons. Orsini had once seen in Brussels some small grenades

2. Charlemagne-Emile de Maupas, *Mémoires sur le second empire*, 2:80.
3. Adrien Dansette, *L'Attentat d'Orsini*, p. 59.
4. *Gazette des Tribunaux*, 26 February 1858; and Pierre de La Gorce, *Histoire du second empire*, 2:212–15.

designed for the art of murder and had had a cabinetmaker devise a wooden model for him. In October of 1857, Dr. Bernard had the susceptible Thomas Allsop write to a Birmingham mechanic named John Taylor, sending him the specifications and an order for six bombs. Taylor, uninformed of their intended use, presumed that they were samples being prepared for the British military.[5] Allsop also gave his British passport to Orsini, who traveled under that unpresumptuous name. When the bombs were delivered, for some reason there were only five of them; but they were deemed adequate for the imperial demise.

Orsini was the first to leave England, sailing for Ostend on 28 November 1857. He carried with him the fulminate of mercury to load the bombshells. He took the precaution of sending the bombshells, partly disassembled to avoid detection, to Brussels with a Swiss café waiter, Joseph Georgi, who was instructed to tell Belgian customs officials he was carrying new devices for the manufacture of gas. In Brussels, Orsini hired a second emissary named Zeghers to carry the bombshells through French customs at Valenciennes with the same ruse, and to deliver them to him at the Hôtel Albion in Paris—for where else would a proper Englishman stay? The bombshells had been divided into two packages, and Zeghers had evidently been so little impressed with the value of his burden that he managed to leave one package in Brussels.

Receiving only the second package, Orsini remained at the Albion only three days, moving on 15 December into a furnished apartment at 10, rue Monthabor. He pretended to the life of an English tourist, taking long walks and riding horseback, while quietly communicating with Dr. Bernard in London. Bernard gave Pieri and Gomez their final instructions on 6 January 1858, and the two sailed for Calais where they landed shortly after midnight, leaving immediately for Lille. Pieri's passport had been altered to convert him into a German (Joseph-Andreas Pierey), and poor Gomez was posing as an English servant named Swiney.

From Lille, Pieri went alone to Brussels in search of the missing package and used the opportunity to call on a former friend, Rosine Hartmann. He could not resist boasting to her about his participation in a great affair that might cost him his life, and soon after, the French minister in Brussels had word of Pieri's presence and telegraphed the Ministry of the Interior of a probable conspiracy to assassinate the emperor. Pieri in the meantime, unaware that he had been detected or betrayed, rejoined Gomez in Lille on the eighth for the trip to Paris. Gomez assumed his role as Orsini's servant, while Pieri took separate quarters in the Hôtel de France et de Champagne, 132, rue Montmartre.

5. Dansette, *L'Attentat*, p. 60.

Carlo di Rudio was the last to leave England, dispatched by Dr. Bernard directly to Paris and traveling as a Portuguese named Da Silva. The team was reunited on 10 January 1858, the same day the Paris police were alerted to be on the watch for Pieri, whose face was known to them because he had been arrested and deported from France in 1852.[6]

The wonder is that Pieri was not promptly located. A municipal policeman who specialized in watching furnished rooms for political refugees was alerted to report anyone arriving from London or Belgium who rented a room on 8 January; and certainly Pieri's alias was transparent. Indeed, confident of his disguise, he made no attempt to hide, taking his meals in the hotel diningroom, lingering in the lobby to read the newspapers. Though the address of Pieri's wife who lived in nearby Montrouge was known, evidently no surveillance was ordered, or Pieri, who visited her briefly three times between the eighth and the fourteenth, would certainly have been spotted. The apparent casualness of the police response to the warning of trouble was probably nothing more than routine inefficiency, but there would be those who would later hint darkly of collusion between some police officials and the conspirators—for surely it is incumbent upon the truly sophisticated to reject the obvious in favor of the labyrinthian explanation of human affairs.

The official gazette, *le Moniteur,* had reported that a gala would be held honoring the retirement of a popular baritone on the evening of 14 January, but with no mention of the imperial couple. They customarily attended the opera two or three times a month, but had not been there for several weeks. Special preparations for their arrival were never begun before six o'clock in the evening. Yet, on the fourteenth, the conspirators either had some prior hint of the imperial couple's intention to attend the gala, or they simply gambled on its probability. Late in the day, Pieri and Rudio reconnoitered the vicinity of the opera, and shortly after six o'clock the four conspirators met in Orsini's room. He divided three hundred francs among them, gave each one a bomb, keeping the two smallest ones himself. It was understood that Gomez was to throw his bomb first; Rudio, second; after which Pieri and Orsini would heave their bombs.

The night of 14 January was unseasonably mild and clear, bringing out an unusual number of promenaders. Early in the evening, the policeman assigned to find Pieri, while strolling near the old opera, saw him standing at the corner of the rue le Peletier and the rue Rossini. As he was being hauled off to the neighborhood police station, Pieri tried to signal Orsini that he had been arrested, but was not understood. The police found Pieri in possession of a bomb, a knife, and a six-shot revolver. Though the police for the

6. *Gazette des Tribunaux,* 26 February 1858; Louis Canler, *Mémoires de Canler, ancien chef du service du sûreté,* p. 438; and La Gorce, *Histoire du second empire,* 2:216–18.

previous six months had been receiving tips of possible assassination attempts by Mazzinian Italians,[7] Pieri's arrest did not provoke serious alarm. Assassination attempts were usually made by individuals, and the arresting officials did not assume that Pieri might have accomplices. No attempt was made to clear the people from the square before the Opera House. Had the prefect of police, Pierre Piétri, been notified of the arrest, he likely would have insisted that the imperial couple remain in the Tuileries; for he, at least, had been uneasy about the hints of trouble and had been urging the emperor not to go to theaters, advice that the empress had been disputing.[8] But Piétri, unaware of events, was dining at the home of a cabinet minister; while Hyrvoix, the officer charged with the emperor's personal security, was at home ill.[9]

In those days the opera faced the rue le Peletier, just north of the boulevard des Italiens, thus a few blocks east of the present opera. As was the custom in most Parisian theaters, a special entrance was provided near the main door for distinguished guests. A private staircase led up to a salon, beyond which was the imperial box. To its right was another box reserved for members of the imperial household, while on the left a stagebox was provided for the imperial guests who might wish to view backstage activity between acts. Upon their arrival, the imperial couple would be met at the door by the first chamberlain, then Félix Bacciochi, and by the director of the opera, Albert Royer, who would light their way up the stairs with a candelabra. On the night of 14 January, since the program honored the baritone Massol, who was retiring after thirty years on the stage, some of the leading French singers and dancers were participating, and tickets had been much in demand.

The imperial procession approached the Opera House escorted by thirty men of the Garde de Paris, the force we call today the Garde Républicaine.[10] Outside the opera the street was lined with policemen, the normal precaution; but there were no security agents mingling with the crowd, which would have been the case if the chief of the *Sûreté* had been informed of Pieri's arrest.[11] The explosions, three of them at approximately ten-second intervals, began as the procession slowed for the halt. Gomez and Rudio, in other words, performed as planned. Orsini, wounded by a fragment from his own first bomb, fled bleeding from the scene, in his haste

7. *Gazette des Tribunaux*, 17 January 1858.

8. *Gazette des Tribunaux*, 26 February 1858; Blanchard Jerrold, *The Life of Napoleon III*, 4:164; Dansette, *L'Attentat*, p. 71; La Gorce, *Histoire du second empire*, 2:218–21; and Canler, *Memoirs*, 438–44.

9. Dansette, *L'Attentat*, p. 13.

10. François Cudet, *Histoire des corps de troupe qui ont été spécialement chargés de service de la ville de Paris depuis son origine jusqu'à nos jours*, p. 106.

11. Canler, *Memoirs*, p. 441.

dropping the remaining bomb and his revolver, both of which were quickly seized by police. Despite the case that would be made for him at his trial as the patriotic hero with vast conspiratorial experience, when the chips were down Orsini had proved to be an amateur at best—and in truth, a flop.

The door of the imperial carriage had been dented in fifty places with occasional holes, but the emperor received nothing more than a scratch on the end of his nose, the empress a glass splinter on the inner corner of her left eye. General Roguet, riding with them, found that his overcoat had been pierced, but he was untouched save for a bad cut on his jaw. In the confusion, which was greatly increased because the explosions had extinguished the gas lights on the square, the party was helped to descend from the carriage. Although frantic attendants tried to rush them indoors, the imperial couple refused to leave the scene until they were assured that the wounded were receiving attention, for the wounded were lying on all sides.[12]

The explosions had been heard inside the opera toward the end of the first number on the program, a selection from Rossini's *William Tell*. Almost at once a *commissaire de police* appeared to ask all physicians in the house for assistance, and the remainder of the audience waited in apprehension. When the imperial couple finally appeared in their box, the audience exploded in cheers and applause.[13] The empress seemed especially composed and said later that, though she had been upset, she would have expected to have been more frightened than was the case.[14]

In the meantime, the neighborhood *commissaire de police* sent word of the incident to the principal police authorities. It happened that Lagrange was attending the gala, and he mobilized his agents to search the buildings adjacent to the opera. Piétri, his dinner interrupted, presented himself at the imperial box shortly after nine o'clock. Said the emperor, his usual phlegm absent for the moment, "Well, Monsieur Piétri, of what use are the police?" And Piétri, equally irritated and aware of the casualties outside, replied, "Sire, they serve by getting themselves killed for Your Majesty."[15] As yet, in fact, none of the wounded had died. They numbered 156: many of them simple bystanders, but including 31 policemen and 11 of the Gardes de Paris. Two of the wounded would die on the following day, and six more on succeeding days.[16]

In less than an hour, Piétri returned to the imperial box to report that some progress was at last being made. For one thing, Pieri, who had not been thoroughly questioned immediately, now received intense attention

12. Esprit-Victor de Castellane, *Journal du maréchal de Castellane*, 5:200–1.
13. J. M. Thompson, *Louis-Napoleon and the Second Empire*, p. 177; and E. A. Vizetelly, *Court Life of the Second French Empire*, pp. 112–14.
14. *Lettres familières de l'impératrice Eugénie*, 1:149.
15. Alfred Darimon, *Histoire d'un parti: Les cinq sous l'empire* p. 144.
16. Dansette, *L'Attentat*, p. 18.

from the police. Shown that the bomb in his possession at the time of his arrest was quite similar to the one found abandoned on the street, Pieri revealed his hotel address in the rue Montmartre, saying he shared it with another individual. The police went to the room at once to find "Da Silva" in bed, fully dressed. He soon admitted to being Rudio.

Anthony Gomez, meanwhile, his feeble rapport with reality unable to cope with the confusion following the blasts, had not returned to Orsini's apartment, but had sought refuge in the nearby Broggi Restaurant, where his accent and agitated behavior immediately attracted attention. Interrogated by agents searching the buildings, he pleaded that he was simply the servant of Mr. Thomas Allsop of 10, rue Monthabor. There the police found the wounded Orsini, who had taken to his bed.[17]

THE OFFICIAL REACTION

Orsini's attempt may have ended in fiasco, but it inaugurated several of the most peculiar months in the history of the Second Empire, and culminated in the assassins' trial. Historians have commented on the extremism of the official reaction to the Orsini attempt; but it has not been emphasized that all the contradictions, all the principles, all the tensions Bonapartism encompassed were churned to the surface in the aftermath. Public outrage, moreover, was quite genuine, and officeholders had been horrified by their brush with unemployment. As it became only too apparent that the Orsini attempt had failed through no fault of the police, that the police had been undeservedly lucky in capturing the four suspects so quickly, public apprehensions mounted.

Several days after the attempt, the emperor had to speak at the opening of the parliamentary session of 1858. "If I live," he said, "the Empire lives with me, and if I succumb, the Empire would in fact be strengthened by my death, as the indignation of the people and the army would become a new support for my son's throne."[18] However necessary the words may have been, no one, including the emperor, entertained any such optimism; and no one had been more shocked than he. On the night of 14 January, after His Majesty had received the official world which called at the Tuileries to offer congratulations on his escape, and after the household had settled down for the night, the emperor had gone to the Prince Imperial's bedroom, knelt beside the crib of the heir who was not yet two years old, and wept bitterly. The English nurse, Miss Shaw, who slept in the room, witnessed the scene.[19]

---

17. *Gazette des Tribunaux*, 16 and 26 January 1858; and La Gorce, *Histoire du second empire*, 2:221–24.
18. *Oeuvres de Napoléon III*, 5:58–59.
19. Jerrold, *Life of Napoleon III*, 4:155.

It was a moment of truth for Napoleon III. He had established a dicta-torship in 1851 and had been thereafter surrounded by officials primarily au-thoritarian in sentiment. Unlike them, however, he believed that the em-pire, to survive, must ultimately promote the libertarianism of the French Revolution, and he said so quite clearly that day in January in opening Par-liament: "What is the Empire? Is it a reactionary regime, an enemy of enlightenment, trying to obstruct the good and the civilizing things that the great principles of '89 can do in this world? No, for the Empire has inscribed those principles at the beginning of its constitution."

He added, on the other hand, that the empire must be strong enough to defeat those obstacles placed in its way. "I welcome enthusiastically, and without second thoughts about their antecedents, all those who accept the national will. But as for trouble-makers and organizers of plots, let them clearly understand that their time is past!" [20] Long since, the emperor had indicated that his dictatorship could not be relaxed until the danger from conspirators at home and abroad had been checked. [21] Even though the French government had no proof that Orsini's plot had been part of a vaster conspiracy involving French Republicans, it was a fact that refugee radicals of various nationalities had gathered together after 1848 in sanctuaries like England and Switzerland, and reports of their effective cooperation had been exaggerated into a red specter.

The Orsini *instruction* revealed that not only had the assassins been Italian, whose cause had always aroused the emperor's sympathy, but that they had come to France from Britain, and that their grenades had been manufactured in Britain—the very country whose friendship was the key-stone of the emperor's foreign policy. The outburst of Anglophobia within the French government and press, as a result of the Orsini attempt, gave the emperor little choice but to take an official hard line. But privately he sought to undermine his own official policies to protect his long-term sym-pathies and goals, a governing technique confusing not only to his contem-poraries, but thereafter also to historians sifting official records.

In explaining the emperor's decision to give way to pressure and adopt uncongenial measures, it needs to be added that the Orsini attempt was re-ally a last straw. For Anglophobia was hardly new to France, and the Cri-mean alliance had been something less than popular. Russian diplomacy, having worked patiently for a revision of the Treaty of Paris, took immediate steps to fan anti-British sentiments in France. Claiming the Orsini attempt to be part of a much larger conspiracy against the social order, the Russians assured Napoleon III of support for whatever measures he deemed necessary

20. *Oeuvres de Napoléon III*, 5:56–58; and *Gazette des Tribunaux*, 18–19 January 1858.
21. Howard C. Payne, *The Police State of Louis Napoleon Bonaparte, 1851–1860*, p. 157.

to meet the threat,[22] thus providing French officialdom with alternatives to the emperor's British alliance.

On the home front, Napoleon's conservative ministers had been arguing for stronger measures against political opposition ever since the national elections of 1857 had returned five Republicans to the *Corps législatif*. Although two of them had resigned their seats rather than take the oath to uphold the constitution, the remaining three took the oath, albeit with ostentatious reluctance—an illustration of the potential disloyalty of the opposition. Though the emperor preferred reforms to repression, he also presided over a regime founded upon popular sovereignty, which made him susceptible to public opinion.[23]

The presence of French political refugees in Britain had been, from the French point of view at least, an unresolved issue since the beginning of the Second Empire. Given the Orsini attempt, Napoleon III asked the British if they would henceforth deport refugees intriguing against him. This would be, the answer came back, condemnation without a trial, and no government would dare propose such a thing to parliament. On the other hand, Palmerston was anxious to preserve the French alliance and promised he would devise a legal alternative. Meanwhile, the uproar in France forced the government to consider openly breaking Anglo-French relations, which Napoleon III counterbalanced with a personal letter on 17 January to Queen Victoria: "In the excitement of the moment," he wrote, "the French want to see accomplices in the crime everywhere, and I am having difficulty resisting the extreme measures being urged upon me. But this incident will not deflect me from my usual moderation; and while trying to strengthen my government, I do not wish to be guilty of any injustice." [24]

Palmerston's foreign secretary, the Earl of Clarendon, believed that the emperor did regret the outburst, and that he would check it as best he could to maintain the alliance. Any other French government might well have been driven to an invasion of Britain (especially in view of Britain's military embarrassment over the Sepoy Mutiny in India), but Clarendon was confident in the emperor's good will and political acumen.[25] In this spirit, at least one historian has had the shrewdness to suggest that the emperor's ultimate decision to allow his ministers to introduce a stringent security law at

22. Charles-Auguste Morny, *Un Ambassade en Russie, 1856*, pp. 209–10.

23. T. A. B. Corley, *Democratic Despot*, p. 193; and Dansette, *L'Attentat*, pp. 78–81.

24. Sir Theodore Martin, *Life of the Prince Consort*, 4:155; and La Gorce, *Histoire du second empire*, 2:242.

25. Charles C. F. Greville, *The Greville Memoirs*, pt. 3, *A Journal of the Reign of Queen Victoria from 1852 to 1860*, 2:158. Also see H. Hearder, "Napoleon III's Threat to Break Off Diplomatic Relations with England during the Crisis over the Orsini Attempt in 1858," *English Historical Review* 72(July 1957):474–81.

home reflected his intention to reduce pressure on both London and Turin.[26] That is, he thereby emphasized the collaboration of the domestic opposition with the assassins in order to play down the alleged delinquencies of the British and Sardinian governments.

He had also, to illustrate the point, asked the Sardinians to control refugees, saying that otherwise he might be driven to an understanding with Austria. Prime Minister Cavour, understanding the necessity for the bluff, assisted his king in drafting the proper response: "One does not treat a faithful ally so. I have never tolerated compulsion from anyone; my path is of untarnished honor, and I hold myself responsible to none but God and my people." A delighted Napoleon III told the Sardinian minister that he had liked the answer and to assure his king "that in case of war with Austria I will come and fight beside my faithful ally, and tell Cavour to get into direct touch with me; we shall certainly understand one another." [27] The grounds for their midsummer meeting at Plombières had been laid.

The official bluster having been undercut by these personal assurances, the emperor moved to turn the crisis inward at the expense of the Republican opposition. By decree of 27 January, the country was divided into five large military regions, each under the command of a marshal, to promote the surveillance of radical elements in the population. On 1 February, a General Security Law, prepared in the *Conseil d'état,* was sent to the *Corps législatif.* A week later, even though the law had yet to be voted, the minister of the interior, the moderate Auguste Billault, paid the price for police negligence in the Orsini affair and was replaced by the authoritarian General Charles Espinasse. Pierre Piétri was not replaced at the Prefecture of Police even though his left-wing sympathies irked the authoritarian Bonapartists presumably then in the saddle. The inconsistency was no mere oversight, as we shall see.

General Espinasse, who took the titles Minister of the Interior *and* of General Security, began his crackdown even before the General Security Law became active on 27 February 1858. Under this law, anyone who had been either interned, expelled, or transported for political activity in May–June of 1848, in June of 1849, or in December of 1851, became immediately liable for a renewal of sentence. For those without previous criminal records, the new law provided that anyone who "has undertaken activities or correspondence with the intention of troubling the public peace or inciting hatred or mistrust of the Emperor's government" was liable to prosecution. Though the law had been a response to popular and official clamor, its

---

26. Thompson, *Louis-Napoleon,* p. 177.
27. Corley, *Democratic Despot,* pp. 194–96.

Napoleon III, "The Vulture" (villainy, ferocity). From
La Ménagerie impériale

harshness—and especially Espinasse's ruthless application of it—soon
aroused widespread disapproval, both in and out of the government.[28]

Because of the destruction of police records in 1871, it is impossible to
know accurately how many people were arrested under the General Security
Law, though the estimate is about two thousand. It is reliably known, however, that 428 people were transported to Algeria under that law, most of
them people who had been condemned at the time of the *coup d'état* of
1851. General Espinasse was continually irritated by attempts from above to
restrain him and resigned office in June after a tenure of four months. His
successor, the magistrate Delangle, dropped General Security from his min-
isterial title. Nearly half of those transported in 1858 were back in France
before the general amnesty of August 1859. Thus, though the General Security Law remained on the books for its original term of seven years, it fell
into disuse after its first spring—the last gasp of the spirit of 1851. By 1859,

28. Vincent Wright, "La Loi de sûreté générale de 1858," *Revue d'histoire moderne et contemporaine* 16(July–September 1969):415–20; and Payne, *The Police State*, pp. 275–77.

the government would be moving not simply toward amnesty and a more liberal climate, but toward armed assistance for Italian nationalism.[29]

Meanwhile, Palmerston had lived up to his promise by introducing a Conspiracy Bill on 20 February 1858. Moderate in tone and preserving the right of asylum, the bill would have defined conspiracy to murder as a felony. Ordinarily, such a bill would have passed without much question, but this bill was compromised by its proximity to the General Security Law in France. Reacting to the wave of Anglophobia in France, the Opposition was able to defeat the bill and turn Palmerson out.[30] And who within Palmerston's own party took the lead in joining the Opposition on the issue but Alexander William Kinglake—the rejected suitor of yesteryear, who had an abiding hatred of Louis-Napoleon. Even the rejection of the bill, however, did not lead to the rupture of Anglo-French relations, making it even clearer that for the emperor the post–Orsini extremism had been a calculated expedient rather than a matter of principle. What is more, during the preparations to prosecute Dr. Bernard and the Orsini foursome, French and British police cooperated secretly as if no genuine crisis existed.[31]

THE TRIAL

Meanwhile, the *instruction* had been proceeding, if in an unedifying manner. Gomez had been trying to save himself by insisting that he had been nothing more than Orsini's domestic, that he had done nothing more than obey orders. Rudio pleaded poverty as his motive, saying he had had no political interest in the attempt, in fact, no political interest at all. Pieri, when asked precise questions, came on with lengthy outbursts, mostly lies of indecent transparence delivered with superb theatricality. Orsini, increasingly outraged by his colleagues' deviousness and want of Italian patriotism, finally denounced them all and feigned ignorance of them. On the other hand, he had not been entirely ingenuous himself. For a time, while admitting complicity in the attempt, he denied having thrown a grenade, gradually changing his story until he offered himself as the lone conspirator and assassin.[32] The marquis Villamarina, Piedmontese minister in Paris, who followed the proceedings closely for the benefit of Cavour, saw Gomez and Rudio as common knaves, Pieri as a skillful thief, and Orsini as a mediocre conspirator who had assumed the airs of a great political figure.[33] Perhaps only an Italian, experienced in opera, could have seen so clearly.

Recognizing the likelihood of an indictment, Orsini sought an attorney.

29. Payne, *The Police State* pp. 278–79.
30. F. A. Wellesley, *Secrets of the Second Empire*, pp. 151–61.
31. Payne, *The Police State*, p. 275.
32. *Gazette des Tribunaux*, 27 February 1858; and La Gorce, *Histoire du second empire*, 2:238–39.
33. Dansette, *L'Attentat*, p. 142.

He evidently saw the necessity of a *political*, rather than a criminal, defense from the outset and initially considered engaging Emile Ollivier, one of the three Republicans who had taken a seat in the *Corps législatif* in 1857—and the only one of those three who was an attorney. For reasons unknown, Orsini opted instead for Jules Favre, whose reputation as a political lawyer had increased markedly after the *coup d'état* of 1851. It may be Orsini was aware that Favre had been an effective defense lawyer for Lieutenant Aladenize in 1840, but it seems more likely he would have been aware that Favre had supported the cause of the Roman Republic in the Legislative Assembly in 1849. "I ask you," he wrote to Favre on 21 January 1858, "to be my defender in the political cause which is soon to become agitated and in which I find myself involved." [34]

Favre did not immediately accept, and while he hesitated, a letter arrived from Pieri asking him to take his defense. The upshot was that Favre accepted only Orsini's defense on 11 February, concluding that he could conduct a proper defense for only one man. He saw in the case the true *cause célèbre* that could give him, at age forty-nine, political thrust as a great defender of liberty. [35] Giuseppe Pieri then turned to Emile Ollivier; [36] but Ollivier, if tempted to plead the cause of liberty with the General Security Law as his backdrop, failed to reach an agreement with Pieri, who wanted his defense based upon an attack on Orsini. [37] In the end, the court had to appoint attorneys for the remaining defendants: Nogent-Saint-Laurens, who had had the doubtful pleasure of defending Verger the previous year, for Pieri; Nicolet for Gomez; and Mathieu for Rudio.

Favre was at once flooded with letters from Orsini's friends in London recommending modes of defense. A number of them merely urged that Orsini be instructed to lie about his presence in Paris. He was to say he had been there on personal business, and that the grenades had been thrown by individuals not yet caught by the police. Given the sensational, and still mysterious, nature of the ultimate line of defense in the trial, one letter stands out. Its writer urged Orsini to deny any knowledge of a plot to execute Napoleon III. Orsini should be portrayed as part of a far larger conspiracy to deliver Italy from foreign domination (including Pius IX). Since France was imposing the pope upon the Italians with bayonets, "we are," he concluded, "in a state of open warfare with France, and this state of war has been created by the oppressors and not by the oppressed." [38]

34. Alberto M. Ghisalberti, *Lettere di Felice Orsini*, p. 252; and Dansette, *L'Attentat*, p. 128.
35. Maurice Reclus, *Jules Favre, 1809–1880*, pp. 204–5.
36. Ghisalberti, *Lettere*, p. 253. Pieri's letter was dated 17 February 1858.
37. Theodore Zeldin, *Emile Ollivier and the Liberal Empire of Napoleon III*, p. 55.
38. Reclus, *Jules Favre*, pp. 206–7.

The four prisoners were officially notified on 13 February that an indictment had been obtained, and that they had been bound over for trial. Accordingly, they were transferred from Mazas to the Conciergerie to await trial.[39] A curious feature of the indictment was its charge of parricide. On the night of 14 January, 156 people had been wounded, 8 of whom had subsequently died. Moreover, Dr. Tardieu, having examined all the wounded, had told the judicial authorities that some of the wounded would be permanently afflicted. Even so, the four defendants (and the fugitive Dr. Simon Bernard) were simply charged with an attempt upon the life of Napoleon III.[40]

The trial opened on 25 February under the presidency of the Bonapartist Claude-Alphonse Delangle before a packed house, the same Delangle who had presided at the Verger trial. First came the indictment, a lengthy review of the details of the crime and its investigation, including a survey of Orsini's prior revolutionary activities dating from 1845. One may judge the tone of the indictment by its remark that "the atrocious nature of the crime suggested that its authors had been men exulting in the savagery of demagogues who are in revolt against all laws; and the investigation has confirmed that prediction." [41]

After the indictment had been read, President Delangle exercised his right to question the defendants further; and he was at pains to give Orsini, who had changed his version of events repeatedly during the *instruction*, the opportunity to settle finally on one story. Dressed impeccably in black, including black gloves, his jet-black hair whitening at the temples, Orsini appeared as the graceful Italian of charming manner, half priest, half condottiere—to the intense pleasure of that portion of the gallery present for reasons other than a passion for justice—wearing his crime proudly, a murderer for patriotism. "I freely admit," he said, "that I considered [Napoleon III] to be an obstacle. And I said to myself: He must be removed. I acted as Brutus did. He killed my country; I decided to kill him." [42]

One would think that the public prosecutor's task in such a trial would not have been difficult, despite the anticipated eloquence of the defense attorney or the breathless partisanship of the aristocratic geese in the gallery. In fact, the public prosecutor, Charles Chaix-d'Est-Ange, was new to his post and inexperienced in that role, though in his fifty-eighth year. He had been a member of the bar since the Restoration and, though not a man of attractive appearance, had early won a reputation for his elegant and intel-

39. *Gazette des Tribunaux*, 14 February 1858.
40. F. Tennyson Jesse, *Murder and its Motives*, p. 196.
41. Gustave-Louis-Adolphe-Victor-Charles Chaix-d'Est-Ange, *Discours et plaidoyers*, 1:404–27.
42. *Gazette des Tribunaux*, 26 February 1858; and Taxile Delord, *Histoire du second empire*, 2:354–55.

lectual eloquence as a fine courtroom lawyer, especially when defending criminal cases. His decision to accept appointment to the magistracy in 1857 came as a shock to the legal profession, partly because French lawyers prepared either for the magistracy or for private practice and rarely passed from one realm to the other; partly because most courtroom attorneys were hostile to the Second Empire. His appointment was seen as the defection of an Orleanist to the imperial regime. His first performance as public prosecutor was awaited by his former colleagues with a malevolent curiosity.[43]

He took the floor on the second day of the trial, launching into a detailed review of the case, too detailed for an audience already familiar with it. Worse, his speech was larded with official platitudes that could only bore and that called attention to his recent apostasy. Even his appearance, never prepossessing, became a topic of malicious comment: he had no style or taste, his head moved ceaselessly, his mouth hung open, he had simian eyes, he seemed to be petty and spiteful and always on guard, and resembled no one so much as Louis XI.[44]

So prejudiced were his listeners in the gallery against him, so concerned were they to see him as a mediocre windbag, that some of his telling observations were quite overlooked. As to the motives of the would-be assassins, he said to the jury: "You will be told that this conspiracy was inspired by love of country. *Love of country* is an expression favored by all ambitious men. Did love of country motivate Pieri? You know what Pieri said: He hoped that his personal situation would improve! Love of country in Rudio? He held out his hand and took blood money! Love of country in Gomez? He, too, held out his hand and said 'give me money.' Love of country in Orsini? Ah, you cannot allow such a plea."

"It is true that in Antiquity, some barbarous sects appealed to assassination in the name of patriotism"; but since that time, the doctrine of justifiable assassination has become universally disapproved for the reason that there can be no society if the state is the scene of perpetual bloody conflict, if every citizen has the right to be executioner. "Would we not then come necessarily to a point," he concluded, "where even the common murderer, who slips into a room and cuts a woman's throat in order to rob her, could then say that, 'If I committed a murder, it was because society was faulty in construction?' "[45]

When Chaix-d'Est-Ange had concluded, the court recessed for twenty

43. Pierre Jacomet, *Avocats républicains du second empire: Jules Favre—Léon Gambetta*, p. 47; and Dansette, *L'Attentat*, pp. 126–27.

44. Anatole Claveau, *Souvenirs politiques et parlementaires d'un témoin*, 1:19; and Félix Platel, *Portraits d'Ignotus*, p. 422.

45. Chaix-d'Est-Ange, *Discours*, 1:439–60; and *Gazette des Tribunaux*, 27 February 1858.

minutes, after which it was Jules Favre's turn for the defense. Favre was reputed not to be Chaix-d'Est-Ange's intellectual equal, but he was a man of imposing appearance which could command attention and admiration. Without doubt he was a fine speaker and a virtuoso performer, so that his professional talents were esteemed. Doubt about his integrity, however, was the shadow over his career. Fellow Republicans had not forgotten his political equivocation in 1848. Though he may well have had a genuine compassion for the oppressed, there remained a suspicion within his profession that, being preoccupied with form, he too often took cases that offered opportunity for great speeches without any personal concern for the legal questions at stake or the outcome of the trial. During a trial, moreover, as Chaix-d'Est-Ange would soon experience, Favre had a penchant for needling his adversary with sarcasm or a snide remark, earning him, in legal circles, the title Maître Aspic. A man admired, in other words, but not much loved or trusted.[46]

Favre's speech for Orsini's defense may well have been the greatest of his career; but its length, which may seem extreme by American standards, conformed to the courtroom custom in nineteenth-century France, and it has remained a supreme example of the political use of the courtroom in that era. He opened his speech with an extended preface entirely political in character: [47] "I should like for a moment to ignore the distressing emotions that have besieged and dominated my mind in order to render sincere public homage to the ability of the eminent speaker [Chaix-d'Est-Ange] you have just heard. He graced our ranks for a long time. His absence is regretted, and his place remains vacant. He brings a great reputation to the demanding functions he has assumed, his prestige lending singular authority to his words. Yet, gentlemen of the jury, if he finds a stumbling block in this trial, it will lie in the fact that, in this dismal debate, he is without any obstacle, without a real adversary.

"Indeed, gentlemen of the jury, he did not need to make his eloquent appeal to our compassion or his fervent appeal for respect for human life to get us to be as horrified as he is by the recital of this bloody tragedy in which so many victims fell wounded. Who among us has *not* shuddered over the description of this new hecatomb offered to political fanaticism? Even before entering this room, *all* of us were ready to lament the fate of our country—too often vulnerable to the recurrence of such crimes.

46. Charles Limet, *Un Vétéran du barreau parisien, quatre-vingts ans de souvenirs, 1827–1907*, p. 225; and Claveau, *Souvenirs*, 1:61–62.
47. It was noted by Claude Gével in 1934 that the text of Favre's speech in his published works differs in some respects from contemporary newspaper accounts. It seems likely that the discrepancies were the work of Mme. Favre, who edited his works after his death in 1880 to commemorate and defend his legal and political career. Therefore, I follow Taxile Delord's verbatim account, as Delord was a journalist sympathetic to Favre.

Jules Favre. From *The Graphic*, 24 September 1870 (courtesy of The New York Public Library, Astor, Lenox and
Tilden Foundations)

"Certainly, different views on a variety of subjects *can* be found in this
room: As for me, if the Public Prosecutor will permit me to say so, I am far
from bowing to all his principles, to all his actions, or to all the men he
upholds. Yes, gentlemen of the jury, despite the times in which we live,
which prevents free expression of my thoughts, I guard them jealously in the
depths of my heart, that sacred storehouse of my beliefs and sentiments.[48]
But neither sword nor dagger has ever been their servant. I am among those
who detest violence, who condemn the use of force in any situation other
than the upholding of the law. I believe that a nation is regenerated by
moral principles and not by blood. If [a nation] has been unfortunate
enough to fall under the yoke of a despot, an assassin's steel will not sever
the chains. Governments perish through their own mistakes, and God, who
numbers their hours among the secrets of His wisdom, knows how to pre-

48. Favre here refers to his republicanism. In that decade, whether or not to take the oath to
support the Empire in order to take one's seat in the *Corps législatif* was a hot issue in
Republican ranks, though not yet personally faced by Favre.

pare unforeseen disasters for those who ignore His eternal laws, catastrophes even more terrible than the explosion of a deadly device invented by conspirators." [49]

Favre next focused upon his client's cause, though hardly eschewing politics: "When Orsini called upon me, I did not rebuff him, though I felt the weight of this dreadful task; and I was aware of the magnitude of his endeavor and his vanity. I was haunted by the visions of those lamented ghosts. At the same time, I surmised that so great a crime could have had neither envy, hatred, nor ambition as a motive. The motive for such a deed had to be the aberration of an ardent patriotism, a feverish aspiration for the independence of his fatherland—the dream of all lofty souls. I said to Orsini, 'I condemn your crime, and I shall say it openly. But your woes touch me; your perseverence in fighting your country's enemies, this desperate struggle you have undertaken, this sacrifice of your life, all these I understand and feel in my heart.

" 'Italian, could *I* have but suffered for my country as you have, to offer myself in a holocaust, to spill my blood for liberty, everything except these murders which my conscience rejects. But you confess your crime; you are going to expiate it; you are going to give your head to the law which you violated; you are ready to die to pay the penalty for your attempt upon the life of another. Very well, I shall help you in this supreme moment, not by presenting a useless defense, not by glorifying you; but by endeavoring to see to it that a ray of the truth, which alone will protect your memory from unwarranted charges, will shine upon your immortal soul—soon to return to God's care.'

"Therefore, I am here, gentlemen, not to make excuses, but to explain the criminal temptation this unfortunate man was unable to resist. It does not belong to me—nor have I the liberty—to do history's work in your presence, to seek out the reasons why our country has so frequently witnessed such acts [of violence]. But in this solemn hour, when society is about to take its vengeance, may I be allowed a few moments to extend my feeble hand to the unfortunate Orsini's head and to examine with you the self-interest and the motive for the act for which expiation is demanded—in the hope that some part of the feelings which have smitten my heart will be felt in yours.

"The Public Prosecutor is mistaken. Orsini's crime was not dictated by envy, nor by hatred or ambition. Nor by sowing death and destruction around him did he mean to achieve power. He had no wish to rise to power on bloody steps. Whose story is that? Mister Prosecuting Attorney, for it is

49. If one accepts Jules Favre's prescription here, it must then follow—given his own wretched political end—that God also prepares disasters for self-righteous windbags, something unforeseen by Favre.

not Orsini's.[50] What did he want? To free his country—he tells us that. Accuse him of madness, but do not doubt the honesty of his statement, as his whole life stands as its guarantee. I do not know of a more rigorous logic. He has given his life entirely to an energetic and ceaseless struggle against the foreigners who tread upon his country. He could not be otherwise, gentlemen of the jury, as hatred of the foreigner was imbibed in his infancy from his mother's milk, from his father's blood."

At this point, Favre launched into a detailed and lavender recitation of Orsini's long participation in the Italian nationalist movement, pausing to remind the jury that the independence and unity of Italy had also been the goal of Napoleon I. He noted that in 1849 Orsini had been elected to the Roman Constituent Assembly, "born of universal suffrage like our own institutions at that moment," an assembly "dispersed by French guns." Thereafter, Orsini had gone about Italy "organizing resistance and whipping up hopes." Arrested once in Switzerland and later in Vienna, Orsini twice escaped from prison; and to hear Favre tell of the escapes was to hear a suggestion of divine intervention, though he stopped short of that bold claim.

"After what I have just made known to you [about his career]," Favre continued, "do I need a further defense? Must I discuss the evidence and the witnesses? Should you not already be convinced that Orsini had only one thing in mind: the delivery, the emancipation of his noble and beloved country! I repeat, this idea, this desire, cannot excuse such an attempt nor justify the death of those unfortunate victims whose lives—as Orsini testified yesterday—he would like to restore at the cost of his own blood. *But it explains*. His arm was fortified by overwhelming, imperious sentiments.

"Have not we ourselves, gentlemen of the jury, given way to the rule of such fearful sentiments? In government, sometimes royal advisers try to order the life and power of other nations. [France] was subject to one such attempt in the recent past: Do we not find the bloody memories of 1815 on the pages of our recent history? Was not Napoleon I ejected from power by the Allies despite the prestige of his name and his power? Did not the [Bourbon] government that replaced his remain unpopular because it had been imposed? Was it not attacked by conspirators who made a fierce and endless war against it? Finally, was not our country, if not glorified, at least inspired by the victims who fell in this patriotic struggle? Well, gentlemen, you have before you an Italian who wanted to do for Italy what they did for France. Look into his heart and see the motive for his crime. You will not mistake it. In particular you must not add to his crime the blood of the unfortunate victims involved in this terrible incident. He will bear responsibility for *that*

50. He means, of course, that it is the story of the *coup d'état* of 1851 and Napoleon III's rise to power.

bloodshed before God; but that responsibility cannot weigh against him in a court of law, as the law forbids it.[51]

"Must we discuss at length the disingenuousness with which Orsini believed he must cloak his explanations, his contradictions, and the denials contained in the interrogations? Does anyone here doubt that this unfortunate man *now* offers his head in expiation for his crime? He denied his crime at first—that is true. But as the other accused were also denying it, he did not want to compromise them. They denied [the crime], and he followed their route. Do not be tempted to believe that he was afraid. The moment of justice finally comes, the day when he finds himself confronted by a jury, and thus the moment when he must give you his final explanation—and he does. Did he conceal anything? Did you hear any hint of boasting or of fear? No! He testified frankly and courageously, admitting his plans and his error. Here he is, gentlemen, before you and ready to die, but still hopeful that his blood can be useful in the cause of Italian independence. He has formalized this hope in a last testament, in a piece of writing addressed to the Emperor from the depths of his dungeon. Having obtained permission from the recipient, I must now read this document to you; and you will once again see revealed, gentlemen of the jury, Orsini's ideas and his entire life:

> To Napoleon III, Emperor of the French: The depositions that I have made against myself during the political trial begun in the aftermath of the January 14 attempt are sufficient to send me to death. I shall submit to it without asking for pardon, partly because I shall never abase myself before him who has killed the budding liberty of my unhappy country, partly because death is a benefit in the situation that I find myself.
>
> Even near the end of my career, I want to make one last effort to come to the aid of Italy, whose independence has led me up to this moment to risk every peril, to anticipate every sacrifice. She was the continual object of my every affection, the ultimate sentiment I want to convey in the words I address to Your Majesty.
>
> To maintain the present equilibrium in Europe, Italy must either become independent or the chains which bind her in slavery to Austria must be strengthened. To free her, shall I ask that French blood be spilled for the Italians? No, I do not go that far. Italy asks that France not intervene against her; she asks France not to allow Germany to support Austria in the struggles that may soon begin. For that is precisely what Your Majesty can do if he so wishes; and upon that wish depends either the well-being or the misfortune of my country, life or death for a nation to whom Europe is in great part indebted for its civilization.
>
> Such is the prayer that I dare to address to Your Majesty from my cell, anticipating that my feeble voice will be heard. I implore Your Majesty to give back to Italy the independence that her sons lost in 1849 thanks to the French. May Your Majesty remember that the Italians, among them my father, gladly shed their

---

51. As noted earlier, Orsini was being tried solely for his attempt upon Napoleon III. Favre means here that the fate of the innocent bystanders cannot legally weigh in the case.

blood for Napoleon the Great wherever it pleased him to lead them; and that they remained faithful to him to the moment of his downfall. May Your Majesty remember that so long as Italy be not independent, both Europe's and Your Majesty's peace will be an illusion. May Your Majesty not reject the last wish of a patriot on the threshold of the gallows. Let him free my country, and the blessings of twenty-five million citizens will be his in posterity.[52]

"Such, gentlemen, is the last word of this man who is quite resigned to his fate. You can see that it is consistent with every action in his life.

"I realize, of course, that there is a certain temerity in petitioning the very one whom he had wanted to destroy as an obstacle to the fulfillment of his plans. Yet, ever faithful to his principles and to his life's whole passion, he does not want his blood spilled without benefit to his country. Yes, gentlemen of the jury, Orsini . . . now bows down; but he ignores the fact that he is going to die. From the edge of the grave he addresses this solemn request to the man for whom he feels no personal hatred, to the man who has been his country's enemy, but who can be its savior: 'Prince, you who pride yourself as having risen from the people, come to the aid of oppressed nationalities; help a people who are friendly to France; raise again the banner of Italian independence as your valiant ancestor did! Prince, do not allow this beautiful, noble, but unhappy country to be forever the victim of the northerners who enchain her. Do not be taken in by the hypocritical testimonials from the old monarchies who would mislead you! Prince, the roots of your dynasty are of revolutionary origin. Be strong enough to give independence and liberty to Italy, be great and magnanimous, and you will be invulnerable!'[53]

"Those are his words, gentlemen of the jury. It does not belong to me to comment on them, nor have I the power or the liberty to do so. But these last words from Orsini clearly give you the idea and the goal behind his action. I have finished, gentlemen, my task completed. You do not need the pleas of the Public Prosecutor to do your duty objectively and firmly. But God, who will judge us all, God before whom the powerful of this world, deprived of their courtiers and their flatterers, appear exactly as they are, God who alone weighs the extent of our sins, the degree of the temptations that lead us astray, and the expiation required to wash them away, God will pronounce his verdict after yours. And perhaps He will not refuse a pardon that men on earth find to be impossible."[54]

52. The original of this letter, written in Italian, dated 11 February 1858, and Orsini's letter asking permission to use it in his defense, dated 16 February 1858, were found in the imperial archives in Farnborough. See Ghisalberti, *Lettere*, pp. 254–55.

53. This final "solemn request," ostensibly from Orsini to Napoleon III, is obviously Favre's wording and provides clear evidence that Favre knew and shared some of Louis-Napoleon's most fundamental principles and sensibilities, and that, as a Republican, Favre was quite aware that Bonapartism, too, was of revolutionary origin.

54. Taxile Delord, *Histoire du second empire*, 2:355–61.

The gallery had listened to this fervent appeal, amazed that the emperor had permitted Orsini's letter to be read in open court. Astonishment only increased when Favre's entire speech was reproduced the following day in the official gazette, *le Moniteur*. But the most astounded of all were the members of His Majesty's cabinet, who had had no inkling of Orsini's first letter, not to speak of his second letter requesting permission to use the first one in court. The ministers customarily dined together each Friday evening, and it happened that the day of Favre's speech, 26 February, was a Friday. Word of that speech, including the use of the letter, was given to them at dinner, considerably unsettling them.

Two ministers went at once to call on Favre to ask *how* he had obtained Orsini's letter to the emperor and *if* its reading had been approved. Favre assured them that he had been given the letter and the necessary approval from the prefect of police himself, Pierre Piétri. In their annoyance and confusion, the ministers publicly criticized both Piétri and President Delangle: Piétri for having allowed the emperor to see the letter in the first place without informing the cabinet of its existence, and Delangle for having allowed it to be read in court. The Austrian ambassador, however, felt sure that he knew the true source of the initiative in the matter and understood that the ministers were necessarily refraining from criticizing the emperor himself. As he put it: "Delangle is highly intelligent and Piétri a slippery customer—altogether a suspicious business." [55] The conservative ministers, in other words, who had been placated after the Orsini attempt with the General Security Law, were being hoodwinked by the emperor as he sought to revivify his liberal ambitions.

When the Austrian ambassador wrote of *initiative* in the affair, he meant to imply that Napoleon III had supplied the defense with the letter out of sympathy for the Italian cause. But from where had come the idea for writing the letter in the first place? The letter was written in Italian and in Orsini's hand, and Italian historians have never doubted that Orsini himself was its inspirer. [56] Certainly that was the impression Jules Favre sought to propagate at the time. He had waited nearly three weeks before accepting Orsini's invitation to conduct the defense, not visiting him in his cell at Mazas until 11 February, when he took the case. Thereafter, Favre told several legal colleagues that Orsini had given him a letter, asking him to deliver it to the emperor. (And, indeed, the letter was dated 11 February.) While Favre did not actually show the letter to his friends, he gave them its tenor quite accurately. [57]

55. Alexander von Hübner, ed., *Neuf ans de souvenirs d'un ambassadeur d'Autriche à Paris, 1851–1859; comte Joseph de Hübner*, 2:71–72.

56. Ghisalberti, *Lettere*, p. 255.

57. Darimon, *Histoire*, pp. 120–21.

Most of those who have written about Favre's career, therefore, noting that the Orsini letter had been revealed at the moment of Favre's first visit to Mazas, have been convinced that Favre must have dictated the letter to provide the basis for the only possible defense for Orsini. It would follow that Favre was also the inspirer of the second letter, which was necessary to make the first one usable in court.[58] We can quite understand that Favre would not at the time have claimed responsibility for the letters, since the effectiveness of the letters required Orsini's authority. On the other hand, it is a matter of some moment that Favre was never heard to take credit for the letters *after the trial.* That claim was later made by his relative, Paul Maritain, who published some of Favre's papers, but who never offered proof.[59] In sum, the best conjecture today is that the letters were dictated by Jules Favre, that Orsini wrote them in his own hand, but that the inspiration for the letters had come through Pierre Piétri, the prefect of police. Given the almost unseemly amount of time that transpired before Favre responded to Orsini's appeal for aid, it seems probable the defensive strategy was being privately negotiated between Favre and Piétri, and that the emperor had been in on the game from the start.

It is known that Piétri had been visiting Orsini regularly in his cell and had been at some pains to convince Orsini that Napoleon III was a true friend of Italy. We know, furthermore, that though the police had been compromised by their failure to smoke out the Orsini conspiracy, Piétri had survived the initial dismissals, despite the fact that, as a man of the Left in 1848, he remained suspect to most of the conservative ministers surrounding the emperor.[60] While it is true Piétri would resign office on 16 March 1858, a few days after the conclusion of the Orsini case ("for reasons of health"), the emperor had asked Piétri to see the Orsini matter through before retiring.[61] Since any police official could have performed the duties that remained in the Orsini case, one is driven to the conclusion that Napoleon III needed Piétri as a private and trustworthy link with Orsini. Piétri's intense personal loyalty to the emperor were as well known as his Italian sympathies.

Further circumstantial evidence would be offered in the summer of 1859, when Piétri accompanied the emperor during the Italian campaign and acted as an intermediary between the emperor and Louis Kossuth, leader of the Hungarian nationalists. Piétri would talk freely to Kossuth of the Orsini affair, revealing his efforts to convince Orsini that he had nearly killed the

58. Reclus, *Jules Favre*, pp. 209–10; and Michael St. John Packe, *Orsini: The Story of a Conspirator*, p. 269.
59. Dansette, *L'Attentat*, pp. 151–52.
60. Darimon, *Histoire*, p. 145.
61. Police Dossier for Pierre-Marie Piétri (1810–64), E. A/22–25.

one European sovereign on whom the Italians could count for aid. His discussions with Orsini, Piétri would claim, led to the first Orsini letter; and he would add that the emperor knew how to exploit the letters as propaganda for his true Italian policy.[62]

The Orsini jury, in the meantime, having heard Favre's eloquent defense, deliberated for two hours and twenty minutes before returning a verdict of guilty for all four defendants. The judges then retired for thirty minutes to consider the sentences. They awarded Gomez life imprisonment at hard labor, but sentenced the remaining three defendants to suffer death as parricides, meaning that they had to go to the scaffold in bare feet, a white sheet covering their clothes, and their heads veiled in black. They were given three days to file an appeal.[63] All three did so the next day, Orsini remarking he merely wanted to gain time to settle his personal affairs. The three were then removed from the Conciergerie to La Roquette.[64]

Orsini remained calm and polite during his remaining days, carefully drawing up his last will and a political testament. In the will he left eight hundred francs for a gold watch and chain with instructions that the watch should be engraved *Felice Orsini à Jules Favre, souvenir.*[65] When the time drew near for the appeals to be heard before the *Cour de cassation*, both Favre and Orsini wrote letters to the emperor. Favre's letter, dated 10 March, begged imperial clemency for his client.[66] Orsini's letter, dated 11 March, thanked Napoleon III for having permitted the initial letter to be used in the trial, adding that it was proof of the emperor's generosity and a sign that the emperor had been touched by, and evidently shared, Orsini's Italian patriotism.

Here again there has been controversy about who inspired the third of Orsini's letters. One well-known historian, apparently unaware of Piétri's revelations to Kossuth in 1859, saw in the particular wording of this last Orsini letter the proof that Napoleon III had inspired all of Orsini's letter-writing. The first letter had included the sentence: "May Your Majesty remember that so long as Italy be not independent, both Europe's and Your Majesty's peace will be an illusion." In the last letter, we find the following: "I declare with my last breath that though by a fatal aberration I organized the attempt of 14 January, assassination—for whatever cause—is not part of my creed. Let my compatriots, instead of relying on this method, take it from me that the liberation of Italy can be achieved only by their restraint, their devotion,

---

62. Count Louis Kossuth, *Souvenirs et écrits de mon exil: Période de la guerre d'Italie,* pp. 40–42.

63. *Gazette des Tribunaux,* 27 February 1858.

64. Ibid., 28 February 1858.

65. Delord, *Histoire,* 2:363.

66. Dansette, *L'Attentat,* p. 156.

and their unity." [67] This notable interpretation would have us understand that the emperor, wishing to grant clemency, but not wanting to encourage further attempts or to seem to be bowing to a threat, had obtained this final statement to counteract the earlier one. [68]

This deduction, if not conclusive, does add strength to Piétri's assertion that the emperor knew how to use Orsini's letters to promote his Italian policy. But when he used the letter in meetings of the cabinet and the privy council in proposing to pardon Orsini, the emperor met solid and determined opposition from an entourage that had been far too shocked by the attempt of 14 January to recommend leniency, and that did not share in the least the emperor's enthusiasm for Italian liberty. Faced with the certain resignation of his ministers and advisers if he pardoned Orsini, the emperor had to retreat. [69] He did revise Rudio's sentence by executive order, commuting it from death to life imprisonment at hard labor. [70]

The Empress Eugénie, meanwhile, had whipped herself into a passion about Orsini, captivated by "the nobility of his language and the heroism of his attitude," weeping over his fate and proposing to visit him at La Roquette. Quite properly the emperor would not permit it, nor did he respond to Orsini's final letter. [71] It remains possible, of course, that Orsini did not personally write that third letter, but that it was concocted by, or for, Piétri; or that the prison chaplain, the Abbé Hugon, had a hand in it. It was Hugon, the chaplain who had attended Louis Verger the year before, who would call upon the emperor a few days later to deliver to him Orsini's political testament. [72]

The *Cour de cassation* heard the appeals on Thursday, 11 March, and found that the legal procedures had been quite proper and the penalties legally applied. Thus, the appeals were rejected. [73] Normally the executions would have been carried out the next morning; but it being Mi-Carême (the Thursday of the third week of Lent, a holiday), the authorities postponed making arrangements until Friday, scheduling the executions for Saturday morning. The condemned men walked to the gallows together dressed as parricides, Orsini accompanied by the Abbé Hugon, Pieri by the Abbé Nottelet. While the place de la Roquette was a sea of humanity, most of the witnesses were troops massed in the square to prevent political demon-

---

67. Ghisalberti, *Lettere*, pp. 257–58.

68. Thompson, *Louis-Napoleon*, p. 180.

69. Darimon, *Histoire*, pp. 141–44; and Dansette, *L'Attentat*, p. 160.

70. *Gazette des Tribunaux*, 14 March 1858; and Delord, *Histoire*, 2:365.

71. Maurice Paléologue, *The Tragic Empress: Conversation of the Empress Eugénie, 1901–1919*, p. 156.

72. Abbé Georges Moreau, *Souvenirs de la Petite et de la Grande Roquette*, 1:78; and Ghisalberti, *Lettere*, p. 257.

73. *Gazette des Tribunaux*, 12 March 1858.

strations.[74] Orsini's death certificate was dated 13 March 1858, 10:15 A.M: "Félix Orsini, *homme de lettres*, deceased this morning at seven o'clock at 168, rue de la Roquette, eighth *mairie*, thirty-eight years old, born in Meldola (Papal States), living in Paris at 10, rue Monthabor, a bachelor." [75] The man of letters had died that Italy might live.

On the following Tuesday, Pierre Piétri resigned from the Prefecture of Police to the great surprise of those in the cabinet who thought he had survived the police scandal of 14 January.[76] His resignation (or dismissal), however, was consistent with the imperial decision to allow Orsini to be executed. It did not mean loss of confidence in Piétri, who would soon again find employment as the emperor's secret emissary; but it meant postponement of the Italian question for the moment.

THE UNTIDY AFTERMATH

The Orsini affair revealed again, as in 1840 and 1848, the proximity of Louis-Napoleon's and Jules Favre's political ideals despite the political gulf that had always separated them. They were virtually the same age, both had dabbled in Saint-Simonian socialism when young, and both were patriots imbued with the liberal nationalism of their generation. Favre had said of Lieutenant Aladenize before the Chamber of Peers in 1840: "He adhered to [Louis-Napoleon's] cause, because he believed this Prince to be destined to recover the country's liberties and to wipe out the marks of humiliation stamped upon France by the former treaties. He wanted France to be great, strong, and respected." These were Favre's own sentiments exactly, and he would vote for Louis-Napoleon for the presidency in 1848.[77]

By 1848, however, Favre's political behavior was already the subject of uneasy comment. In the early months of the Second Republic, when radicals and liberals contested for the national leadership, he had maneuvered for the liberals and earned the enmity of the radicals. Their charge of opportunism was unfair, as Favre had remained consistent with the political and social liberalism he had so often represented during the July Monarchy as defense attorney for *le National*. Younger men in the party, increasingly radical after 1848, were also inclined to suspect the integrity of those with whom they differed. Had Favre really had political ambitions, he would have seen in Louis-Napoleon's presidential victory in 1848 the route to high office; but he stood aloof.[78]

74. Ibid., 14 March 1858; Moreau, *Souvenirs*, 1:77; Jesse, *Murder and Its Motives*, 212–15; and Vizetelly, *Court Life*, p. 119.

75. Charles Nauroy, *Le Curieux*, 2:139.

76. Georges-Eugène, baron Haussmann, *Mémoires*, 2:228.

77. Reclus, *Jules Favre*, p. 96.

78. Georges Weill, *Le Parti républicain de 1814 à 1870*, p. 183; and Reclus, *Jules Favre*, pp. 129–31.

The fact is that, though a Republican whom the party had early found to be a valuable defender of Republican causes in court, Favre had never been inclined to bend to party discipline. He was not a party man, thus escaping the popularity and the reputation for reliability easily earned by those of simple party faith. Moreover, though he may have given most of his time to law and politics, he was also devoted to metaphysical and religious meditation, which showed how much he was out of step with the younger Republicans of the Second Empire, who had forsaken spiritual belief.[79] His well-known asperity was the sign of his isolation and intense individuality, and the references to God, in his speech defending Orsini, were far from being cynical platitudes designed to enthrall the multitude.

The Orsini trial, however, made him a celebrity. He left the Palais de Justice exhausted and overwhelmed by his effort (which he would always consider to be the finest performance of his career) and was ill for several days thereafter. In a short time, he found himself pressured by Emile Ollivier to seek public office. The national elections of 1857 had returned five Republicans to the *Corps législatif*, three of whom (Ollivier, Darimon, and Hénon) had taken the oath to uphold the Empire, to the distress of many older Republicans who had advised abstention from politics for the duration. Two of the elected, Goudchaux and Carnot, had refused the oath and thus vacated their seats. Favre allowed himself to be pushed into standing for Michel Goudchaux's seat, the Sixth District in Paris, in the by-elections of 1858. While beating the government's candidate, Favre did not obtain as great a plurality as Goudchaux had, the returns suggesting that a substantial number of the more radical Republicans abstained from voting.[80]

Favre took his seat on 5 May 1858, but did not give his maiden speech until the following 30 April, after the government had announced military preparations in support of Sardinia–Piedmont. "If you mean to destroy the Austrian despotism," he announced, "to deliver Italy from her plight, then I am with you body and soul. But I reserve the right to ask the victor, after his victory, to consider the timeless principles championed abroad as applicable at home, so that he may give to his own people the liberty that he restores to a friendly nation." [81] Fair enough, one would think; but it did not please the more radical Republicans who favored systematic opposition to the Empire. Favre, in fact, had already augmented his reputation for opportunism and equivocation. At the time he took the oath of office, he had commented by way of explanation: "The Emperor has done some abominable things, but for him personally I feel more kindly than anything else." [82] Beyond

79. J. Tchnernoff, *Le Parti Républicain au coup d'état et sous le second empire*, pp. 153, 232; and Weill, *Le Parti républicain*, pp. 354, 420, 431.
80. Reclus, *Jules Favre*, pp. 210–16.
81. Ibid., pp. 221–22.
82. Tchnernoff, *Le Parti républicain*, p. 280.

that, Favre ought to have admitted that he also *agreed* with the emperor on many matters. Instead, he chose the halfway stand which won him little trust.

The truth of the matter is that Jules Favre did not have political instincts, he had principles. He had neither the patience which permits the politician to temporize until the opportune moment arrives, nor the toleration of dissent which allows the alliances necessary for political success. He liked Napoleon III and some of his policies, but despised his (successful) politics. Favre behaved in the *Corps législatif* as in a court of law, as a place where he could deliver a great speech; but he was unconcerned for the day-to-day politics of his party. It won him the annoyance of the younger generation of Republican radicals, who previously had merely suspected his principles. And since they were as intolerant as he, never the twain would meet.

In 1860, Favre was elected to be *bâtonnier* ("president") of the Parisian corporation of barristers—in recognition of his legal eloquence and his opposition to the Empire rather than out of affection. Nor was his election to the *Académie française* in 1867 a matter of affection, for the *Académie* made it a habit to elect enemies of the regime.[83] Favre's acceptance speech, not given until 23 April 1868, was remarkably free of attacks upon the regime; but like Berryer before him, Favre asked to be excused from the customary call upon the emperor, which the emperor accepted with his usual good grace. In private, however, he said: "I do not want to force anyone to pay homage to the Empire. If these brilliant Frenchmen cannot appreciate the grandeur of the Napoleonic idea, it is their loss. Bonapartism is a historic fact, and the academicians who have not yet learned this are to be pitied. We move on and leave them in the wake."[84] The emperor's toleration and tact, in the face of Favre's discourtesy, was especially noted because of the bad taste left by Favre's behavior at the time of the Morny funeral in 1865. As presiding officer of the *Corps législatif*, Morny had always treated the Left fairly and in good humor; yet, Favre had urged the Left to boycott the Morny funeral, an action that called into question his character and his sense of honor both in and out of his party.[85]

While Favre's biographers have seen the Orsini trial as the incident which opened for Favre the most "successful decade" in his career, one might better argue that the trial removed him from the exclusive practice of law, where he was prosperous and secure, and launched him into a public life that led to personal and political catastrophe. Moreover, what followed was

83. Jacomet, *Avocats républicains*, p. 53.
84. Robert Reichart, "Anti-Bonapartist Elections to the Académie Française during the Second Empire," *Journal of Modern History* 35(1963):42–44; and Maurice, comte Fleury, ed., *Memoirs of the Empress Eugénie*, 1:411.
85. Claveau, *Souvenirs*, 1:21.

not without its ironies, which those same biographers, if not entirely ignoring, certainly neglected to point up.

Later in the nineteenth century, for example, one finds a persistent legend claiming that the Empress Eugénie, contemplating a separation from her husband in the 1860s, had sought Jules Favre's legal advice. He is supposed to have advised her against stirring up a scandal for the sake of the nation and to stick it out in her palace like a *petite bourgeoise*. Though the story might seem to have been designed to demonstrate that Favre had always put the nation above party interest, the story was in fact repeated to show that Favre had necessarily protected the emperor's private life because he knew the emperor had been protecting his.[86]

The Empress Eugénie *did* on occasion consider a separation, but she most certainly never consulted Favre or any other lawyer from the Republican opposition.[87] On the other hand, Favre's private life had indeed been vulnerable. An unmarried man, he had been living for many years with a married woman by whom he had had children. (Divorce was legally impossible in France between 1816 and 1883.) The liaison had evidently begun in the 1840s with Favre endeavoring to keep his personal life as private as possible, making his decision to run for public office in 1858 virtually an aberration. The woman was Jeanne Vernier, née Charmont, whom Favre called Madame Julie.

Their first child, Gabrielle, born on 22 November 1845, was recorded as the daughter of Jeanne Charmont, legally represented by Jules Favre, but with the father unnamed. Their son, Jules, was born 25 August 1849. On his birth certificate, dated from Sceaux, Favre declared himself to be the father, Mademoiselle Jeanne Charmont to be the mother, and thus the child to be illegitimate. The third child, Geneviève, was born 5 November 1855, the birth certificate being registered in the First Arrondissement of Paris. In this case, the parents were listed as man and wife, allegedly having been married in Dijon. On 19 May 1858, Favre had Gabrielle's birth certificate altered in order to recognize her legally as his daughter. All three original birth certificates, in any case, contained deliberate errors.

In mid–1859, the death of Favre's close friend, Alphonse Odiot, threatened to disclose Favre's legal indiscretions, for Odiot left the bulk of his estate to the children "of the lady called by us Madame Julie." When working out the details of the inheritance with the executors of the will, Favre evidently came to the conclusion that the time had come to regularize the children's status, to which end he engaged a legal friend, Laluyé, in addition to his two regular attorneys. In the meantime, the emperor had become

86. Pierre de Lano, *Le Secret d'un empire: La Cour de Napoléon III*, p. 115.
87. Reclus, *Jules Favre*, p. 270. Isabella II of Spain did make such a call upon Jules Favre, perhaps the source of the confusion.

aware of Favre's legal dilemma, the information perhaps provided by police informers or even by Favre himself after the Orsini trial. Consequently, when a private hearing took place in civil court on 14 February 1860, the imperial magistrates had been informed that they should overlook Favre's earlier false declarations, which could have been so embarrassing to a lawyer and a deputy. He was quietly recognized as the legal representative of his natural children, all of whom were still minors.[88]

Toward the very end of the Second Empire, a newspaper friendly to the government got hold of the details of Favre's private life and intended their publication to ruin the regime's bitter enemy. Once again the emperor interfered to protect the Republican deputy,[89] but the incident should have been a warning that Favre's privacy was in jeopardy. A few months later, 10 June 1870, Madame Julie died unexpectedly at the age of fifty-eight. As a final tribute to the mother of his children, Favre described her in the death announcements as Madame Jules Favre, one last erroneous claim to cap the others.[90]

Within a few weeks came the war with Prussia that sealed the regime's doom at Sedan, and Jules Favre was among the first to propose the formal overthrow of the Second Empire. He was also among the liberal Republican deputies who comprised the provisional Government of National Defense on 4 September 1870, taking the Ministry of Foreign Affairs. These liberals were continually harassed by the more radical Republicans in Paris over matters of defense and diplomacy, several times to the point of insurrection; and Favre's inexperience in diplomacy, his lack of political acumen, equipped him poorly for the desperate tasks he and his government faced.[91] To the fury of the radicals, he finally secured an armistice on 28 January 1871, which provided for national elections as a prelude to a peace settlement.

He stood for reelection in Paris on 5 February, but was badly beaten thanks to radical hostility. On the other hand, he was hopeful of election in rural France where the voting was scheduled for 8 February and where opinion was known to favor the armistice he had secured. On the morning of that day, Félix Pyat's newspaper, *le Vengeur*, published a lengthy article signed by Jean-Baptiste Millière, exposing Favre's intimate life in documentary detail. Both Pyat and Millière had been prominent radical critics of the Government of National Defense after 4 September, had helped to organize insurrections, and had both just been elected to the National Assembly from

88. Ibid., pp. 104, 196, 226–27; and Emile Ollivier, *L'Empire libéral, études, récits, souvenirs,* 4:80.
89. Paul Guériot, *Napoléon III,* 1:218.
90. Reclus, *Jules Favre,* p. 312.
91. See Roger L. Williams, *The French Revolution of 1870–1871,* pp. 81–112.

Paris on 5 February. (Pyat would also be a leading member of the Paris Commune some weeks later.) They now sought to crush their political opponent with scandal. If too late to affect the provincial elections, they could at least undermine him as a negotiator for peace.

Millière's article amounted to extracts from fifteen legal documents with his commentary upon them. The first document was Geneviève's birth certificate showing that Favre and his "wife" had been married in Dijon. Then a letter from Mayor Joliet of Dijon, dated 14 August 1869, attesting that no such marriage had ever taken place in his city—the date revealing that someone in the left wing had been preparing to expose Favre even before the parliamentary elections of 1869.

Next was presented the birth certificate of Berthe Vernier, a girl born on 5 March 1839 to Louis-Adolphe Vernier and his wife, Jeanne Charmont. As additional proof that Vernier was indeed Jeanne Charmont's husband, Millière added the legal record of Berthe's marriage to François Sain on 24 March 1860. This document noted that the father of the bride, Adolphe Vernier, then a resident of Algiers, had given his consent to the marriage through a *notaire*; but that the mother, Jeanne Charmont, had been present and had given her approval.

The next two documents were birth certificates: that of Gabrielle in 1845, in which Favre had failed to register his paternity; and that of Jules in 1849, which suggested illegitimacy. After these Millière added the statement made in court by Favre on 19 May 1858 legally recognizing Gabrielle as his daughter. Favre's motive, Millière argued, was to make her eligible for a share in a rich bachelor's bequest; for though Odiot did not die until 14 July 1859, he had long suffered from an illness from which no recovery had been expected. The registry of Gabrielle Favre's marriage to P. M. Delrio, on 17 July 1867, was added as further evidence of Favre's paternity.

Millière included Geneviève's baptismal record from the parish church of Saint-Pierre et Saint-Paul for two reasons. Because the document described Favre and Jeanne Charmont as her parents, Millière wanted his readers to understand that what had been initially a "legal forgery" had become a "religious crime." In the second place, since Alphonse-François Odiot was noted as Geneviève's godfather, Millière suggested Favre had been plotting to benefit financially from his matrimonial crimes as early as 1855.

Two letters were introduced, dated 10 September 1869 and June 1870, to prove that Louis-Adolphe Vernier still lived in Algiers; and their wording strongly suggested that Vernier had been receiving periodic sums of money from Favre. Then came Madame Julie's death certificate, registered on 11 June 1870, the day after her death, in which she was identified as the wife of Adolphe Vernier, resident of Algiers. Millière explained that she had died unexpectedly, that Favre had been away at that moment, and thus had been unable to have the death certificate falsified. A copy of the invitation to attend the funeral, which Favre and the children had sent out, was obviously the next document. Monsieur Vernier was not mentioned among the survivors.

The final two documents focused upon the money presumably realized by the Favre family as a result of legitimizing that which had been legally irregular. A quotation from Alphonse Odiot's will showed that most of his money had been left to "Jules, Berthe, Gabrielle, and Geneviève" as children of Madame Julie. Unwittingly, Millière thereby invalidated part of his argument. Since the will included Berthe, who was not Favre's daughter, it followed that there had been no need to legitimize Gabrielle's status in order for her to benefit from the will. That they were all Madame Julie's children sufficed. Millière also cited the civil court action of 26 November 1859, validating the Odiot inheritance in favor of the four children, as further evidence that the imperial judicial authorities had cooperated with Favre to conceal the fraudulent statements of his past.[92] Here, Millière was on firmer ground.

The cruelty of Millière's article was even more wounding in that Favre still grieved for Madame Julie. What is more, having assumed the particular office requiring him to personify the national defeat and humiliation, he could have no illusions about his personal or political future. It hardly required the exposure of his children to ruin him; and in any case, the article had been published too late to affect the provincial voting. He won in six departments and was soon reconfirmed as minister of foreign affairs so that he might complete the negotiations for the disastrous treaty with the Prussians.[93] One of the few to protest against Félix Pyat's mixture of politics with personal matters was Henri Rochefort,[94] certainly no friend of Jules Favre, but a man who had three illegitimate children of his own whose existence had not yet become well-known. And Rochefort, though ultimately sympathetic to the radicals in the Commune of Paris, would soon have to flee from Pyat's vicious wrath.

As for Favre, his hatred for Millière and Pyat may well account for his illiberal behavior thereafter in the National Assembly—behavior that seemed so out of character. When a showdown between Paris and Versailles seemed imminent, Millière was a prominent member of the Parisian committee which sought a compromise. Among the ministers in Versailles,

92. *Le Vengeur*, 8 February 1871.
93. Reclus, *Jules Favre*, pp. 448–49; and Aimeé Dupuy, *1870–1871: La Guerre, la commune et la presse*, p. 246.
94. *Le Mot d'Ordre*, 10 February 1871.

Favre was noticeably intransigent, seemingly eager to punish a Paris "which contains so many detestable elements." [95] Yet, after what he had experienced, it would seem extravagant to expect Jules Favre to have placed much stock in the good faith or in the humanitarian claims of the likes of Millière and Pyat.

Favre had good reason to believe a number of the critical documents published in *le Vengeur* had been provided by Laluyé, his former friend who had become a bitter political opponent. After the Commune, Laluyé was investigated because of alleged sympathy for the Communards, and arrested when letters from notable Communards were found in his home, though he was released without penalty. Claiming that his arrest had been engineered by Favre, Laluyé published a letter on 22 July 1871 in which he stated that all the charges made by Millière the previous February were true. [96] Favre gave his resignation to Thiers the following day, ostensibly over a disagreement on the Roman Question, but clearly to free himself to take legal action against Laluyé. His political usefulness had come to an end in any case, and Thiers accepted his resignation on 2 August.

Favre than brought charges against Laluyé for having defamed a public functionary, and the case was heard the following month in Paris. It gave Favre his first opportunity to account for his dubious handling of his personal past. He claimed he had done what seemed necessary out of love and respect for his companion, and because of his great affection for his children who were his "reason for being and the joy of his life," and that he had been unwilling to sacrifice them to the "fetishism of conventions or to social coersion." But *Favre* was not on trial, and Laluyé's guilt was patent. He was sentenced to a year in jail and to a fine of one thousand francs. [97]

On 6 August 1874, Jules Favre finally married at the age of sixty-four. His wife was Julie Velten (another Madame Julie!), then forty-one, a woman of intelligence and education who was originally from Wissembourg. After Favre's death at Versailles on 19 January 1880, she became director of the École Normale in Sèvres, but gave devoted attention to her late husband's memory and reputation. She published his parliamentary, political, and legal speeches with only the briefest commentary, but she may also have been responsible for occasional alterations in her husband's favor. [98]

The Orsini trial had been a triumph for Jules Favre despite the condemnation of his client and had led to a political career. So political had been his approach to the trial that, in fact, he had never discussed the evidence

95. Emile Zola, *La République en marche*, 1:118.

96. *La Vérité*, 22 July 1871.

97. *Gazette des Tribunaux*, 7 and 9 September 1871; and Reclus, *Jules Favre*, pp. 498–511.

98. *Discours parlementaires*, 4 vols.; and *Plaidoyers politiques et judiciaires*, 2 vols. Paul Maritain, who published *Jules Favre: Mélanges politiques, judiciaires et littéraires*, was also related to Favre.

or the witnesses in the case before the jury. A more politic man, on the other hand, aware of the necessity to protect his privacy, would have resisted all efforts to entice him to seek public office. Perhaps the first of Favre's failures as a politician was that he ran for office in the first place, and thus the Orsini trial proved to be the source of the pride that led to the fall. Humiliated and aggrieved by the events of 1871, he lived thereafter in near-retirement during the formative years of that Third Republic which he had so long aspired to see established. One wonders if he ever faced the fact that the Empire had done better by him!

CHAPTER FOUR

The Thunderhead Murders

ANTOINE-François Claude, chief of the *Sûreté* from 1859 to 1875, departed this earth in 1880. Within a year, the first four volumes of his memoirs were available to readers, and six more volumes crowded hard upon them in the following years.[1] Sophisticated readers, aware of Monsieur Claude's reputation for probity and professional discretion, knew that the disclosures were entirely foreign to his character and that the memoirs were spurious. One reviewer called them "a tissue of fiction and dramatic invention," [2] while another reviewer attributed them to "a fanciful writer." [3] Indeed, the real Monsieur Claude, testifying before a parliamentary committee on 23 June 1871, had said he could not give the committee precise figures on criminals and suspects in Paris, because "all [his] documents had been destroyed." [4]

Many of the criminal cases recalled in the memoirs were reported unvarnished, based upon accounts readily available in the press, and owed their appeal to the public appetite for the lurid and the bizarre. On occasion, however, the journalist responsible for the project—and we know not who he was—embroidered the record to make it fit his conspiratorial theory of history as well as his anti-Bonapartism. A public ready to believe the worst could read the detailed memoirs as being authentic and be gratified to learn that the military disaster of 1870 had been attributable to deviousness in high places and not to any national shortcomings. This journalist's device was especially clever in that the public has always been susceptible to the conspiratorial theory of history, and because anti-Bonapartism was intellectually fashionable. That such matters remain unchanged in France may be suspected from the republication of two abridged editions of "Monsieur Claude's" memoirs in recent years. The second of these contains the

1. *Mémoires de Monsieur Claude, chef de la police de sûreté sous le second empire.*
2. *Le Figaro*, 12 November 1884.
3. *La Nation*, 19 November 1884. Also see Police dossiers for Gustave Macé, B a/1165 and E a/89.
4. *Enquête parlementaire sur l'insurrection du 18 mars*, 2:208.

introductory remark, "Nothing permits doubting their authenticity." [5]

Unlike the trials of Louis-Napoleon in 1840 or of Orsini in 1858—when defense attorneys made direct political appeals in the courtroom—the memoirs of Monsieur Claude now confront us with the covert creation of political myth through the deliberate misrepresentation of legal cases. The Claude memoirs, in sum, reveal the extraordinary lengths to which political ax-grinders would go to insure the damnation of the fallen regime.

This counterfeit Claude reminded his readers that the Second Empire had commenced with the crime of 2 December 1851, when France had been seized by the throat. The regime had been destined to end similarly, with two thunderclaps as he put it: the crime of Pantin (the Troppmann murders), and the crime of Auteuil (the killing of Victor Noir by Prince Pierre Bonaparte). What is more, he saw the murder of an imperial magistrate by Charles Jud in 1860 as the "thunderbolt" which prefaced the first "thunderclap" nine years later, thus signaling the beginning of the regime's downfall—an unusual pause between lightning and thunder, we might think, but clearly necessary for this essay in *grande histoire*.

Both Jud and Troppmann were Alsatian, presumably manipulated for reasons of state: "Jud and Troppmann, though merely debased instruments of an obscure nationality [German], were also frightful omens for that man [Napoleon III] who toyed with national patriotisms solely for the advancement of his dynasty." [6] All this came about because Prussia had not obtained her share of the European cake in 1859, when Napoleon III fought for the expansion of Sardinia-Piedmont in northern Italy, and had coveted Alsace as her proper compensation. The murder of the magistrate in 1860 was the first sign that Bismarck had begun the machinations which would culminate in the events of 1871. Readers were evidently expected to have forgotten that Bismarck only became minister-president of Prussia in 1862, and that in 1860 he had been ambassador to Russia.

THE THUNDERBOLT; OR,
MURDER IN A FIRST-CLASS CARRIAGE

> As Caesar was at sup-
> per the discourse was of
> death,—which sort was the
> best. "That," said he,
> "which is unexpected."
> PLUTARCH

The daily post train from Basle arrived as usual on Thursday morning, 6 December 1860, in the Gare de l'Est at four o'clock, but with an unusual

---

5. In Paris by the Club Français du Livre in 1962, and by Les Amis de l'Histoire in 1968. The introductory remarks in the latter were written by François de Clermont-Tonnerre.

6. *Mémoires de Monsieur Claude*, 4:324.

burden that particular morning. Railway workers soon discovered that one passenger, in the first-class carriage closest to the locomotive, had failed to disembark—for the reason that he was dead. And rather messily so, for a bullet had passed through his head, generously splattering the brain. The immediate impression was suicide, but suspicions of murder were aroused when no identification could be found on the body. A check of the baggage room in the station revealed that only one parcel had not been claimed by the incoming passengers, and it bore the name Poinsot, 12, rue de l'Isly. The railway employees did not recognize the name; but officials from the public prosecutor's office, who had been frantically summoned, were horrified to recognize the deceased as one of their own. He was Victor Poinsot, president of the Fourth Chamber of the Imperial Court of Paris, and was scheduled to preside in court that very morning at eleven.

The *Sûreté* began its investigation at once, and the *instruction* was formally opened the following day. Poinsot had left Paris the previous Saturday on personal business in his native department of l'Aube. He had stayed with his family in Troyes, during which time he had visited properties he owned in the small village of Chaource—in forested country some thirty kilometers south of Troyes—to collect rents that were owed him. On Wednesday evening, 5 December he had gone to the railway station in Troyes several hours before train time, as was his custom, to dine before getting aboard for the return trip.

The autopsy, performed by the famous Dr. Tardieu, ruled out suicide. Two bullets had been fired: one had penetrated Poinsot's overcoat, suit, vest, shirt, and underwear, coming to rest next to his skin near the heart, and the other bullet had passed through his head. The murderer had then mutilated his victim's head with a blunt instrument. Tardieu thought that death had been immediate. As for the time of the assault, a traveler reported she had heard strange cries when the train had been in the vicinity of Nogent-sur-Marne; and the wife of a railway gatekeeper at the crossing in Noisy-le-Sec reported having seen someone jump from the train and run. This implied that Poinsot had been murdered close to Paris, probably within an hour of the train's arrival. In those days, Nogent-sur-Marne was approximately ten miles east of Paris; Noisy-le-Sec, only five miles. The train stopped at neither town, but slowed down to take on mailbags. An examination of the roadbed near Noisy-le-Sec revealed the point where someone had leaped from the slowing train.[7]

The motive seemed to be theft, since the police quickly ascertained that a number of items Poinsot had worn or carried to the train were missing: a

7. *Gazette des Tribunaux*, 7 December 1860; *Annual Register for 1860*, p. 182; and Maurice Garçon, "Le Mystérieux crime de Jud," *Miroir de l'Histoire* 121(January 1960):272.

black and white lap rug; a wallet of black morocco; a gold watch bearing the identification number 2,638 and the name of the watchmaker, Sourian, 10, rue de la Paix; a gold watch chain with key, studded with rubies and engraved with the initial *P*; and most notable of all, a large traveling case of polished leather, the sort often used to carry valuables. It had actually contained Poinsot's property records and receipts, some architectural plans for the improvement of buildings he owned, and a garden book entitled *Le Parfait jardinier*.[8] The murderer had evidently opened the wallet on the spot to check its contents, in his haste had dropped eighteen pennies, and had neglected to pick them up.

The victim had been a member of the magistracy since the earliest days of the July Monarchy, beginning as the king's prosecuting attorney in Troyes. He had moved to Paris in 1833, starting as a substitute on the Civil Tribunal of the Seine, gradually rising in legal rank until he had achieved the presidency of the Imperial Court on 6 April 1857. He was well-regarded for his notable sense of duty and responsibility, and was considered loyal to the Empire.[9]

His funeral on 8 December 1860 brought out many judicial worthies, among whom were noted Chaix-d'Est-Ange, Marie, Favre, and Berryer. The services were held at the church of Saint-Louis d'Antin, where Jules Favre was alleged to have remarked to Berryer during the ceremony, "Well, that is what it costs to be too close to the Chateau [the Tuileries]!"[10] Whether or not such a remark was actually made, it reflected a widespread view in Paris that the murder had necessarily been political in motive and that the imperial government was simply suppressing the evidence. On the other hand, some of the judiciary were more inclined to the view that Poinsot had fallen victim to someone he had previously sentenced, and cases over which he had presided were reviewed in search of clues.[11] It was intolerable that such a glamorous crime should have had so petty a motivation as theft!

Meanwhile, the *instruction* continued. As anyone who has traveled on French railroads knows, railway tickets are not only checked after one boards a train, but are recovered by the company as passengers disembark. This practice provides employment for functionaries, while furnishing the police an additional and unobtrusive means of surveillance. In this case, the police checked ticket sales and recoveries in all stations along the Chemin de Fer

8. *Annual Register for 1860*, p. 182.
9. *Gazette des Tribunaux*, 8 December 1860; and *Annual Register*, pp. 183–84.
10. *Gazette des Tribunaux*, 9 December 1860; and Garçon, "Le Mystérieux crime de Jud," pp. 275–76.
11. Garçon, "Le Mystérieux crime de Jud," pp. 275–76.

de l'Est. On the evening in question, the night of December 5, only one third-class ticket had been sold in Troyes, the destination being Mesgrigny, the first station after Troyes. It happened that the local train, which stopped at Mesgrigny, departed from Troyes within five minutes of the time that the express for Paris departed. This third-class ticket had not been surrendered that night in Mesgrigny; but the following afternoon, a passenger arriving in Troyes gave the ticket taker a Troyes-Mesgrigny ticket, which was refused as invalid. The passenger had then fished through his pocket and had come up with a second ticket—this one the proper Mesgrigny-Troyes ticket. This enabled the police to deduce that the murderer had bought the cheapest possible ticket in order to gain access to the railway platform, but that he had boarded the express close upon Monsieur Poinsot. Then, after jumping from the train as it slowed down near Noisy-le-Sec, he had somehow regained Mesgrigny, from there returning to Troyes.[12]

The police had had no trouble verifying that Poinsot had dined at the Hôtel du Mulet, where he was well-known, before going to the railway station. He had chatted freely and indicated that he was returning to Paris on the night train. A check of the hotel manager soon produced a suspect—a man registered as Jules Matricon. He had come to the hotel on 3 December and had stayed in his room almost continuously, coming downstairs only for meals. On the evening of 5 December he had suddenly informed the manager that he must go to Paris on the night train, but that he would retain his room and leave his baggage therein. Matricon had indeed returned to the hotel the following afternoon about 5:30. He dined, spent the night in his room, and checked out early the next morning, mentioning, as he paid his bill, that he was on his way to Marseille.[13]

Further police investigation provided additional details about Matricon's route after he had jumped from the train. He had arrived in Mesgrigny about noon on 6 December, evidently very fatigued, and had taken lunch at a local hotel. He had then boarded a train for the return to Troyes where the ticket incident took place. Attempts to find Matricon registered in Marseille after 7 December were fruitless, but the police soon learned that a Matricon had stayed the night of the seventh at the Hôtel de Vaucluse in Lyons.

In the meantime, judicial authorities had been noting the similarity between the Poinsot murder and one committed on the same railway line the previous 12 September—in that case on a train from Paris to Mulhouse. A badly injured man had been found along the roadbed between Zillisheim and Illfurth; he had been knifed, robbed of his valuables, and thrown from the train. Unfortunately for all concerned, he never regained his senses sufficiently to tell what had happened; but he was soon identified as a Russian

12. *Gazette des Tribunaux*, 16 October 1861.
13. Ibid.

army physician named Heppe. His bag, known to contain both French and Russian money, was missing.

This case had remained a mystery until 28 November 1860, when police in Ferrette arrested Charles Jud, an army deserter who was wanted to serve a sentence of twenty years at hard labor. Jud was found to possess both Russian and French money, a hunting weapon, and a hunting license and passport in the name of his brother, Jacques Jud, a resident of Paris. During his first night of his detention in Ferrette, Charles Jud had managed to free himself from his chains; and when two unsuspecting guards entered his cell, he knocked them flat, overpowered a third guard outside, and fled from the Ferrette jail.

Given the proximity of Ferrette to the murder scene—about thirty kilometers—the authorities concluded that the powerful Jud was the probable murderer of Dr. Heppe. By December 10, the Public Prosecutor in Paris had come to realize that Matricon was probably an alias. He put out a description of Charles Jud, using the facts given in his military records, as the alleged murderer of Victor Poinsot.[14] Jud was then twenty-seven. He had a noticeable scar above his left eye, several broken teeth, and a long, thin face. His hair and eyebrows were brown, and his beard, which he had on occasion been known to let grow, was reddish-brown.[15]

Jud did not remain long in Lyons, but passed into Switzerland on 9 December under the name Dulin. His presence in Geneva was betrayed when he abandoned Poinsot's black and white lap rug at the Hôtel de la Poste. The Swiss police notified Paris of his presence, but could not find him. Evidently, he spent the next few nights in houses of prostitution, for the Swiss police became aware that a French customer was paying his tab in Russian gold coin. On 18 December, still using the name Dulin, Jud registered for one night at the Hôtel des Vingt-deux-Cantons in Geneva, but had vanished again by the time police checked the registry.

If the Paris police no longer had any doubt that Matricon-Dulin was Jud, and were convinced that the motive for the crime had quite evidently been theft, rumors to the contrary continued to swell, and they were no longer limited to allegations of political homicide. One version, easily swallowed whole, had it that poor old Poinsot had seduced a village girl during his trip to Chaource, and that her brother had sought revenge on the train. The editors of the *Gazette des Tribunaux* repeatedly tried to warn the public against such groundless rumors,[16] but the facts in the case could hardly compete with the public craving for something more sensational or diabolical.

Jud's elusiveness reduced the French police to an intense investigation of

14. *Gazette des Tribunaux*, 10–11 December 1860; and *Annual Register*, p. 183.
15. *Gazette des Tribunaux*, 20 December 1860.
16. Ibid., 19 December 1860, and 16 October 1861.

his background. They returned to the Hôtel du Mulet in Troyes and made a thorough search of his room, turning up one valuable piece of evidence: a pair of regulation gendarmerie handcuffs bearing initials that enabled the police to trace the owner. He turned out to be one of the unfortunate officers of the Ferrette jail. The handcuffs, which had been broken, had been hidden by Jud behind a piece of hotel furniture—more evidence that Jud and Matricon were the same.[17]

As for Jud's background, there was very little to recommend him. He had been born in the village of Bourogne (Haut-Rhin) near Belfort on 7 February 1834, to Jean-Jacques Jud and Françoise Grillon, who had subsequently moved to Ferrette and later to Altkirch. The Juds were a large and respectable family, but at an early age Charles began petty pilfering and later progressed to serious robberies. In 1854, when his class—the class of 1855—became eligible for service under the military recruitment law, he was serving a six-month sentence for theft and could not be present for the local drawing of lots. The mayor drew for him and, whether by chance or design, provided Jud with what the public called a "bad number," but which the government called "good for service." After his release from jail, Jud was ordered to join the Third Squadron of what we would call the Quartermaster Corps (just the place for a thief), which then served in North Africa. He reached his unit on 18 August 1855.

The Third Squadron was transferred to the Crimea on 3 February 1856, after the cessation of hostilities, and returned to North Africa about six months later. From the outset of his military service, Jud had been noted for indiscipline; and from the time his unit returned to Oran, he had been repeatedly suspected of thefts within his outfit, but evidence was lacking. On the night of 15 June 1859, however, he was caught in the storeroom of the unit's master tailor, which he had entered with a passkey of his own manufacture, and was put under arrest in solitary confinement to await trial. On the morning of 18 June he was missing, having managed to dig his way out of the cell. Consequently, he had to be tried *in absentia* for theft and desertion, receiving a sentence of twenty years at hard labor and a dishonorable discharge on 3 September 1859. Approximately one year later the first of the two murders would take place.[18]

In August of 1860, a few weeks before the Heppe murder, Charles Jud went to Paris in search of his brother Jacques, who worked as a tailor in the faubourg Poissonière. Charles had by then acquired several sets of identification papers, including those of a coachman in Algiers which he had used in his escape from Africa, and those of a worker named Matricon whose ap-

17. Ibid., 16 October 1861.
18. Ibid., 27 December 1860.

pearance Jud had recognized as being similar to his own. He now wore dark glasses and a cap, explaining to his brother that he wanted to hide the scar over his eyebrow; he was further disguised by a moustache and a short beard. Charles wanted Jacques to accompany him to London, but Jacques said he could not leave his business even for a few days. Charles insisted, saying that he had plenty of money to pay their expenses, and Jacques gave way and applied for a passport. Once it was obtained, Charles simply made off with it, saying he was going to London alone.

Jacques Jud was then unaware that his brother was wanted by the military. In November, however, he read a newspaper account of Charles' arrest in Ferrette on the desertion charge, of his subsequent escape from the Ferrette jail, and of the suspicion that Charles was responsible for the Heppe murder. Jacques was considerably unsettled by the news, fearing implication from the passport; but before he could make up his mind whether to go to the police, Charles appeared again on his doorstep. A quarrel ensued with Charles endeavoring to calm Jacques' fears, saying that the charges against him were false—except for the matter of desertion—and that he meant to return to Africa to give himself up. Jacques remained unconvinced of Charles' sincerity, and Charles went away within a day of his arrival.

Within a few days the Poinsot murder occurred, after which the police picked up Jacques for questioning, suspecting him of having aided Charles by providing him with a psssport. Jacques insisted he had been tricked into releasing the passport, and that he had been fearful of retaliation by Charles if he had come to the police about the matter. Since Jacques' wife gave similar testimony, he was released after a week of detention.[19]

In January of 1861, rumors persisted that Charles Jud had been captured in Switzerland, but the rumors were false.[20] In February, the Ministry of the Interior put out a new circular on him, repeating his description, listing his offenses, and distinguishing him as a "criminal of the worst sort and with unusual strength." [21] The longer Jud remained uncaught, the more the gossip multiplied, setting the stage for the deliberate distortions later to be perpetrated by the bogus Monsieur Claude and others. By the time the *instruction* closed (31 August 1861) and Jud bound over for trial in contumacy, the case had become for some a ludicrous example of police incompetence. Others had come to believe that no such person as Jud existed.[22]

The case was heard in the *Cour d'assises* of the Seine on 15 October 1861 with Chaix-d'Est-Ange serving as the public prosecutor. In the absence of the accused, the court proceeded without a jury. The indictment, which

---

19. Ibid., 14–15 January 1861.
20. Ibid., 10 January 1861.
21. Ibid., 23 February 1861.
22. Garçon, "Le Mystérieux crime de Jud," pp. 288–92.

was read and published, not only reviewed the details of the case as we know them, but made special mention of the widespread rumors of other motives in the murder—none of them having any foundation. Poinsot had never sentenced Jud in an earlier trial, he had no known enemies, and his legal career had been distinguished by a long and notably fair service on the bench. After a résumé of Jud's criminal biography, the prosecutor recommended a charge of premeditated theft and murder. The court declared Jud guilty and sentenced him to death.[23]

All that remained was to find him. On 24 November 1861 an Alsatian with dubious papers thought to be Jud was arrested in Montélimar (Drôme), and was sent to Paris for interrogation.[24] But the man proved to be substantially older than Jud would have been, and those who had known Jud were unanimous in saying that the suspect was not Charles Jud.[25] Public attention soon faded, having fastened itself to a new sensation, the La Pommerais poisoning; and it seems likely that the Jud case would have been forgotten had not professional gossip-mongers of the postwar period revived it.

Monsieur Claude's "revelations," which turned Charles Jud into a Prussian spy, and which asserted that Victor Poinsot had been murdered for trying to penetrate Prussian state secrets, also implied that Jud had never been found because he had reached the protection of the Prussian police. These allegations even went so far as to say that Napoleon III himself had been conspiring with the Prussians for the restoration of Alsace to Germany as compensation for what France and Italy had gained territorially from the War of 1859. If the French police had failed to trap Jud before he passed into Switzerland, it was because they had received official hints not to pursue the matter with "excessive zeal."[26] Only an audience profoundly distressed by the events of 1870–71 could have been sold such a bill of goods.

After "Monsieur Claude" was in print, Charles Nauroy, a writer who specialized in historical or anecdotal items of interest, and whose books were a mixture of reliable and dubious material,[27] began publishing biweekly pamphlets of a similar genre. In 1885, he professed to know that Auguste Vermorel, a moderate member of the Commune of Paris, who had earlier published several books on the Paris police, had taken the Jud–Poinsot dossier from the police files in 1871 and had never returned it. Therefore, that dossier was not among the records destroyed in the fires that accompanied the end of the Commune. Vermorel himself, wounded defending a barricade, died as a prisoner of the Versaillese. Nauroy now claimed that the

23. *Gazette des Tribunaux*, 16 October 1861.
24. Ibid., 24 November 1861.
25. Ibid., 28 November 1861.
26. *Memoirs de Monsieur Claude*, 2:112–21.
27. For example, Charles Nauroy, *Les Secrets des Bonaparte*.

missing dossier would prove that Charles Jud, in fact, had never existed. He and his career had been fabricated by the imperial government and the police to protect the regime from the scandalous "truth" that Victor Poinsot, the imperial magistrate, had seduced a rural maiden who had been avenged by her brother. Nauroy said that he would be grateful if the current owner of that important dossier would come forward.[28] Since the dossier never reappeared, Nauroy was free to repeat his version of the Jud case in later publications devoted to exposing the secrets of the Bonapartes. The real Monsieur Claude, dead since 1880, was unable to protest the implication that he had collaborated with the imperial government to prevent a scandal.

The dossier had indeed disappeared, apparently one of the many destroyed by fire in the offices of the Prefecture of Police in May 1871. But unbeknownst to these later writers, the real Monsieur Claude, who remained at the *Sûreté* until 1875, by no means regarded the Jud case as closed despite the passage of time, nor was he a partisan of the specious rumors circulating about the case. A new Jud–Poinsot file was opened, and Claude took a personal interest in recovering materials that might lead to Jud's arrest.

A second Jud brother, Edouard, was found in Paris, living in the passage du Grand-Cerf, the very neighborhood of Jacques Jud.[29] Edouard, about thirty years of age, was found to be in the service of a Monsieur Rouzé, who operated buffets at the race track and at the Opera.[30] Both brothers were put under surveillance and were questioned, but neither could give any information about their fugitive brother. Monsieur Claude thought it might become necessary to obtain search warrants to permit the examination of both homes simultaneously in the hope of finding family correspondence that could, if nothing else, suggest whether Charles Jud were dead or alive. As it was, the destruction of the original dossier made anything like a systematic investigation difficult.[31]

A year later, the prefect of police in Paris received word that Charles Jud had been seen on the streets of Basle by the Abbé Couvet, who claimed to have known him in their school days. This identification, given to the police in Basle, had then been forwarded to German authorities in Mulhouse and to French authorities in Belfort; and the Swiss asked the public prosecutor in Belfort whether Jud's extradition would be requested if they should succeed in arresting him. The information was then passed to Paris by a *commissaire de police* named Fleuriel, who was posted in Belfort for railway surveillance.

28. Charles Nauroy, *Le Curieux*, 1:293.
29. Jud-Poinsot dossier, #33064, Archives de la Préfecture de Police, 23 and 24 May, 1873.
30. Ibid., 30 May and 5 June 1873.
31. Ibid., Monsieur Claude to the Chief of the Municipal Police, 8 June 1873.

Both the Swiss and German authorities asked Fleuriel to provide Jud's description and a photograph if possible. All he could offer them was an up-dated description: "Charles Jud, age forty, brown hair, very thick brown eyebrows, high forehead, brown eyes deeply inset, glum or disdainful expression, straight nose, large mouth, tanned complexion, brown beard, a scar above the left eye, powerful build, little given to communication, and careless of attire." He asked Paris to provide the public prosecutor in Belfort with a photograph of Jud.[32]

Monsieur Claude had to tell the prefect of police that the files contained no photograph; but evidently it was known that a photograph of Jud had at some time been made, and agents were sent out to scour the photography stores of Paris. A negative was finally located in a shop in the rue du Louvre; the police met some resistence from the proprietor in obtaining a copy, but ultimately convinced him of the wisdom of cooperation.[33] All this was for naught, however, since the Basle police failed to find Jud. He vanished as he had before in Geneva, and soon after, Monsieur Claude retired. The Paris police never again pursued the matter, and we must assume that Charles Jud finished his life in Switzerland under a successful alias.

Even if that postwar investigation fell short of its goal, the documents it left confirm those journalists of the 1880s who suspected that the rumors about the Jud–Poinsot case were entirely fanciful. On the other hand, who can be certain that such fantasies ever die? May we not look forward to the next abridged edition of Monsieur Claude's memoirs, adorned by a favorable notice assuring us that nothing permits doubting their authenticity!

THE FIRST THUNDERCLAP; OR,
THE CRIME OF PANTIN

It hath been often
said, that it is not death,
but dying, which is terrible.
HENRY FIELDING

On the morning of 20 September 1869 a farmer named Langlois, who worked a field in Pantin near Aubervilliers, immediately northeast of Paris, noticed a mound he had not seen before. Probing it with a spade, he uncovered human remains and was horrified to realize that his property concealed more than one victim. Hastily summoned legal and medical authorities continued the excavation, and unearthed a woman and five children. All had been battered by some heavy object. The horror of the discovery was only increased when the medical examiners determined that at least some of

32. Ibid., Fleuriel to the Prefect of Police, 10 May 1874.
33. Ibid., Monsieur Claude to the Prefect of Police, 19 May and 23 May 1874.

the children had been buried when still living and had failed in their struggle to break free of the earth. The woman was found to have been seven-months pregnant. None of the bodies bore any identification.[34]

The news churned the public into a frenzy of excitement. September was the month government stood still: the ministers went to their country places; the imperial couple, to Biarritz. Nothing transpired to compete with the crime of Pantin for public attention. A swarm of the curious, including the Queen of Spain, swept through the Porte de Pantin, and happy families picnicked in the very field where blood had flowed. Those unable to take the route to Pantin could feed on repulsive photographs eagerly provided by a press emancipated by the reforms of 1868.

One great lady, who had sought the limelight for years, found it in her demand to be invited to attend the autopsies.[35] She was Marie Bonaparte-Wyse—granddaughter of Lucien—by 1869 married for the second time to the Italian statesman Urbano Rattazzi. Decidedly a card, Madame Rattazzi had aspired to be the Madame de Staël of the Second Empire. She was intelligent, beautiful, ambitious, and capricious—one of those people called "wonderful" by those who do not have to live with them. Unwelcome at the Tuileries, like all of Lucien's descendants, she had opened her salon to opponents of the regime, never avoiding an opportunity to associate the name Bonaparte with words or deeds embarrassing to Napoleon III; though she expected to be supported with a substantial pension from his civil list. Her literary career came to something less than Madame de Staël's,[36] and her hope to be present at the autopsies was also disappointed. In like manner the hopes of the unusual numbers of spectators who turned up at the Morgue were frustrated, for the corpses were not immediately put on display.[37]

The police were lucky in their investigation. Had they been unable to identify the victims quickly, the murderer, as we shall see, might well have escaped to America. But an innkeeper, proprietor of the Hôtel du Chemin de Fer du Nord, in the avenue Denain near the railway station, came forward to report that a woman and five children from Roubaix (Nord), registered at his hotel, were missing. Since the labels on several of the deceased boys' jackets were those of a Roubaix tailor, the innkeeper was taken to the Morgue and promptly identified the victims as Madame Kinck, her four sons, and daughter.

The family had come from Roubaix by train and had asked for a Jean Kinck upon their arrival. Jean Kinck was already registered at the hotel, but had since disappeared. A quick check in Roubaix proved that Kinck was the

34. Félix Sangnier, *Plaidoyers de Charles Lachaud*, 2:253.
35. Céleste Baroche, *Second Empire: Notes et souvenirs de seize années, 1855–1871*, pp. 542–43.
36. André Billy, *Sainte-Beuve: Sa vie et son temps*, 2:166–75.
37. *Gazette des Tribunaux*, 22 September 1869.

husband and father of the deceased, but that he, too, along with his eldest son, Gustave, was missing. Since the ages of the Kinck children ranged from two to sixteen, it could be deduced that the young man registered at the hotel as Jean Kinck had been an imposter, that he was the probable murderer, and that there remained two more victims as yet undiscovered.[38]

A second piece of luck, however, led the investigators to Le Havre. Local police there had picked up for questioning a young man reported to be shopping for fraudulent papers that would enable him to embark for the United States. He had registered in two hotels on successive nights: once under the name Fisch, and once as Wolff, pretending to be a Bavarian who spoke no French. He had been overheard, however, speaking French quite fluently. The arresting officer, dissatisfied with the young man's answers to questions, decided to take his suspect to the local public prosecutor. On their way, the suspect broke loose, raced to the waterfront and threw himself into the water, evidently in an attempt at suicide, since he did not know how to swim. A calker named Hanguel dove in after the suspect and pulled him to the wharf despite furious resistance. When the drenched and exhausted man was searched, the police found hidden papers on him that identified him as Jean Kinck. When this news reached Paris, Monsieur Claude left at once for Le Havre.[39]

Subjected to intense questioning, the suspect confessed his true identity as Jean-Baptiste Troppmann, an Alsatian; but he insisted that he had been merely an accessory in the Kinck murders, only assisting Jean and Gustave Kinck in the murder of the wife and children. Monsieur Claude then took Troppmann back to Paris to face his victims in the Morgue. Not even removing his hat in their presence, Troppmann calmly pointed in turn to Madame Kinck, Emile, Henri, Alfred, Achille, and little Marie. He was then asked, according to the usual procedure in an *instruction*, to sign a statement about the confrontation on the spot. Seating himself at a table, he blew from the paper some traces of dust, tried the pen on his fingernail before using it, and signed his name with a careful flourish. Finally, he shook the remaining ink from the pen and replaced it on the inkstand. Veteran police officials and journalists who witnessed the performance were utterly chilled.[40]

Puny rather than robust, his sparse brown beard revealing his immaturity, could Troppmann have possibly committed such murders without accomplices? In short order his nerves, like his story, began to give way. He

38. Ibid., 24 September 1869; and Sangnier, 2:254.
39. *Gazette des Tribunaux*, 23 and 24 September 1869; and *Annual Register for 1869*, ,p. 156.
40. *Gazette des Tribunaux*, 26 September 1869; Sangnier, *Plaidoyers*, 2:254; and Maxime Du Camp, *Paris: Ses organes, ses fonctions et sa vie dans la second moitié du XIXe siècle*, 3:165.

began to weep frequently, *not of remorse*, but about his capture. On 26 September, after persistent archaeology, a seventh body was found in the Langlois field, a knife still plunged into its throat and a pickax buried nearby. This discovery considerably distressed Troppmann. When he was taken to view the corpse, that of the eldest Kinck boy, Gustave, Troppmann tried to preserve his story by saying of Jean Kinck: "The swine! He has now killed his remaining son." [41]

It was now of the utmost importance to find Jean Kinck to learn whether he had been an accomplice or a victim. As the Langlois field contributed nothing further, police informers were placed near Troppmann in Mazas. For a time they could get nothing out of him; but little by little he began to talk about himself and the Kincks. He was then nineteen, a mechanic by trade, and had been born in Cernay (Haut-Rhin), just west of Mulhouse. The Kinck family, though residing in Roubaix, was originally Alsatian. Troppmann said that he had met Jean Kinck quite casually in a Roubaix *brasserie*, finding him to be a man who had made money and was anxious for more. Kinck had, according to Troppmann, taken him to Alsace to an alleged site of gold, silver, and mercury deposits.

Ultimately, out of Troppmann's garbled babbling, an agent of the *Sûreté* named Souvras secured a confession from Troppmann that he had poisoned Jean Kinck in Alsace, and obtained a fairly precise description of where the body had been concealed. Troppmann himself had manufactured the fatal prussic acid, added it to a wine flask, and had given it to Kinck in a remote area where he could easily dispose of the body. [42] And indeed, the body was found buried in a wooded area near the village of Wattwiller (just north of Cernay).

Troppmann further assured authorities that if they would now recover Kinck's briefcase buried nearby, they would find in it the names of his [Troppmann's] accomplices. Troppmann's earlier story, that he had cooperated with Jean Kinck in murdering his wife because Kinck suspected his wife of infidelity, had now evolved into an admission that he had cooperated with those who sought to exploit the secrets of mineral wealth that Kinck had possessed.

Naturally the police doubted these various versions of events, yet were bemused by several anonymous letters addressed to Troppmann in Mazas, threatening reprisals against his family should he reveal his accomplices. It seemed to some that so young a man would have been incapable of such horrendous crimes without assistance, and it remains entirely possible that he had had accomplices. On the other hand, such letters more often than not come from cranks who are always with us; and the briefcase was never

---

41. *Gazette des Tribunaux*, 27–28 September 1869.
42. Ibid., 18 November 1869; and Du Camp, *Paris*, 3:97.

found, not to speak of the accomplices. Rumors even began to circulate that the imperial government had engineered the crimes to distract public attention from domestic affairs and, in particular, to delay further the liberalization of the regime.[43] The political opposition, in other words, in seeking to undermine the government, initiated the rumors in the fall of 1869 that later would become gospel truth for the left wing.

After Jean Kinck's internal organs had been removed and sent to Paris to determine if poison had in fact been the cause of death,[44] the judicial authorities were able to complete the *instruction.* The *Chambre des mises en accusation* indicted Troppmann for murder, theft, and fraud, and bound him over for trial before the *Assises* of the Seine. He was thereupon transferred from Mazas to the Conciergerie to await trial.[45]

The trial, which would require three days, opened on 28 December 1869 under the presidency of Thévenin. Admission to the gallery was by ticket only—the president having received over three thousand requests. To accommodate as many spectators as possible, a few seats for distinguished people were provided behind the bench. The audience contained many women, but also a scattering of diplomats and aristocrats; and Alexandre Dumas *fils* and Emile Augier were there in the name of literature. Among the exhibits prominently displayed before the bench was a glass tube containing the innards of Jean Kinck, wrapped in cotton to prevent indecent exposure.[46] The packed chamber resembled a steambath, hot and sticky, even before the trial got underway, and was tense in anticipation of Troppmann's appearance.

Troppmann had not been shaved since the beginning of his captivity. He was thought to be suicidal, given his plunge at Le Havre, and the authorities feared he might in some fashion throw himself on a razor to inflict a fatal wound. His defense attorney, Charles Lachaud, had been insisting that Troppmann had the right to appear in court as he had looked on the day of his crime; and after some resistance the prison official gave way. Troppmann was put into a strait jacket, tied firmly to a chair, his head held by three policemen, while a fourth person did the shaving. Flattered by the attention, Troppmann seemed to thrive on his importance. But he insisted that the precautions were useless: "I could die if I wanted to, for I have ways they don't know about. But I don't want to kill myself, not wanting to dishonor my family." [47]

It was soon evident what Lachaud's motive had been in demanding the

43. *Gazette des Tribunaux,* 26 November 1869; *Annual Register for 1869,* pp. 156–57; and Sangnier, *Plaidoyers,* 2:255–56.
44. *Gazette des Tribunaux,* 27 November 1869.
45. Ibid., 11 December 1869.
46. Ibid., 29 December 1869; and Sangnier, *Plaidoyers,* 2:258–59.
47. Du Camp, *Paris,* 3:173–74.

shave: Troppmann, rather puny, hollow-chested, with sloping shoulders, looked even more innocent and helpless when shaved; as if he were a mere youth of fifteen years rather than the twenty he had just become, a baby-faced appearance that was quite feminine, hardly suggesting brutal strength. Yet, he had demonstrated considerable muscular strength, and his hands, in sharp contrast to the rest of his body, were almost grotesque in size and asymmetry. There was an unusual space between the thumb and the index finger, with the thumbs being longer than normal, extending to the second joint of the index fingers. The fingers were spatular. The backs of the hands were remarkably hairy considering the sparseness of the beard: the hands of a monster attached to a child.[48]

According to custom, the indictment was read at the opening of the trial. It featured a detailed description of the victims and their wounds, attesting to the ferosity of the assaults. Madame Kinck, for instance, though probably killed instantly by a knife-blow in her back, suffered an additional thirty wounds administered by a pickax. Gustave Kinck, the eldest boy, had evidently fought desperately for his life until knifed through the throat. Troppmann's arrest in Le Havre was described, as were the papers and personal effects belonging to the Kincks that were in his possession; and his impassivity when confronted with his victims was duly noted.

In addition to having obtained Troppmann's confession, the *instruction* had reviewed his brief career. Born 5 October 1849 in Cernay (Haut-Rhin), Troppmann had at an early age been apprenticed to Troppmann et Kambly, a company which built industrial equipment and which was managed by Troppmann *père*. In December of 1868, the firm had sold some machinery to a Parisian manufacturer, and Troppmann *fils* had been sent to Paris to supervise its installation. He had resided at Quatre-Chemins in Pantin until May 1869, and those who met him during that period testified to his preoccupation with money, and his desire to become rich. Thereafter, he had been sent by his father to install machinery in Roubaix, at which time he had become acquainted with the Kinck family.

Jean Kinck, the *instruction* revealed, had been a simple industrial laborer whose "virtue and hard work" had enabled him to prosper and rise until he had become the owner of a business. His marriage had apparently been happy, and the children had been receiving a formal education. Only one dispute persisted to mar their serenity: Kinck, an Alsatian, still owned a house in Bühl, which he wanted to improve and ultimately to occupy. Madame Kinck, a native of Roubaix, however, resisted that idea and opposed any investment in the house. Evidently, Kinck had been considering reestablishing his business in Guebwiller, just north of Cernay. Troppmann

48. Sangnier, *Plaidoyers*, 2:259; and Major Arthur Griffiths, *Mysteries of Police and Crime*, 1:310.

had presumably worked on Kinck's Alsatian ambitions in order to get Kinck to accompany him to Cernay; and it is possible that he had encouraged Kinck with stories of lost gold and silver mines in that vicinity.

Once Troppmann had disposed of Kinck in a wooded ravine, he had endeavored to cash a 5,000-franc bond made out to Kinck, but had been foiled despite his possession of Kinck's identification papers. In desperation for the money, Troppman had then written to the eldest son, Gustave, asserting that Jean Kinck had had to go to Paris on business before his money had reached Alsace; and that Gustave should come to claim the money so that it could be taken to the father in Paris. The unsuspecting Gustave did as bidden; but he, too, failed to obtain the money from the Guebwiller post office and went to Paris—and to his doom—empty-handed.

It remained for Troppmann to summon the rest of the Kinck family to Paris. Numerous letters were written between Troppmann and Madame Kinck to make the complicated arrangements. Troppmann avowed that he was writing on behalf of Jean Kinck, who had injured his right hand. She must bring the children to Paris to meet her husband at the Hôtel du Chemin de Fer du Nord, and, of course, she must bring a substantial sum of money. By some fluke she arrived at the railway earlier than arranged and, not finding anyone to meet her, had gone on to the hotel. Again no one was there, so she had evidently taken the children and returned to the station at the appointed hour to meet her husband and had there found Troppmann. He explained that he had instructions to take the family to Pantin, so they boarded a carriage and took the road to Pantin. By then, the early winter darkness had descended, and Troppmann asked the coachman to wait at the edge of a field while he accompanied Madame Kinck and two of her children across the field in the direction of a lighted house. About twenty minutes later, he returned for the remaining three children. So ended the house of Kinck.

In conclusion, the indictment brought five charges against Jean-Baptiste Troppmann: that he had murdered Jean Kinck by poison in Haut-Rhin; that he had defrauded Kinck's heirs by stealing Kinck's watch-and-chain, his papers, and approximately 6,000 francs; that he had murdered Gustave Kinck in Pantin; that he had defrauded Gustave's heirs by taking valuable objects; and, finally, that he had murdered Hortense-Juliette-Joseph Rousselle (Madame Kinck) and her five children in Pantin.[49]

Various witnesses were heard on the second day of the trial, among them handwriting experts who agreed that the critical letters and signatures, ostensibly Jean Kinck's, had all been written by Troppmann. From testimony by hotel employees, the jury learned that when Troppmann had completed his

---

49. *Gazette des Tribunaux*, 29 December 1869; Sangnier, *Plaidoyers*, 2:265–74; and *Annual Register for 1869*, p. 157.

tasks in Monsieur Langlois' field on the night of 19 September, he had returned briefly to the Hôtel du Chemin de Fer du Nord and had attempted to wash himself and his clothing, finally abandoning his efforts and leaving behind in his room bloodstained clothing and weapons. The third day of the trial opened with the testimony of François-Zacharie Roussin, a professor of chemistry at the Val-de-Grâce, who had examined the state's exhibits, including Jean Kinck's stomach and intestines. He verified Troppmann's confession.[50]

The evidence gathered by the state was overwhelming, as the public prosecutor, Michel Grandperret, pointed out in his brief speech for the prosecution. In summing up, he emphasized not simply Troppmann's obvious guilt, but also that Troppmann could have acted, and *did* act, without accomplices. Throughout the summation, Troppmann maintained the passivity he had shown throughout the trial.[51]

Finally, it was the turn of Charles-Alexandre Lachaud, the defense attorney. Eloquent and theatrical, primarily a defense lawyer and a great fighter for his clients, Lachaud was in the first rank of Parisian attorneys and virtually the only one on good terms with the Second Empire. Unlike many of his breed, Lachaud took pains to be correct and polite in court, and he never carried his legal battles beyond the courtroom. That he was generally on good personal terms with perennial courtroom adversaries and political opponents he owed largely to his own good nature, which won him not just affection but also the respect due to an ideal professional. Consequently, his political enemies were his best friends: Jules Grévy, Jules Favre, and Léon Gambetta. Lachaud had several times stood for public office, but never successfully. In the elections of 1869, he had been overwhelmed by Jules Favre in the Eighth Parisian electoral district. Even after 1871, Lachaud would remain a convinced and ardent Bonapartist. Jules Favre was often his legal adversary; and if a case took them to the provinces, they would travel together and take adjoining rooms in a hotel. Lachaud had a reputation for taking even the most hopeless cases (he would accept the Bazaine case in 1873 after Edouard Allou refused it), so it was anticipated that Troppmann would turn to him even before he actually did so.[52]

What possible defense could there be for such calculated and brutal murders? Lachaud received several letters, anonymous of course, asserting that no defense should be provided, much less by a distinguished lawyer. One line of defense, however, was prescribed by a physician who hit the streets with a nineteen-page pamphlet the day before the opening of the trial. He

50. *Gazette des Tribunaux*, 30 and 31 December 1869; and Sangnier, *Plaidoyers*, 2:276–78.
51. *Gazette des Tribunaux*, 31 December 1869; and Sangnier, *Plaidoyers*, 2:279–81.
52. Henri Robert, *Lachaud*, pp. 18–23. Originally a lecture, this piece was reprinted in Robert's *Les Grands procès de l'histoire*, pp. 233–53.

peddled this tract for one franc, clearly hoping to influence the outcome of the trial by describing his own system for explaining madness and its cure. This physician, Dr. Amédée Bertrand, made no pretense of having seen or examined Troppmann. He had simply studied the case in the newspapers and had become convinced that Troppmann had been a victim of what Bertrand called *monomaine raisonnante.* That is to say, he had been possessed by a fixed idea, which he had obtained by reasoning, and to such a point that neither other ideas nor further evidence could in any way influence him. In such a state of mind, he had become maniacally possessed with working resolutely toward the one goal that had become fixed in his mind. He had become a madman.

In Troppmann's case, Dr. Bertrand continued, the madness had not only suggested the crime, but had enabled him to carry it out in a cold and calculated manner, and thereafter to view what he had done as simply the logical way to go about achieving his goal. At Le Havre, according to Dr. Bertrand, Troppmann had inadvertently begun a period of cure. Consequently, one should anticipate that he would become increasingly aware of the horror of his deeds, understand for the first time the likely penalty, and try to develop a defense. If the madness had been genuine, it would only be temporary.

Dr. Bertrand believed in five principal treatments for madness and listed them in the order of their efficacy: hydrotherapy, saline purgatives, a violent emotion or shock, isolation, and finally the moral influence of good counseling. He pointed out that Troppmann had been subjected to all five treatments: the first two when he threw himself into the harbor; the third when he was recognized by the arresting officer; the fourth because of his necessary isolation as a prisoner; and the fifth, as a result of *exhortations sages et raisonnables,* when he had given indications of repentance.[53] None of Bertrand's other published works have anything to do with insanity, revealing, if the point needs to be made, that his medical expertise lay elsewhere. Yet, Lachaud's speech for the defense reads as if he had taken a cue from Bertrand, though the matter is entirely circumstantial. Lachaud gave the court the portrait of a young man who, from the age of fourteen, had had one ambition: to get rich. No evidence at all that he had taken any pleasure in life was available. An abnormal youth with a fixation on money, he had engaged in no frivolities, not even a love affair. He had worked for his father, and he read books: on chemistry, and, in addition, the most insalubrious of novels. The only good and normal thing about Troppmann was his love for his mother: "He idolizes her." Troppmann dropped his head at this statement and wept, and did not raise his head again during Lachaud's speech.

53. Dr. Amédée Bertrand, *Etude médico-légale au sujet de Troppmann,* pp. 5–19.

We can imagine that one hundred years later a defense attorney of La-chaud's skill would have been less persuaded that Troppmann's adoration of his mother, in view of his particular abnormalities, was a "good and normal thing." Troppmann's excessive introversion, his demonstrated indifference to human beings, and the self-confidence he would reveal after the trial surely suggests a schizoid personality; and even the attempt at suicide would be consistent with schizoid behavior.[54] While such terminology could not have been used in 1869, a more sophisticated medical testimony could have strengthened the case for Troppmann's emotional immaturity or illness.

Lachaud sought to weaken the prosecution's case in two ways. First, he tried to raise doubt about Kinck's "noble nature." Evidently he had gone to Alsace in search of quick wealth, and Lacaud questioned whether Jean Kinck was really as innocent of any conniving in this bad business as the state had implied. Secondly, Lachaud brought up the matter of Tropp-mann's still undiscovered accomplices. "That," said Lachaud, "is the central question in the debate." The jury must not vote for Troppmann's death until convinced that *he alone* was guilty as charged. No doubt Troppmann *had* lied about many things during the *instruction*, Lachaud admitted; but Troppmann had sometimes told the truth. The police, for instance, had not found Jean Kinck's body until Troppmann gave its location. He truthfully reported the cause of Jean Kinck's death. Why would he not name his ac-complices? Lachaud professed not to know. All Troppmann would say was, "Find the briefcase and you will have the rest of the story."

Now *why* had the briefcase not been found? Lachaud speculated at some length to the effect that perhaps it had been found, but that the judicial authorities had discovered in it matters too delicate to reveal. Thus did the Bonapartist Lachaud, clutching for any straw on his client's behalf, inadver-tently open the way for the conspiracy theory later to be advanced by the anti-Bonapartist "Monsieur Claude." Lachaud also rebutted the state's con-tention that Troppmann could have acted alone, deducing in some detail that there must have been at least three additional murderers. The argument was seemingly effective since it played upon the adult predilection to believe in the innocence of children; and for those of such predisposition, it did strain credibility to be told that such a complex of crimes had been planned and executed by one juvenile.

The original idea for the crime, Lachaud proposed, had come from read-ing, from authors who put bad ideas into people's heads; he pointed espe-cially to Eugène Sue's *Wandering Jew*, where the reader will find Rodin coveting Rennepont's fortune, and for which an entire family of six is dispat-

54. H. Guntrip, "A Study of Fairbairn's Theory of Schizoid Reactions," Reed, Alexander, and Tomkins, eds., *Psychopathology: A Source Book*, pp. 362–67.

ched. Troppmann, said Lachaud, became "fixed" on that theme to the point of becoming ill.

"Look at his hands," Lachaud added, "the hands of a wild animal. Just look at him—look at the bizarre in his build. On the other hand, if this is a matter of a ferocious animal, he ought to be muzzled, not killed. This is a case of criminal madness." Finally, he reminded the jury that society had been drifting toward the abolition of capital punishment on the grounds that society has the right to protect itself, but not the right to seek vengeance. And in any case, he concluded, Troppmann certainly ought to be spared until his accomplices could be arrested.[55]

The jury left the courtroom about six-thirty in the evening and remained out for three hours. They found Troppmann guilty on all counts. The court then retired to consider the penalty, returning in ten minutes with a sentence of death. Its pronouncement brought a burst of applause from the gallery. Troppmann gave no sign of emotion on hearing the verdict, saying, "Oh, I quite expected it."[56] Once in his cell, he added, "All those people [in the courtroom] are angry at me, and I do not know why since I've not done anything to them."[57]

Troppmann was immediately transferred to La Roquette to await execution. He seemed in good spirits and was able to sleep well, avowedly confident that Lachaud would have the verdict reversed.[58] Lachaud naturally filed an appeal with the *Cour de cassation*, but he also took advantage of his good relations with the Tuileries to address an appeal for clemency to the emperor. He said not a word about insanity in his letter, but simply stressed Troppmann's youth and the probable accomplices who had not yet been located.[59]

In truth, Lachaud had not for a moment believed in the existence of the briefcase or the accomplices. At the time of the trial, he had attended a reception at the Ministry of Foreign Affairs and had been engaged by Richard von Metternich in a long, private chat. Afterward, everyone sought out Metternich to hear what Lachaud had revealed about the Troppmann case. The foxy Lachaud had told Metternich that he had been unable to get Troppmann to give him the accomplices' names, and that he must therefore seek to prolong the case until he could get the truth out of his client. Later, after Troppmann's execution, Lachaud would admit to Metternich that he had known all along there had been no accomplices; but that he had cer-

55. Sangnier, *Plaidoyers*, 2:285–315.
56. *Gazette des Tribunaux*, 31 December 1869.
57. Du Camp, *Paris*, 3:184.
58. *Gazette des Tribunaux*, 1 January 1870.
59. Pierre Bouchardon, *Troppmann*, pp. 235–36.

tainly not wanted any juror to get wind of that fact while the trial proceeded.[60]

The movement toward the abolition of capital punishment, to which Lachaud had referred when seeking mercy from the jury, was something less than a ground swell. Earlier in 1869, the Republican Jules Simon had published an attack upon capital punishment,[61] but Troppmann's bloody performance had rather undermined the cause. The well-known Catholic polemicist and dandy, Jules Barbey d'Aurevilly, sneered at Simon on 4 November 1869, calling him a papier-mâché philosopher, in an article entitled "Les Assassins contre les rhéteurs, Troppmann contre Jules Simon." Despite the free-thinking philosophers who have proclaimed an inviolable respect for life for even those who have not respected it, Barbey d'Aurevilly wrote, "the one hundred seven blows from Troppmann's knife" have shown the people that the death penalty is "the necessary penalty."[62] Whether or not Troppmann was God's response to the philosophical argument, as Barbey d'Aurevilly would have us believe, the drama of Troppmann's execution would suggest that Barbey d'Aurevilly had been closer to the popular pulse than Jules Simon had been.

Even when informed that the emperor had rejected the plea for clemency, Troppmann indicated to Monsieur Claude that he was quite confident the high court would quash the verdict.[63] The *Cour de cassation* had the case on its agenda for 13 January. In the meantime, a new murder was announced, that of Victor Noir, shot by "Prince X who lives in a town neighboring on Paris."[64] This opaque reference was clarified the following day by an imperial decree, countersigned by Emile Ollivier, providing for the prosecution of Prince Pierre Bonaparte, another nuisance for His Majesty from Lucien's line. The new sensation began to shove Troppmann off the front pages.[65] His appeal was heard as scheduled, but the court found that all the legal procedures in the case had been correct, and that the death penalty was consistent with what the law provided and with the jury's verdict. The appeal was rejected.[66]

Prince Pierre's *instruction* proceeded as Troppmann awaited his execution, unaware that he was doomed, since the law forbade prisoners to be told that their appeals had been rejected until the last moment.[67] A prison

60. Pauline de Metternich, *Souvenirs d'enfance et de jeunesse*, pp. 223–24.
61. Jules Simon, *La Peine de mort*.
62. Jules Barbey d'Aurevilly, *Polémiques d'hier*, pp. 328–29.
63. *Gazette des Tribunaux*, 6 January 1870.
64. Ibid., 10–11 January 1870.
65. Ibid., 12 January 1870.
66. Ibid., 14 January 1870.
67. Ibid., 19 January 1870.

chaplain, the Abbé Crozes, induced Troppmann to confess himself on the afternoon of 15 January, and Troppmann attended Mass in a strait jacket the following morning and took his last communion. He seemed entirely calm, certainly calmer than those who observed him.[68] Crowds had been gathering each night outside La Roquette in anticipation of the execution, but Troppmann was unable to hear their noise and received no inkling of his fate. Cheerful and confident, he asked for books and magazines, notably *le Magasin pittoresque* and *la Revue des deux mondes.*[69]

The true story of Troppmann's last hours was not revealed until after a dozen years, when the officials charged with the execution were either retired or dead. It would appear that both Monsieur Claude and the prefect of police, then Joachim Piétri, had agreed to permit a group of writers to be present within La Roquette to witness Troppmann's preparation for execution. Evidently this impropriety was arranged by Maxime Du Camp, who was a friend of Monsieur Claude. In addition to Du Camp, the party included Albert Wolff, Victorien Sardou, and Ivan Turgenev.

Though the execution was set for seven in the morning on 19 January 1870, the literati arrived at the prison before the preceding midnight, for they might otherwise have been unable to penetrate the mob that would swarm for the spectacle. They came prepared on that bitterly cold night with bread, ham, two bottles of Bordeaux, and cigars. But their precautions were unnecessary, because, as Monsieur Claude explained, a stuffed turkey had been prepared for them in the prison pharmacist's apartment; and they were received in the prison director's apartment where servants passed sandwiches, ham, chicken, pâté de fois gras, tea, wine, and punch. Officers commanding the attendant regiments (the troops being present because of the agitations resulting from the Noir murder) were also invited in for refreshments, while coffee was served to the troops in the courtyard.[70] Ivan Turgenev, opposed in principle to capital punishment, was soon smitten with the grotesquerie of the entertainment and regretted that he had accepted Du Camp's invitation. To assuage his conscience, he would later write of his experience in the hope of aiding opponents of capital punishment.

The prison director, Laroche d'Oisy, assured his guests that Troppmann was also eating well, showed no fear, and continued to claim he had accomplices whom he would not name. Despite this apparent confidence, Troppmann had written a letter to the prison pharmacist in an attempt to obtain poison, and he had sought the cooperation of several prison officials in plotting an escape. The literary guests were shown a pile of letters ad-

68. Abbé Georges Moreau, *Souvenirs de la Petite et de la Grande Roquette*, 2:225–26.
69. *Gazette des Tribunaux*, 20 January 1870.
70. Albert Wolff in *Le Figaro*, 15 January 1882; and Moreau, *Souvenirs*, 2:235–37.

dressed to Troppmann, which he had refused to read. Most of them were from cranks, but a few writers begged him to make an honest confession and to repent. A Methodist minister had sent him a twenty-page dissertation on the theological points relating to his case, which understandably went unread. Inevitably, there were the notes in feminine handwriting, enclosing violets and marguerites. Monsieur Claude told them about the Jud case and how Jud had evaded arrest, saying he had virtually lost all hope of ever capturing Jud, if indeed he were still alive. Finally, they met "Monsieur de Paris," the headsman Heindreicht, an Alsatian whose name was pronounced "Indric" by the prison authorities. Suddenly it was 6:20, and Monsieur Claude said to the group, "It is time."

In addition to the literary guests, the party now included the prison director, the Abbé Crozes, Monsieur Claude and his secretary, Souvras. Down they went to Troppmann's cell, separated from the street by three thick walls. Troppmann had already awakened and was seated at his table when the party entered. Monsieur Claude removed his hat and spoke: "Troppmann, we have come to tell you that your appeal for pardon has been denied and that the moment for expiation has arrived." The condemned man remained calm, seemingly unmoved, and chatted about his accomplices who had actually struck the fatal blows. He offered no resistance as a strait jacket was put over him, nor did he cry out or show any signs of an impending collapse. Where did this moral strength come from, Turgenev wondered? Was Troppmann eager to play his great role before an appreciative audience, or was this proof that Troppmann was not in full possession of his mental faculties? He went through the religious ceremony, receiving absolution, though his religious feelings were obviously slight.

When the party reached the outer dressing chamber, Heindreicht and his assistant worked swiftly to prepare Troppmann for the ax. The strait jacket was removed and the victim heavily bound, his hands crossed behind his back. He was then seated so that his hair could be cut by the assistant, and the shirt collar was snipped away. Asked for his last request, Troppmann had nothing to say. Once again Monsieur Claude asked him whether he still insisted on those accomplices, and again he said yes. "Very well," said Claude, "let us go!" The crowd let out a howl of satisfaction at the sight of its prey. He went easily to the scaffold; but once in position for execution, he forced his head to the side and managed to bite a finger of the hand that struggled to hold the head in place. After the body had been removed, several men were seen to approach the guillotine and soak their handkerchiefs in the pool of blood, until the police chased them away. The Troppmann family claimed the body for burial.[71]

71. Ivan Turgenev, *Devant la guillotine*, pp. 5–59; *Gazette des Tribunaux*, 20 January 1870; and Alister Kershaw, *A History of the Guillotine*, pp. 72–73.

During the Troppmann affair, left-wing gossip held that the emperor had paid Troppmann to murder the Kinck family in order to divert public attention from domestic politics, presumably to avoid the liberalization of the regime. Thousands of people, ready to believe anything sensational, were victims of the rumor. Others argued, for the same reason, that Troppmann was a myth, that the murders had never taken place, but had been invented by the regime to occupy public attention. One woman wrote to the Abbé Crozes on 27 March 1870 asking for a definitive statement as to whether it had really been Troppmann who was executed on 19 January; or whether he had been set free and shipped abroad, a substitute kneeling in his place that day. Lachaud himself, though a loyal Bonapartist, had contributed to the mystery by wondering in court if the celebrated briefcase had contained state secrets necessarily concealed by the judicial authorities. In the early years of the Third Republic, it would become absolutely fashionable to believe that the Troppmann case had been invented by the police for the convenience of the late regime.[72] The utter inanity of such rumors was veiled, because many of the chief rumor-mongers were regarded as intellectuals in possession of superior insights into political realities. In fact, their sophisticated skepticism was the mother of a naïve gullibility.

How easy, therefore, was the task of the counterfeit Monsieur Claude, especially after 1870! The reason for Troppmann's silence about his accomplices, he would have us believe, allows us to understand the Jud case: all of Alsace had become honeycombed with Prussian agents, military observers in particular, studying the terrain in preparation for invasion, and protected and encouraged by the local Protestant population. Poinsot had been murdered because he had tried to penetrate Prussian state secrets; Kinck *père* lost his life because he had discovered enemy secrets. Jud and Troppmann were hired killers interested solely in money, but acting for the enemy—petty crooks whose crimes were planned and directed from beyond the Rhine.[73] What would poor old Poinsot, clutching his *Parfait jardinier*, have made of that!

Of all the well-known game birds, the poppycock is surely the hardest to bring down. It neither dies nor fades away. It can, indeed, be readily tamed and rendered a household pet by one whose cause might thereby be served. Troppmann, as Frank Jellinek tells us,[74] would have caused little public stir had not Paris been living in an "atmosphere of approaching calamity." His arrest, only the result of a series of flukes, merely demonstrated the inefficiency of the costly and hated imperial police. The "fortuitious crimes of

---

72. E. A. Vizetelly, *Court Life of the Second French Empire*, pp. 326, 386; and Moreau, *Souvenirs*, 2:253–54.
73. *Memoirs de Monsieur Claude*, 5:45–61.
74. Frank Jellinek, *The Paris Commune of 1871*, pp. 48–49, 95.

Troppmann and Pierre Bonaparte," he concludes, "hastened the fall of the Second Empire." That has been the latest version of "Monsieur Claude's" hokum.

THE FINAL THUNDERCLAP; OR,
THE CRIME OF AUTEUIL

> All happy families
> resemble each other, each
> unhappy family is unhappy
> in its own way.
> LEO TOLSTOY

The Bonapartes were never the happiest of all possible families. Napoleon I had found the conduct of his four brothers and three sisters a continual irritation. Napoleon III would say, when accused of having nothing of the first emperor in him, that, alas, he shared his family.[75] Given the variety of caprices and incompetences represented in the clan, it is probably risky to assert that Lucien's branch was the most troublesome. Lucien himself had early become hostile to Napoleon I, suspicious that Napoleon had abandoned the Jacobin ideals of their youth for personal advancement. In 1803, Lucien made the rift public by marrying a commoner despite Napoleon's objection, which later won Lucien exclusion from the imperial family. He accepted a papal title, and the annoying suspicion that Napoleon's political career had entirely hinged on Lucien's intervention on the Eighteenth Brumaire remained for both brothers. It is true that Lucien rallied to Napoleon during the Hundred Days—a moment when Napoleon reasserted his Jacobinism—but the reconciliation came too late to benefit either brother.

By the time of the Second Empire, several branches of the family were extinct and several more were inconsequential in size. Otherwise, the familial burden might well have been more than either public funds or His Majesty's patience could have borne. Napoleon I's own legitimate issue had ceased with the death of the duc de Reichstadt in 1832. Pauline, princesse Borghese, had escaped childbirth entirely, despite rumors of ample opportunity. Of King Joseph's two daughters, only Julie survived long enough to see the birth of the Second Empire, and she died in 1854. Elisa, wed to that outstanding nullity, Félix Bacciochi, had only one daughter who survived into the Second Empire—Napoleone-Elisa, by marriage a Camerata. (The chamberlain named Bacciochi was Elisa's nephew.)

When Napoleon III reconstituted the imperial family, it included only the imperial couple; old King Jerome and his children, Jerome-Napoleon and Mathilde-Letitia-Wilhelmine; and ultimately the Prince Imperial.

---

75. Dr. Prosper Ménière, *Mémoires anecdotiques sur les salons du second empire*, p. 31.

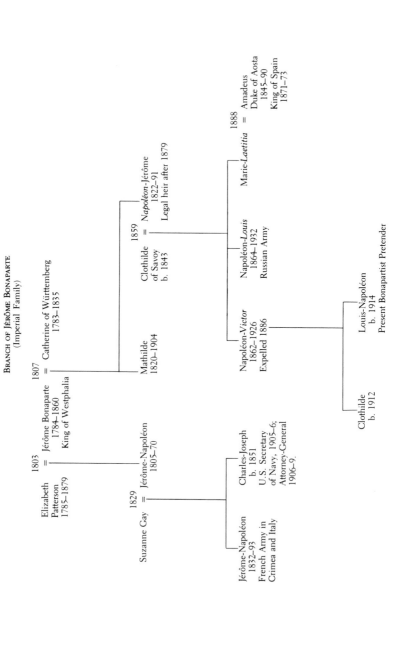

BRANCH OF JÉRÔME BONAPARTE
(Imperial Family)

Elizabeth
Patterson
1785–1879

1803
=

Jérôme Bonaparte
1784–1860
King of Westphalia

1807
=

Catherine of Württemberg
1783–1835

Jérôme-Napoléon
1805–70

1829
=

Suzanne Gay

Jérôme-Napoléon
1832–93
French Army in
Crimea and Italy

Charles-Joseph
b. 1851
U.S. Secretary
of Navy, 1905–6;
Attorney-General
1906–9.

Mathilde
1820–1904

Napoléon-Jérôme
1822–91
Legal heir after 1879

Clothilde
of Savoy
b. 1843

1859
=

Napoléon-Victor
1862–1926
Expelled 1886

Napoléon-Louis
1864–1932
Russian Army

Marie-*Laetitia*

1888
=

Amadeus
Duke of Aosta
1845–90
King of Spain
1871–73

Clothilde
b. 1912

Louis-Napoléon
b. 1914
Present Bonapartist Pretender

BRANCH OF LUCIEN BONAPARTE
(Civil Family)

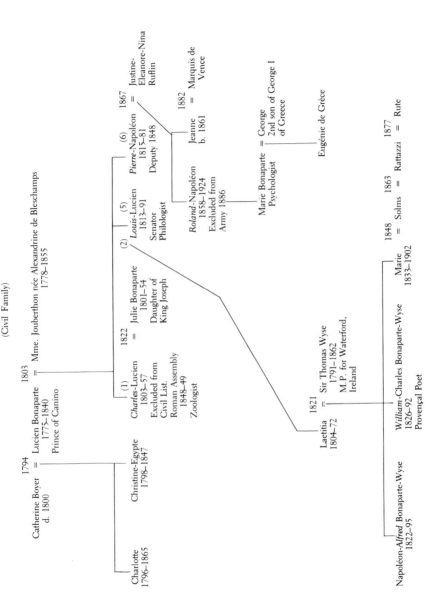

Catherine Boyer = Lucien Bonaparte = Mme. Jouberthon née Alexandrine de Bleschamps
d. 1800   1775–1840   1778–1855
1794   Prince of Canino   1803

Christine-Egypte
1798–1847

Charlotte
1796–1865

(1)
Charles-Lucien
1803–57
Excluded from
Civil List.
Roman Assembly
1848–49
Zoologist

1822
Julie Bonaparte
1801–54
Daughter of
King Joseph

(2)
Louis-Lucien
1813–91
Senator
Philologist

(5)

(6)
Pierre-Napoléon
1815–81
Deputy 1848

1867
Justine-
Eleanore-Nina
Ruflin

Roland-Napoléon
1858–1924
Excluded from
Army 1886

Jeanne
b. 1861

1882
Marquis de
Vence

Marie Bonaparte = George
Psychologist   2nd son of George I
                 of Greece

Eugénie de Grèce

Laettitia
1804–72

1821
Sir Thomas Wyse
1791–1862
M.P. for Waterford,
Ireland

William-Charles Bonaparte-Wyse
1826–92
Provençal Poet

Marie
1833–1902

1848   1863   1877
= Solms   =   Rattazzi   =   Rute

Napoléon-Alfred Bonaparte-Wyse
1822–95

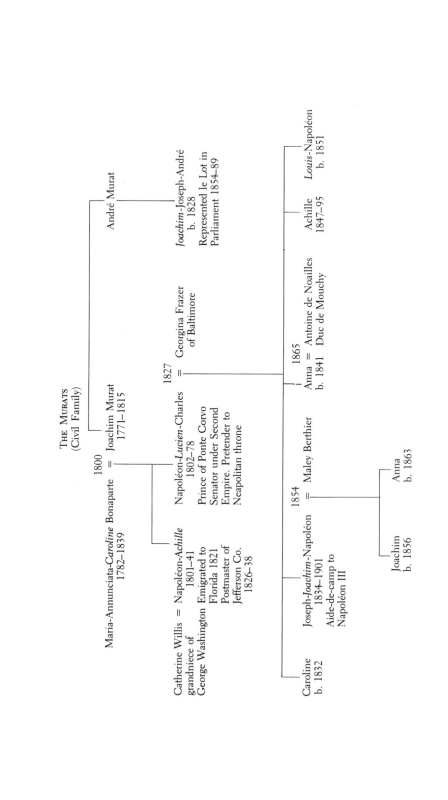

The Murats
(Civil Family)

André Murat

Maria-Annunciata-*Caroline* Bonaparte = Joachim Murat
1782–1839   1800   1771–1815

Catherine Willis = Napoléon-*Achille*   Napoléon-*Lucien*-Charles   1827   Georgina Frazer
grandniece of   1801–41   1802–78   of Baltimore
George Washington Emigrated to   Prince of Ponte Corvo   =
                   Florida 1821   Senator under Second
                   Postmaster of   Empire. Pretender to
                   Jefferson Co.   Neapolitan throne
                   1826–38

Joachim-Joseph-André
b. 1828
Represented le Lot in
Parliament 1854–89

Caroline   Joseph-*Joachim*-Napoléon   1854   Maley Berthier   1865   Anna = Antoine de Noailles   Achille   *Louis*-Napoléon
b. 1832   1834–1901   =   b. 1841   Duc de Mouchy   1847–95   b. 1851
            Aide-de-camp to
            Napoléon III

Joachim   Anna
b. 1856   b. 1863

Thus, he perpetuated the exclusion of Lucien's branch from the succession and forbade them to use the title "imperial highness." Napoleon III did create a civil family to provide for Bonapartes not included in the imperial family, giving them a claim on pensions from his civil list. The civil family included the Murats as descendants of Caroline, and all of Lucien's descendants save Charles-Lucien, the firstborn.[76]

Prince Pierre-Napoleon was Lucien's third son, born in Rome on 11 October 1815. It became apparent early that he was his father's son: by temperament a man of action, but condemned by events to political and military inactivity. In 1831, when an insurrection broke out in Romagna, the sixteen-year-old Pierre joined the Italian nationalist movement against the wishes of Lucien, who had him arrested and confined. Released later in the year, Pierre was no longer welcome in the Papal States. Lucien then sent him off to New Jersey to visit his uncle Joseph. There he met Francisco de Paola de Santander, a friend of Joseph and close associate of the late Simon Bolivar. With Joseph's permission, Pierre took service during the remainder of 1832 with Santander in Colombia; but, unable to obtain the exalted military rank to which he aspired, he returned to New York and from there to Italy.

Quarrelsome and adventurous, Pierre seemed to be forever in trouble until 3 May 1836 when he was seized by police at Canino, and sent to Rome to imprisoned in the Castel San Angelo. Before he could be taken, however, he put up a vigorous fight against his thirty arresters, one of whom he killed. His trial, on 24–26 September 1836, ended in a sentence of death, but the sentence was commuted to exile in February 1837. There followed many months of wandering which took Pierre to New York (where he met his cousin Louis-Napoleon, in exile after the Strassburg fiasco), London, Greece, Corfu, and Albania; finally, toward the end of 1838 he settled down on an isolated, rented farm near the Belgian village of Mohimont, deep in the forest of the Ardennes.[77]

Ten years later, the February Revolution brought him out of retirement. As a good Republican, he hastened to Paris to offer his services. Not until 15 April was he notified by Louis Blanc that the Provisional Government had appointed him to the rank of battalion commander in the Foreign Legion, though no command was immediately available for him. The lack of enthusiasm for his service was rather transparent.

A few days later, however, he found himself elected to a seat in the Constituent Assembly from Corsica, though he had never visited his constitu-

76. *Papiers secrets et correspondance du second empire* (Paris: Auguste Ghio, 1873), p. 42; and E. A. Vizetelly, *Court Life of the Second French Empire*, pp. 210–11.

77. Eugénie de Grèce, *Pierre-Napoléon Bonaparte, 1815–1881*, pp. 18–167; and Emile Ollivier, *L'Empire libéral, études, récits, souvenirs*, 12:396–97.

ency. He sat with the Republicans, but voted for measures helpful to Louis-Napoleon and aided his cousin in the presidential campaign. On the other hand, his conduct in the assembly was erratic, until he was trusted by no faction including the Bonapartists; on one occasion he assaulted an aged deputy, renewing his reputation for a violent temperament. Louis-Napoleon concluded that it would be the better part of wisdom to send Pierre to Algeria on military assignment. This was accomplished in September 1849, to Pierre's great chagrin. In November, he returned to Paris without leave and was dismissed from the service for indiscipline.

While Pierre approved the *coup d'état* of 1851, seeing in it the restoration of universal suffrage and the preservation of the Republic, he was considerably less pleased by the revival of Empire in 1852. Yet, he did not reject the Empire, but was himself rejected. His annual pension from the civil list amounted to 100,000 francs, but he was denied official employment despite his repeated requests and was never invited to court. With his mistress, Justine-Eléanore-Nina Ruflin, an attractive woman of common origin, he retired once again, buying a house in Auteuil. He retained his retreat in the Ardennes for hunting, for he was passionately fond of arms. (Pierre always carried a revolver in his pocket and placed it under his pillow at night, a habit formed in his Italian days.) The house at 59, rue d'Auteuil had belonged to Helvétius in the eighteenth century and had been the scene of regular Tuesday dinners attended by the Diderot-Holbach-Lespinasse set. It had, as the saying goes, seen better days.[78]

In 1863, Prince Pierre announced that he would stand for election in Corsica to regain the seat he had held from 1848 to 1851. Napoleon III let him know that his presence in Parliament would be an embarrassment and asked him to withdraw. Pierre refused. The emperor then reminded him that, while he could not prevent him from seeking office, he could, as head of the family, legally prevent him from taking his seat. That proved to be unnecessary. The government sponsored an official candidate, Séverin Abbatucci, who won the election.[79]

The next rebuff grew out of Pierre's belated decision to marry his mistress in order that he might legitimize their two children: Roland, born in 1858; and Jeanne, born in 1862. But Napoleon III was as firm in the matter as his uncle had been with Lucien. Refusing to recognize such a marriage, Napoleon III wrote to Prince Pierre that "when one has the honor to bear your name, there are proprieties that have to be respected. The barrier they impose [to such a marriage] is, after all, a small price to pay for the envied ad-

78. Ollivier, *L'Empire libéral*, 12:397–400; and Alexandre Zévaès, *L'Affaire Pierre Bonaparte* (*le meurtre de Victor Noir*), p. 24.
79. Eugénie de Grèce, *Pierre-Napoléon Bonaparte*, pp. 292–99.

vantages which, I would suppose, you would not want to give up." [80]—the 100,000 francs, for instance.

So matters stood at the beginning of 1870 when, as Troppmann awaited his execution, the announcement was made that Victor Noir had been shot by "Prince X who lives in a town neighboring on Paris." [81] The incident was the last act in what had been a quarrel between two newspapers: *La Ravanche*, a radical, anti-Bonapartist sheet, which was the organ for a republican-socialist group in Corsica headed by Louis Tomasi; and *l'Avenir de la Corse*, a conservative Corsican paper published in Paris, but founded for the express purpose of answering *la Ravanche*. The editor was Jean de la Rocca, an employee of the Ministry of the Interior. In 1869, these two newspapers had been debating the merits of Napoleon I and, by extension, the Bonapartes, while exchanging insults.

The nominal editors aside, a key figure in the quarrel was a Republican pamphleteer of Corsican origin, Paschal Grousset, who served as the Paris correspondent for *la Ravanche*, who had been one of its founders, and who had often inspired the articles signed by Louis Tomasi. Paschal Grousset had also been hired as a journalist by Henri Rochefort, who had been permitted by the regime to return from exile to take his parliamentary seat after the elections of 1869. Rochefort at once founded a new polemical journal called *la Marseillaise*. Articles inspired by Grousset in *la Marseillaise* were sometimes signed by Ernest Lavigne. As such arrangements permitted a rich confusion when it came to literary or editorial responsibility for articles, it is a matter of some curiosity that Alexandre Zévaès, long the authority on the Noir murder, neglected to emphasize Grousset's double association. [82]

Prince Pierre entered the picture on 30 December 1869, by writing a letter to *l'Avenir de la Corse* to congratulate the paper on its campaign against *la Ravanche*. He characterized its editors as "cowardly Judases, traitors to their country, whose own relatives in earlier days would have put them in bags and tossed them into the sea." He called them traitors simply on the grounds that the causes of Corsica and the Bonapartes had always been united. [83]

To this feeble argument came two responses. The first, from Louis Tomasi in *la Ravanche*, stated that the Corsican Republicans, having taken at face value the Bonapartes' professions of republican faith in 1848, had given the Bonapartes electoral support. Who had subsequently betrayed whom? Was not Prince Pierre, in fact, a liar? [84] These were grounds for a duel with

80. Ibid., pp. 304–5; and *Papiers secrets*, pp. 36–38.
81. *Gazette des Tribunaux*, 10–11 January 1870.
82. Zévaès, *L'Affaire Pierre Bonaparte*, pp. 11–18; Eugénie de Grèce, *Pierre-Napoléon Bonaparte*, p. 315; and Pierre de La Gorce, *Histoire du second empire*, 6:11.
83. *L'Avenir de la Corse*, 30 December 1869.
84. *La Ravanche*, 4 January 1870.

Tomasi, concluded Pierre, and on 8 January he asked Jean de la Rocca and Paul Granier de Cassagnac to serve as his seconds.

The second response came the following day in *la Marseillaise:* "In the Bonaparte family there are some strange individuals whose wild ambitions cannot be satisfied, and who, seeing themselves systematically relegated to the shadows, burn with spite at being nothing and having reached no power. They resemble those old girls who have never found a husband and who weep about the lovers they have not had either. Let us rank Prince Pierre-Napoleon Bonaparte in this category of lame unfortunates. He makes war on radical democracy, but achieves more of a Waterloo than an Austerlitz. . . . Scratch a Bonaparte, find a ferocious beast." The article's conclusion reminded readers, in the vein of *la Ravanche,* that Prince Pierre had betrayed his republican principles of 1848.[85] Though the article was signed by Ernest Lavigne, the style was Henri Rochefort's, and Prince Pierre knew it.

Pierre issued, therefore, a second challenge on 9 January, drawn up with Cassagnac's aid: "After having abused each member of my family, you now insult me with one of your penned contrivances. My turn must come. Only I have an advantage over the others of my name: being a private citizen while being a Bonaparte. . . . Thus, I ask if your pen is backed up by your chest. . . . I live—not in a palace—but at 59, rue d'Auteuil. I promise that if you present yourself, you will not be told that I am out." [86] Rochefort thereupon appointed two seconds of his own, J.-B. Millière (the same Millière who would expose Jules Favre's private life in 1871) and Arthur Arnould, both staff members at *la Marseillaise.* [87]

Pierre was taking on even more than he yet realized, for Paschal Grousset, as a staff member of *la Ravanche,* regarded himself insulted by Pierre's initial letter of 30 December. On 9 January, Grousset appointed two seconds to represent him—Ulric de Fonvielle and Victor Noir, both of *la Marseillaise*—and instructed them to ask reparation from Pierre.[88] While it is quite clear that Prince Pierre had instigated the tangle with his gratuitous and intemperate letter of 30 December, it remains unclear why Grousset waited until 9 January to appoint and instruct his seconds. The effect, whether planned or coincidental, was to associate his challenge to Pierre with Rochefort's letter in *la Marseillaise,* to refocus the quarrel from Corsica to Paris, and to involve a remarkably large number of staff members from *la Marseillaise* in the showdown with a Bonaparte, albeit one of no official sta-

85. *La Marseillaise,* 9 January 1870.
86. Eugénie de Grèce, *Pierre-Napoléon Bonaparte,* pp. 319–20; La Gorce, *Histoire du second empire,* 6:12; and Ollivier, *L'Empire liberal,* 12:402.
87. Henri Rochefort, *Les Aventures de ma vie,* 2:132.
88. Eugénie de Grèce, *Pierre-Napoléon Bonaparte,* p. 323.

tion. What followed certainly encourages the suspicion that the gentlemen of *la Marseillaise* were in collusion.

Pierre's letter to Rochefort arrived at the offices of *la Marseillaise* on the morning of 10 January and was opened by Millière, whose task it was to open all correspondence. He took it at once to Rochefort. Since a challenge is not properly delivered by the challenger but by his seconds, Pierre's letter was technically a provocation. Rochefort, therefore, asked Millière and Arnould to call upon Pierre to deliver the formal challenge.

Grousset, while he would later insist that he had acted without Rochefort's knowledge, dispatched his own seconds that same morning. Indeed, in defiance of the customs governing duels, he accompanied his seconds and took along an additional friend, Georges Sauton of *le Réveil*, another opposition newspaper. This party of four reached the house in Auteuil before Rochefort's seconds did, though only Fonvielle and Noir went to the door.[89]

Fonvielle, then thirty-six, was a man of some experience, having seen military service in the Italian campaign of 1859, with Garibaldi in 1860, and thereafter in the American Civil War.[90] On the other hand, Victor Noir, who would become the victim of the piece, was a mere twenty-one. Though he has usually been described as an editor at *la Marseillaise*, Victor Noir was simply an aspirant writer who had little skill and whose education had been neglected. Born Yvan Salmon to a Jewish family, in Attigny (Vosges), he had changed his name to ape his brother, a writer of serialized stories, who used the name Louis Noir—Noir being their mother's maiden name. Victor had been a hanger-on at several newspapers before he drifted to *la Marseillaise* in December 1869. Burly, generally good-humored, given to a kind of mindless radicalism, he could also be aggressive—a St. Bernard puppy. A Rochefort-directed newspaper was a natural home for him, and he was evidently posted near the entry to cope with outraged readers who might seek direct redress after experiencing Rochefort's unique version of events. Noir's name had several times been signed to articles written by others, which pleased him; but he was really the doorman and very nearly a bystander in the political hassle that cost him his life.[91]

When Fonvielle and Noir arrived at 59, rue d'Auteuil on the afternoon of 10 January, Prince Pierre, suffering from either a bad cold or the flu, was resting in the salon. The calling cards were brought in by the maid. Pierre did not recognize the names, but as he was expecting the arrival of Rochefort's seconds, he went to his bedroom to put on a jacket (which had the ha-

89. Ollivier, *L'Empire liberal* 12:403–4.
90. Zévaès, *L'Affaire Pierre Bonaparte*, p. 19.
91. Anatole Claveau, *Souvenirs politiques et parlementaires d'un témoin*, 1:353; Zévaès, *L'Affaire Pierre Bonaparte* pp. 5–6; and La Gorce, *Histoire du second empire*, 6:11.

bitual revolver in a pocket). Upon his return to the salon, the two visitors introduced themselves as representing Paschal Grousset and handed him the letter in which Grousset asked for reparation.

Prince Pierre moved to the window and read the message quickly, growing angry as he construed the letter to be a Rochefort trick: "I am going to fight with Rochefort," he cried out, "not with one of his hacks!" (Fonvielle would later claim that Pierre had said "not with his swine!") At that, Victor Noir advanced and struck Pierre on the left cheek with his right hand. Pierre fell back several steps, drew out his revolver and fired. Noir staggered, then fled from the room and out of the house. Fonvielle, who also carried a concealed pistol, tried to load it, but ended by fleeing when he was fired at by Pierre.[92]

Noir collapsed outside the house and was carried to a neighborhood pharmacy, where he quickly expired. Rochefort's seconds had arrived on the scene by then, and Millière in vain tried to organize a gathering crowd of the curious to take the house by assault. Prince Pierre, expecting an attack, put his children in the summerhouse at the bottom of the garden, secured the house as best he could; and, with his wife (both of them armed), took a position on the stairs to meet the assault. The police soon arrived to put an end to further warfare.

Next came Dr. Morel, Pierre's physician, who had promised that morning to call again in the afternoon to check on Pierre's cold. He now found him with an additional ailment, a cheek puffed up from the blow. Pierre, who obviously believed himself to be in the right, freely described the incident for the police. Dr. Morel added that the blow was recent, not having been apparent when he had called that morning. Finally, Pierre sat down to write a report of the incident to the emperor's private secretary. Far from attempting to avoid arrest as a Bonaparte, he asked to be detained; and by six that very evening, he was accordingly lodged in the Conciergerie.[93]

The order for Prince Pierre's arrest was issued by both Joachim Piétri, the prefect of police, and by Emile Ollivier, the new minister of justice. Ollivier also gave the order to begin the *instruction* at once. The emperor, returning that evening from a hunt, was met at the station by Piétri and given the news. So shocked was he that he required assistance to gain his carriage. Once at the Tuileries, he received Emile Ollivier and tearfully approved the initial measures which had been taken. The emperor had, of course, no affection for Prince Pierre; but after the installation of the liberal ministry on 2

92. Ollivier, *L'Empire liberal*, 12:405–6; Eugénie de Grece, *Pierre Napoléon Bonaparte*, pp. 323–24; and Dr. Balthazard, "Le meurtre de Victor Noir," *Revue médicale française* 14(1933):120.

93. Ollivier, *L'Empire liberal*, 12:407–8; and Eugénie de Grèce, *Pierre Napoléon Bonaparte*, pp. 327–32.

January 1870, he had appeared to be greatly relieved and confident in the future. Conversely, the Republicans had dismally recognized that a liberal empire would doom their political chances. Now, on 10 January, "a child of the people" had been killed by a Bonaparte, and the emperor was too realistic not to see his peril. His liberal ministers were inexperienced, the opposition had a martyred corpse, and the revolutionaries among them would hardly miss the opportunity to undermine the liberal regime and destroy the reforms.

Though the new government had moved swiftly in the case and in evident good faith, its first embarrassment was the realization that the ordinary judicial procedures could not be applied. Prince Pierre had asked for trial before a jury in a common-law court, and Ollivier would have preferred that arrangement; but the *Senatus-consulte* of 4 June 1858 had provided for special criminal jurisdiction for members of the Bonaparte family. In such a case, the High Court had to be summoned, and its jury had to be drawn from the general councils of each department, a kind of national grand jury. Would such a trial be fairer or more partisan than one before a simple Parisian jury? Though no one actually knew, the special jurisdiction in itself was open to suspicion, and both the government and its opponents knew it.[94]

In any event, before the night of 10 January was over, the murderer had been jailed, the emperor had signed the decree convoking the High Court,[95] and the *juge d'instruction* had questioned both Prince Pierre and Fonvielle. The former gave as his version of the murder the story to which he would stick throughout the process, whereas Fonvielle damaged his integrity as a witness from the outset and inadvertently revealed information useful to the defense. When he had been in the presence of Victor Noir's body in the pharmacy, Fonvielle had been overheard to say: "He [Prince Pierre] killed my friend, but *c'est égal*; he got a hard slap!" Yet, having had time to calm down, Fonvielle told the *juge d'instruction* that, in response to Pierre's question, Noir and he had admitted that Grousset and Rochefort were in collusion; and that Pierre had then struck Noir, then stepped back to draw his revolver and fire. The medical examiners, however, had found no trace of such a blow on Noir's face when examining the body in the pharmacy, such as that Dr. Morel had found on Pierre's face. After that initial medical examination had been completed, the *juge d'instruction* ordered the body removed for an autopsy on 11 January, to be performed by Doctors Tardieu and Bergeron.[96]

94. La Gorce, *Histoire du second empire*, 6:15; Claveau, *Souvenirs*, 1:352, 357; Ollivier, *L'Empire libéral*, 12:409–10.

95. M.-G. Lemarchand, *Procès du prince Pierre-Napoléon Bonaparte devant la haute cour de justice*, p. 4.

96. Ollivier, *L'Empire libéral*, 12:411–14.

The next steps were Rochefort's. On the morning of the eleventh, his *Marseillaise* appeared, framed in black with bold headlines: VICTOR NOIR ASSASSINATED BY PRINCE PIERRE-NAPOLEON BONAPARTE; and ASSASSINATION ATTEMPT BY PRINCE PIERRE-NAPOLEON BONAPARTE AGAINST ULRICH DE FONVIELLE. In the lead article Rochefort wrote: "I have been so weak as to believe that a Bonaparte could be other than a murderer!

"I dared to suppose that a straight-forward duel was possible in this family where murder and traps are tradition and custom.

"Our collaborator, Paschal Grousset, shared my error, and today we weep for our poor and dear friend, Victor Noir, murdered by the bandit Pierre-Napoleon Bonaparte.

"For eighteen years France has been held in the bloodied hands of these cutthroats, who, not content to shoot down Republicans in the streets, lure them into wretched traps in order to slit their throats in private.

"Frenchmen, have you not had quite enought of it?" [97]

Rochefort's election to the *Corps législatif* in 1869 had been regarded by the revolutionary left as a declaration of war against the Second Empire. "In electing you," Millière had said to him, "we knew quite well that you would not be a legislator, but an enemy of the Empire." [98] They saw in this article the call to arms and Victor Noir as the war's first casualty; [99] and they would see Prince Pierre's courtroom as a battlefield that was as legitimate as the streets of Paris.

Rochefort's second step was to put in an appearance at the *Corps législatif* on 11 January with a demand to interpellate Minister of Justice Ollivier. The presiding officer, Eugène Schneider, granted the request, whereupon Rochefort asked Ollivier if he intended to subject the prisoner to the same justice applied generally by the "high dignitaries of the Empire." As a spokesman for "the people," he noted that the murdered man had been "a child of the people," and that the people insisted on judging the murderer themselves. Therefore, he was demanding a common-law jury trial. A trial before the High Court would be a mockery since the judges would be devoted to the imperial family.

Schneider interrupted, telling Rochefort that it was improper to doubt the integrity of judges whom he could not yet know. Rochefort answered that he certainly could doubt them in view of the calibre of justice meted out during the Second Empire—a rather impolitic sally considering the large number of lawyers who sat in the *Corps législatif*. He had, in fact, wondered whether they lived under the Bonapartes or under the Borgias, concluding that it was

97. *La Marseillaise*, 11 January 1870.
98. *Le Figaro*, 2 December 1869.
99. Gustave Flourens, *Paris livré*, p. 5.

Pierre Bonaparte, "The Wild Boar" (savagery, brutality). From
La Ménagerie impériale

time for all citizens to arm and to take justice into their own hands.
Schneider cut him off.[100]

Ollivier then went to the rostrum to reply. He defended the judicial process; he asserted the independence of the magistracy; and he remarked that it
was highly unusual to predict, as Rochefort had done, the outcome of a case
still in process. The government deplored the murder and would tolerate no
interference in the carrying out of justice. The defendant's rank would not
excuse him. Though the cabinet regretted the exceptional jurisdiction, the
Senate decree would have to be obeyed; and he hoped that the decree would
be abrogated in the future.

Ollivier's conclusion was the response of a man who knew he was being
threatened by subversion: "A murder has been committed by a highly-placed

100. Rochefort, *Les Aventures*, 2:140–41.

person. We have begun the prosecution, and we are demonstrating that, faithful to democratic principles, we subject the great as well as the small to the country's justice. As for these efforts to inflame popular feelings by speaking of 'a man of the people killed' and by publishing in newspapers gross descriptions designed to kindle imaginations and excite the people, we view them without fear. We are the law, we are the prerogative, we are moderation, we are liberty, *and*, if you stand in our way, we shall be force." [101]

Rochefort called these words "threatening." To underscore them, Ollivier handed Schneider a request from Public Prosecutor Michel Grandperret, who wanted authorization to begin proceedings against Rochefort under Article 86 of the Penal Code and Article 2 of the Law of 17 May 1819 for offenses against the emperor and for inciting revolution and civil war. What Grandperret needed was an official opinion as to whether Rochefort's parliamentary immunity covered him as a newspaperman. The question was immediately referred by the chair to an *ad hoc* committee chaired by the attorney Nogent-Saint-Laurens. [102]

Victor Noir's funeral, meanwhile, had been scheduled for 12 January. The body had been moved to Louis Noir's home in the rue du Marché in Neuilly. In Noir's body the radicals had the classic instrument for an emotional demonstration; but the left was far from united. Their divisions had been painfully exposed in the elections of 1869; and in the chamber on 11 January, when Rochefort launched his maladroit attack upon Ollivier, he found himself shunned by the leading liberal Republican deputies (Favre, Gambetta, and Picard) to his great irritation. [103] Moreover, they showed no interest in exploiting the funeral for political ends. Even among the radicals, the Blanquists refused to participate, certain that the government was going to be handed the opportunity for an easy victory over radicalism; and those radical leaders who gathered at the Noir home on the twelfth were unsure how to proceed. Gustave Flourens and Auguste Vermorel were for parading the corpse eastward across Paris for burial at Père Lachaise, whereas the Noir family preferred a simple burial in the Neuilly cemetery. Rochefort, increasingly impressed by evidence of official determination to bar the way to Père Lachaise, suddenly preached caution, having done the most to raise a mob for the occasion. [104]

101. Ollivier, *L'Empire liberal*, 12:417–20; and La Gorce, *Histoire du second empire*, 6:16–17.

102. Céleste Baroche, *Second Empire: Notes et souvenirs de seize années, 1855–1871*, p. 580; Rochefort, *Les Aventures*, 2:142–43; and Ollivier, *L'Empire liberal*, 12:420.

103. Rochefort, *Les Aventures*, 2:143.

104. Emile Ollivier, *Journal, 1846–1869*, 2:418; Eugénie de Grèce, *Pierre-Napoléon Bonaparte*, pp. 340–41; Rochefort, *Les Aventures*, 2:143–44; and La Gorce, *Histoire du second empire*, 6:17–18.

The government had no intention of preventing a proper funeral or of impeding the crowd that might gather to do homage to the dead. It *did* mean to obstruct any attempt to use the occasion for political purposes. During the Second Empire, when disturbances were anticipated, troops were readied but were kept out of sight. In this instance, Ollivier asked the emperor's consent to have cavalry and infantry deployed in the open as fair warning to the radicals, and the maneuver was probably decisive in preventing a bloody clash. The troops were massed before the Palais de l'Industrie in the Eighth Arrondissement.[105]

Accounts differ on the size of the crowd that gathered for the funeral from 80,000 to 200,000. It seems likely, whatever the true numbers, that a great share of the mob was merely curious, full of those who rallied for any lugubrious occasion. The radicals endeavored to improve the theatricality of the exhibition by providing a young fiancée in mourning for the procession. The savage Corsican had struck down not simply Youth but Love! It is doubtful that Victor Noir had ever seen the woman.[106] When the procession reached the avenue de Neuilly, Flourens tried to direct the hearse to the left toward Paris. The more moderate heads prevailed, Charles Delescluze in particular, and the procession veered right toward the Neuilly cemetery. In the crush, Rochefort vanished. His own explanation was that he had fainted from lack of food. But the other radical leaders were beginning to see him for what he was: a bogus revolutionary, a man who made a career of stirring up trouble, but who thought himself to be above and beyond the consequences.[107]

Napoleon III had recognized at the outset that the murder of Victor Noir by a Bonaparte was the kind of incident that brings down regimes. Having survived the crisis on 12 January, he told Ollivier that in all probability an authoritarian empire could not have survived: "Without any doubt I could not have got through this crisis without my [liberal] ministry." The revolutionaries would later pride themselves on having given the Second Empire its death blow that day, and the counterfeit Monsieur Claude and many subsequent historians took them at their boast. Emile Ollivier, however, saw more clearly that the crisis had given the liberal regime occasion to prove its ability to be firm and strong—something the conservative Bonapartists had doubted. Far from giving the regime a death blow, the revolutionaries had failed; and their failure was confirmed by the plebiscite in April, which overwhelmingly ratified the Liberal Empire.[108]

105. Ollivier, *Journal*, 2:419; and La Gorce, *Histoire du second empire*, 6:18–19.

106. Claveau, *Souvenirs*, 1:359–60.

107. Rochefort, *Les Aventures*, 2:145–46; Eugénie de Grèce, *Pierre-Napoléon Bonaparte*, pp. 343–46; and Roger L. Williams, *Henri Rochefort, Prince of the Gutter Press*, pp. 54–55.

108. Ollivier, *L'Empire libéral*, 12:441–42.

The committee to study Rochefort's immunity reported on 13 January. Its recommendation was based upon a parliamentary decision of 3 July 1849, which had defined parliamentary immunity as the intention to give both the individual deputy and the assembly as a whole a guarantee of political independence and dignity. The intent was *not* to confer *personal privilege* upon deputies, which would amount to an intolerable inequality. As the proposed prosecution was aimed not at Rochefort as deputy, but at Rochefort as private editor, the committee unanimously found his prosecution to be entirely legal.[109]

The issue was put on the chamber's agenda for 17 January. Rochefort was, as usual, ineffective in responding to the committee's recommendation when a reasoned response was required from him. He argued that any prosecution of him would convince the people that the government was simply trying to rid itself of an embarrassing and annoying member of the chamber, as an admission that the government had not been able to manage him in any other way. Ollivier, who had much the better of the debate, responded to that ploy by reminding the chamber that the government, far from trying to exclude Rochefort, had permitted him to return from exile in 1869 to stand for election and had not pressed the charges pending since 1868 from which he had fled.

The key issue was something quite different, Ollivier concluded: Rochefort had published an article, not merely outraging the sovereign, but containing an unequivocal appeal for insurrection. A government committed to liberal reforms really had no fear of revolution and knew that the nation had no wish for one. "We would be sorry to have to repress [a revolt] since repression would mean bloodshed." He said that the government also intended to prevent what the revolutionaries called "Days." "Everyone must understand that we shall prosecute those who provoke them." Freedom of opinion and of expression, even of extreme criticism, would be defended by the government; but every appeal for civil strife would be prosecuted. The chamber sustained Ollivier 222 votes to 34, Thiers and some members of the Center Left abstaining.[110]

Rochefort's trial took place in the Sixth Correctional Court. He did not trouble to attend, saying that its jurisdiction did not apply to him as a deputy. At Olliver's suggestion, the public prosecutor only asked for a six-month sentence and a fine of three thousand francs; for, as Ollivier himself explained to Rochefort in the corridors of the chamber, "we have not wanted to appear to be too hard." In fact, Rochefort had been anticipating much worse, at least a five-year sentence. He asked if the sentence meant

109. Police dossier E a/14, a Rochefort dossier, 13 January 1870.
110. Ollivier, *L'Empire libéral*, 12:451–55; and La Gorce, *Histoire du second empire*, 6:26–27.

the loss of his seat and suppression of *la Marseillaise*. Told *no* on both counts, he laughed and said, "Oh, then I don't give a damn." [111] He was given ten days to file an appeal, but did not. Thus, the judgment became effective on 3 February. Yet, he refused official invitation to surrender himself at Sainte-Pélagie, hoping to embarrass the government by making an arrest necessary. [112]

In the meantime, some of Rochefort's rather reluctant defenders in the chamber had been joined by a few Bonapartists in a motion to the effect that Rochefort's arrest and confinement would be impolitic. The legal point having been made, it would now be better to let this representative of the people complete his parliamentary term at his desk. But the motion was defeated 191 to 45 with 20 abstentions. [113] The police followed Rochefort as he left the chamber in the dark of the late afternoon on 7 February, but he evaded them. [114] Since it had been announced that he would appear that evening at a public meeting in the rue de Flandres (the Nineteenth Arrondissement), the police were on hand to seize him as he attempted to enter the hall. In less than an hour, he took up residence at Sainte-Pélagie. Informed of the arrest, Gustave Flourens proclaimed the revolution and sought to have barricades raised in the Belleville district; but mounted Paris Guards dispersed the would-be insurgents before midnight. [115]

In all the excitement, Prince Pierre had almost been forgotten, except by the government, which not only intended his prosecution, but hoped he would be sentenced to at least several years in prison. [116] The trial was set for Monday, 21 March, in the Palais de Justice in Tours, by an imperial order dated 19 February, far enough from the passions of Paris to insure a reasonable climate. [117] The presiding judges were all members of the *Cour de cassation*, and the *haut jury* included general-counselors from each department except la Seine, which had no general council. Of the eighty-eight prospective jurors, six did not answer the roll call and were excused for illness or age. The remaining eighty-two then retired to the juryroom to draw lots in order to reduce their number to an actual jury of thirty-six with four additional substitutes.

The four judges and the defendant then entered the court—the judges in crimson robes, and Prince Pierre in a black suit with the rosette of the Legion of Honor, carrying his hat and a large sheaf of notes. [118] After the

111. Rochefort, *Les Aventures*, 2:147–50; Ollivier, *L'Empire libéral*, 12:451–55; Ollivier, *Journal*, 2:419; and Baroche, *Second Empire*, pp. 587–88.
112. Rochefort, *Les Aventures*, 2:152–55.
113. Claveau, *Souvenirs*, 1:366–67; and Zévaès, *L'Affaire Pierre Bonaparte*, pp. 76–79.
114. *Le Paris-Journal*, 10 February 1870.
115. *Le Figaro*, 8 February 1870; and Police Carton B a/1246, a Rochefort dossier.
116. Ollivier, *Journal*, 2:419.
117. Lemarchand, *Procès*, p. 5.
118. Ibid., pp. 1–10.

clerk of court had read the indictment, which had been signed by Michel Grandperret, the president opened the questioning by recalling an unsavory incident from the past. Had not Prince Pierre received a fine of two hundred francs in 1849 for assaulting Monsieur Gastier in the Constituant Assembly? Pierre replied that he had been provoked by insults, not only to himself, but to those close to him. President Glandaz then read the verdict of the Sixth Correctional Court, dated 16 August 1849, which showed that Pierre had indeed been provoked, but that the regrettable act of violence had been deemed inappropriate for a member of the assembly.[119]

Next, from the detailed questioning of Prince Pierre and Fonvielle about their differing version of the murder emerged two critical matters of contention. Pierre admitted that it was his custom to be armed (and the *instruction* had found ample evidence to verify him), a custom which the court deplored. But neither the *instruction* nor the interrogation in court extracted from Fonvielle a satisfactory explanation for his having gone armed to Pierre's house, and he was reproached by the court for this. Nor would Fonvielle explain why Paschal Grousset had accompanied his own seconds to Pierre's house. The second major matter left unresolved for the moment was whether Prince Pierre had struck Victor Noir "a very violent blow with his left hand" as Fonvielle claimed and Prince Pierre denied—though the *instruction* seemed to support Pierre's version.

Paschal Grousset was then introduced as a witness. When asked the customary question as to whether he was in any way related to the defendant, he answered, "His mother [sic], Madame Letitia, had so many lovers that I cannot be sure." Called to order by the president, Grousset did nothing to erase this initial bad impression. He persisted in avoiding direct testimony, simply making speeches to confuse the issues. Finally, he had to be removed from the courtroom, and his original deposition from the *instruction* was read aloud by the clerk for the record. Its last words purported to describe his feelings when he had been told that Victor Noir was dead: "Until that moment I had never realized to what degree of baseness eighteen years of Empire had reduced France."[120]

After that editorial opinion, which might strike the reader as remarkably free of grief for the fallen "dear friend," the court called Dr. Jean-Louis Morel of Auteuil, Pierre's physician. He was an expert witness, but also a friend of Prince Pierre. He repeated what he had said during the *instruction*, adding that on the morning of 10 January, when he had given the prince a prescription for his cold, Pierre had said he needed to be cured quickly as he was expecting "an affair with Rochefort," in which case he would like Morel

119. Ibid., pp. 15–24.
120. Ibid., pp. 61–66.

to accompany him as a doctor.[121] A number of neighborhood witnesses, also somewhat suspect as being favorable to Pierre, appeared as witnesses to say that in the heat of the moment Fonvielle had been heard to say that Noir had struck a good blow. Fonvielle, who had subsequently asserted that it had been Pierre who had struck Noir, grew increasingly angry and abusive, until he, too, had to be removed from the courtroom. On the other hand, Mortreux, the pharmacist in whose shop Victor Noir had died, supported Fonvielle's version of the blow.[122]

A neighborhood doctor, Pinel, who examined Noir in the pharmacy immediately after death, related that Victor Noir's abdominal hair had been saturated with urine, indicating violent emotion. Pinel meant to illustrate that Noir had evidently lost control of himself at the time of the incident. Such evidence may have been telling at the time; but we would understand today that the emission of urine or even of semen is a common occurrence in violent death and thus proved nothing in the case at hand.[123]

Next came the turn of Dr. Ambroise Tardieu, professor of medicine from Paris, who had presided at the autopsy. He had found no marks of violence on the body save for one gunshot wound. He had found no sign of a blow to the face. Though he could not say precisely from what distance the shot had been fired, the nature of the wound showed that the shot had *not* been fired at extremely close range—that is to say—at a distance of less than one meter, for there was no skin burn. This served as further evidence, in other words, that Prince Pierre had not been close enough to strike a blow with his hand. The top of Noir's heart had been struck by the bullet; there had been a heavy loss of blood and a quick death. He had also examined the bullet holes in Fonvielle's clothing, which showed that Fonvielle had not been facing Prince Pierre when the latter had fired, suggesting that Fonvielle was endeavoring to flee.

As for the blow allegedly delivered by Victor Noir, Tardieu testified at length about Noir's hands and his tight, buttoned gloves. Reviewing the medical evidence previously given by Morel and Pinel, Tardieu concluded that Noir had not struck Prince Pierre with the hand open, but rather with his gloved fist, the button making its mark. Thus, he had delivered a hard blow, not a slap. In short, Dr. Tardieu gave important testimony for the defense.[124]

Though the trial was primarily a criminal affair, and has been so remembered by historians, a civil suit had been adjoined by the Salmon-Noir family to press for financial damages from Prince Pierre for the loss of a son. It

121. Ibid., pp. 116–18.
122. Ibid., pp. 159–71.
123. Dr. Balthazard, "Le meutre de Victor Noir," pp. 120–21.
124. Lemarchand, *Procès*, pp. 127–30.

seems probable that some of the earlier misinterpretations of the trial have resulted from a failure to distinguish between the criminal and civil aspects of the case. Two well-known Republican lawyers, Charles Floquet and Clément Laurier, were in the courtroom to represent the family; and their partisan behavior went considerably beyond a proper concern for their clients.

As soon as the witnesses had completed their testimony, Floquet took the floor and made a skillful attempt to prejudice the jury against Pierre by emphasizing his social rank and his Corsican origins. He quoted a statement ostensibly written by Victor Noir's father, but which still smacks of an editorial: "Even though quite ill, I left my house on the day of my son Victor's burial, alone, at eight-thirty in the morning with the intention of seeing him one last time. . . . I went up alone [to the death bed], and after looking at him for a moment, I placed a kiss on his forehead; and I spoke these words, the *only* words I spoke in the mortuary room: 'Hear me, Victor: Your father asks only one thing—justice! Not the justice princes give a man of the people, but a legal justice, straight-forward and genuine. Otherwise, I would claim my prerogative. A Corsican has struck you down, I should act in the Corsican fashion.' " Even though Floquet's proper mission was to obtain an equitable financial settlement for the bereaved family, he proceeded as if he were the prosecuting attorney, announcing that he was going to review all the facts in the case in order "to prove to you that Monsieur Pierre Bonaparte is only a common murderer." [125]

When Floquet's lengthy review was completed, Laurier took the floor to comment further. Whatever the ultimate verdict may be, he said to the jury, "the people" had already rendered their verdict by their massive attendance at the Noir funeral— "200,000 jurors!" "[Victor Noir] has acquired from this large jury, by the verdict of democracy, a martyr's immortality. And alongside this verdict, another verdict has also been rendered; and this one has created for the murderer the immortality of infamy." [126]

The court at once reprimanded Laurier for having presumed the defendant's guilt in the criminal case before a verdict had been handed down. But the even greater impropriety, the president added, was for the attorneys in the civil case to assume the public prosecutor's role in the criminal case. When applause from the gallery greeted these words, Floquet shouted, "Corsicans, be quiet!" [127]

Since brief accounts of Prince Pierre's trial habitually stress the court's apparent prejudice in favor of the defendant, it bears remarking that the insolent and improper behavior of the various Republicans in court, whether as witnesses or attorneys, forced the court to expel or reprimand them. Their

125. Ibid., pp. 229–31.
126. Ibid., p. 323.
127. Ibid., p. 324.

very rhetoric reveals that they were in court to pursue political goals, and they succeeded to the extent that they goaded the court into punitive actions, creating the impression of partiality for a Bonaparte for whom even loyal Bonapartists had little sympathy. In the above reprimand, the president referred to Floquet and Laurier as "the defense," which has often been construed to show that the president inadvertently revealed his partiality toward Prince Pierre. In the context of the civil suit, where the remark was made, when Floquet and Laurier were ostensibly there to *defend* the financial interest of the Salmon family, the terminology was not improper.

Moreover, the speech by Public Prosecutor, and Bonapartist, Michel Grandperret, which followed those by Floquet and Laurier, obviously contributed to the Republican tradition of partiality in the case; Grandperret, in reviewing the facts of the case as they had emerged from the *instruction*, found fault on both sides of the quarrel, not in Prince Pierre alone. Since his most caustic words were reserved for those who had been proclaiming their absolute innocence in the incident—he contrasted these to Pierre's confession and his request for an ordinary trial—Grandperret may well have influenced the jury more than he intended. Clearly, both Grandperret and Ollivier hoped for Pierre's condemnation.[128]

Victor Noir, Grandperret argued, had not been merely the unfortunate victim of a bullet, but of that group of fire-eaters in the midst of whom he had lived. What is the responsibility, this loyal Bonapartist asked the jury, of a press specializing in invective, a press dedicated to fomenting hatred, a press that threatens not simply the social order, but *"l'élan intellectuel, l'esprit, le goût, la loyauté, ces choses éminemment françaises!"* [129]

As for Prince Pierre, the prosecution held that he had fired at Victor Noir to avenge the insult he had just received, *not* in self-defense. His indignation and anger caused him to fire, *not* fear for his life. Fonvielle may have drawn a revolver, but not until after Pierre had drawn his and fired at Noir. Could Prince Pierre have seriously believed that the two men had come to kill him, in broad daylight, with several servants nearby to protect him? Under French law, no legitimate case could be made for self-defense. The murderer, in sum, may have been provoked; but his guilt, if *attenuated* by that fact, still remained.[130]

Finally, on Saturday afternoon 26 March came the moment for the defense attorneys, Emile Leroux assisted by Charles Demange.[131] Leroux opened by stressing his desire to eliminate all politics from the defense. Not only would he defend Pierre Bonaparte as if he were an ordinary citizen, but

128. Ollivier, *Journal*, 2:419.
129. Lemarchand, *Procès*, pp. 325–39.
130. Ibid., 350–53.
131. The same Demange who would represent Captain Alfred Dreyfus in 1894 and 1899.

he would avoid the abusive language already heard in the courtroom. There followed a long and documented history of Prince Pierre's career, much of it meant to refurbish his character; one of the principal problems the defense faced was to overcome Pierre's unsavory reputation. Leroux became more convincing when he turned to the gentlemen of *la Marseillaise* to probe their motives and tactics. Why, he asked, had Paschal Grousset chosen Victor Noir—a man only in his twenty-second year and "known in the world of letters for his Herculean strength!"—to be his second?

To answer the question, Leroux introduced an interesting legal complaint against Rochefort which had been signed by printer Alfred-Eugène Rochette on 20 July 1868. On 9 July of that year, at a moment when Rochefort was enjoying great notoriety as the publisher of *la Lanterne*, he had gone to Rochette's printery, accompanied by two seconds, to provoke a duel, regarding himself as having been insulted by the publishers of *l'Inflexible*, which was printed by Rochette. Though Rochette had protested that he was merely the printer and not the author of the outrages, Rochefort had struck him several blows with a leaded cane, and then had run to his carriage protected by his two seconds, Victor Noir and Emile Blavet, both of whom had carried canes. In his complaint, Rochette stated that he believed Rochefort had chosen to come to the printery at an hour when there would be no workers or employees present to defend him [Rochette].[132] His charges had been verified by an *instruction* completed on 7 August 1868. Rochefort was sentenced to four months in jail, though *in absentia* since by then he had fled to Brussels to escape charges against *la Lanterne*. Was this not the very pattern, Leroux asked the jury, for the incident of 10 January 1870? [133]

Leroux next touched on Victor Noir's growing reputation for violence, citing a twenty-five-franc fine levied against him in Bordeaux on 27 February 1869, for having threatened a policeman with a knife. As for the polemics that had preceded the murder of Victor Noir, Leroux reviewed them in a manner which implied that Prince Pierre's opponents at *la Marseillaise* had not only worked in collusion to provoke the incident, but had done so in a way that would shield Rochefort from the consequences. Leroux emphasized the fact that both seconds had been armed: Fonvielle with a revolver, and Victor Noir with a sword cane. Millière and Arnould, who arrived shortly after the murder, were both armed: Millière with a revolver, Arnould with a cane; and Grousset and Sauton were also on the scene. Why should Prince Pierre have not suspected the collusion of his opponents and sus-

---

132. For a sweetened version of this assault, see Alexandre Zévaès, *Henri Rochefort le Pamphlétaire*, p. 52, where Zévaès says that Rochefort "administered a correction" to Rochette. This is a fair measure of Zévaès' reliability.
133. Lemarchand, *Procès*, pp. 356–94.

pected that he was being trapped in his own home? Did not the blow Victor Noir gave Prince Pierre prove the existence of a conspiracy?

In passing, Leroux pounced upon the contradictions in Fonvielle's testimony. Then he turned to the jury to ask if it did not agree that any man, if hit by a giant armed with a cane, would have believed himself to be in danger and would have fired in self-defense—especially a man of courage, a soldier, conscious of the name he must protect! "Pierre Bonaparte, imperiled by two aggressors, did what was his right." Leroux asked for acquittal.[134]

Charles Demange closed out the afternoon with a few brief remarks for the defense. He aimed his fire primarily at the attorneys representing the Salmon family in the civil suit, characterizing their insulting treatment of the defendant as entirely contrary to the spirit of liberty that they, as Republicans, feigned to espouse, for they would deny him the liberty of a fair defense.[135]

On Sunday, 27 March, the president exercised his obligation to give a résumé of the entire proceedings, after which he explained to the jury that it must decide whether Prince Pierre had been provoked to commit the murder "by blows or serious threat to his person." If the jury found this to be a legitimate matter of self-defense, that would remove his guilt. If not, then he must be found guilty. The jury was out for an hour and a quarter, returning with a verdict of "not guilty." The president then pronounced Prince Pierre as acquitted in the criminal case. As for the damages in the civil suit, the jury recommended that Prince Pierre be ordered to pay Victor Noir's parents 100,000 francs. The court reduced the penalty to 25,000 francs, but also assessed him the costs of the civil suit.[136]

It may be that justice was done. The trouble was, as Anatole Claveau pointed out, that despite the best intentions of the Ollivier government and the judicial authorities, neither the *instruction* nor the prosecution got everything satisfactorily straight, lacking absolute proof of the collusion of Rochefort's staff in the case. No one knew in 1870—or thereafter, it must be added—the whole story.[137] The verdict satisfied neither the regime nor its opposition, both preferring a condemnation, although for different reasons, all of them political.

It will not do, however, to repeat the old Republican cliché that the murder and the acquittal undermined the regime. Even if the verdict had been guilty, it would have done nothing to reconcile the Opposition to the

134. Ibid., pp. 395–414.
135. Ibid., pp. 414–22.
136. Ibid., pp. 424–46.
137. Claveau, *Souvenirs*, 1:352.

Liberal Empire. For that matter, there is even reason to believe that the verdict was not so generally unpopular as the Opposition would have us believe. When Prince Pierre returned from the Tours prison, where he had signed the register for his release from custody, to his hotel in Tours, he was cheered by many people *en route;* and he had to appear on a balcony to greet a friendly crowd.[138] But intellectuals write the history of a period, and they are prone to the notion that when *they* oppose a regime, it is about to crumble.

The immediate victim of the verdict was Dr. Tardieu. When he returned to his medical classroom in Paris, his students, having recognized the importance of his testimony for the defense, greeted him with a tumult and showered him with pennies. When the dean of the faculty, Adolphe Wurtz, was unable to put a stop to the demonstrations, all medical courses were suspended.[139]

As for Prince Pierre the emperor wrote to him on 2 April to say that, despite the acquittal, the incident in Auteuil had been "a great scandal" and an embarrassment for the family, and that it would be well if Pierre went abroad for some time. Pierre resented the word *scandal* (preferring the word *malheur*), saying that in view of the verdict by a national jury he would only leave the country if removed by force. Napoleon III then withdrew the word *scandal* and simply asked Pierre to leave Paris, not France. When war with Prussia came in July, he applied to the emperor for service but was refused. Nor was he welcome at Camden Place in England where the defeated emperor lived in exile. His financial resources now sharply reduced, Pierre lived in Belgium until 1877, when he returned to France and took up residence in Versailles. There he died in 1881 and was buried in a simple grave,[140] a properly obscure end.

The gentlemen of the Third Republic, however, had the final word. Through funds raised in a national subscription, a monument to Victor Noir was unveiled in Père Lachaise on 18 July 1891. Later, the municipal council of Neuilly renamed a street for him, as it remains today, the one-block street bounding the north side of the Neuilly cemetery[141]—the apotheosis of a bully.

138. Baroche, *Second Empire,* p. 617.
139. Taxile Delord, *Histoire du second empire,* 6:69.
140. Eugénie de Grèce, *Pierre-Napoléon Bonaparte,* pp. 378–81, 407–8.
141. Zévaès, *L'Affaire Pierre Bonaparte,* p. 123.

CHAPTER FIVE

General Trochu v. "Le Figaro"

> Let him go for a scape-
> goat into the wilderness.
> LEVITICUS XVI, 10.

*O*N 9 February 1872, General Louis-Jules Trochu signed a complaint against *le Figaro*, a popular Parisian daily newspaper, specifically naming Hippolyte-Auguste Delaunay de Villemessant as owner-publisher and Auguste-Charles-Joseph Vitu as author of two articles offensive to Trochu. The first article, published on 23 January 1872, had been entitled "Les comptes du 4 septembre," and had been followed four days later by "Le Général Trochu." In his complaint addressed to the public prosecutor, Trochu held that he had been libeled relative to the exercise of his public obligations, a violation of Article 20 of the Law of 26 May 1819.

An *instruction* was immediately opened on the complaint, after which the charges were forwarded to the *Chambre des mises en accusation* for an indictment. This court, however, threw out the complaint for being insufficiently detailed as to precisely where the libel lay. Trochu had to redraft his complaint, submitting it again on 28 February. This time he secured an indictment. It specified seven counts of libel: three from the article of 23 January, and four from the article of 27 January.[1]

1. A reference was made to 19 January 1872 as the first anniversary of the battle of Buzenval, "a day when the purest blood was shed in a dubious enterprise which the public conscience has called murder." Though Trochu had made a formal announcement that he would never surrender, the article continued, he knew in fact that within ten days he would not only surrender Paris and her arms, but would agree to armistice terms that would mean the loss of Alsace and Lorraine. The governor of Paris [Trochu] ought then to have followed Paris in her heroic suicide. Instead, he had merely given his resignation from the government. The unfortunate dead of 19 January were the price of his military honor.

---

1. *Procès du Général Trochu contre MM. Vitu et de Villemessant du Figaro*, pp. 3–4.

2. Vitu had claimed that in France power is always secured through intrigue, treason, or insurrection. The country is seized by the collar and drained of blood, wealth, and confidence; then it is simply rejected by the master, having been reduced to a quivering mass, overcome by poverty and shame. The leader, meanwhile, prides himself on having saved the fatherland, and laughs as if "punishment is neither of this world nor of the next."

3. In 1851, the article alleged, Trochu had been an aide-de-camp to General Saint-Arnaud and one of his collaborators in the *coup d'état*. In this capacity, Trochu had been responsible for carrying out the [repressive] decisions of the mixed Commissions and was known for his indifference to those decisions.

4. On 16 August 1870 [during the Franco-Prussian War], Vitu claimed Trochu reached Châlons, the same day that Napoleon III arrived there from Metz. The two met the next day, Trochu telling the emperor that the military crisis might well provoke a revolution in Paris, that everything possible must be done to prevent a revolution, and that he [Trochu] would take the responsibility. Several times he pledged his fidelity to the emperor. Returning to Paris, Trochu told the empress-regent that she must name him governor of Paris at once. When she replied that she could not act alone because of the responsible ministry, he warned her that the greatest misfortune could result from her refusal, explaining that 12,000 *mobiles de la Seine* (Parisian reservists) under his command were on their way to Paris from Châlons, and that he could not guarantee their behavior if they found that he had not been named governor of Paris. This forced the empress to give way.

5. By letting it be known that these 12,000 pretorians, who had been unruly in Châlons, were now camped in Paris, Trochu himself forecast the revolution by enabling the parliamentary left to realize that its time had come. In fact, the article continued, close relations were established between the revolutionary left and this military chief who had sought the confidence of the imperial government.

6. Trochu told the empress that, while her police had undoubtedly informed her that left-wing deputies had held several meetings at his home, she should not be alarmed, as his devotion to her was based upon a triple guarantee: "Je suis Breton, catholique et soldat." Trochu had, in other words, been playing both sides, preparing for either the success or the failure of the left. Meaning that he had also been ready *to betray* both sides, all while putting himself under the holy aegis of the one who was sold out by Judas.

7. Whereas the empress had told Trochu that the Chamber, rather than the Tuileries, was the building most endangered by an insurrection and that it required defense, he did little to provide it. Instead he worked out an arrangement with Jules Favre: if given the presidency [Trochu] would serve

the Republic; if no presidency, he would save the regency. When the Tuileries was later in danger and the empress sent for the general who had offered to die for her, she was told that he had passed by the Tuileries on his way to take a seat at the Hôtel de Ville where a republic had been proclaimed. His "treason had just guaranteed the success of the uprising."

A second section of the indictment charged Vitu and Villemessant, through *le Figaro*, with having committed the offense of disrespect for General Trochu in his public capacity—disrespect for his office and functions. In the article of 23 January, Vitu had written: "In Versailles yesterday, I recognized the person I had seen in Madame Tussaud's wax museum in London, between Dumolard and Troppmann. It was General Trochu!" In the article of 27 January, Vitu wrote: "The first [characterization of Trochu] came from General Changarnier: 'He is Tartuffe in Mangin's helmet.' The second came from Marshal MacMahon before the parliamentary commission: 'I believed him to be a man of integrity.' "

These offenses, in sum, were indictable under articles 1, 13, and 16 of the Law of 17 May 1819; under article 6 of the Law of 25 March 1822; under articles 1 and 3 of the Law of 15 April 1871; and under articles 59 and 60 of the Penal Code.[2] The stage had been set for a political trial in the guise of a civil case.

Villemessant, who called himself Cartier de Villemessant in his thirst for aristocratic origins, was in fact the illegitimate son of an army colonel. Though not a writer (even his memoirs have been attributed to Phillipe Gille), Villemessant was a professional journalist—an organizer and manager of newspapers. *Le Figaro*, which he founded in 1854, was his greatest financial success. He had a talent for finding and hiring writers who could attract readers and ought to be remembered as one of the early patrons of sensational journalism. He was a paper merchant whose interests were commercial before they were political or ethical. He would have recognized that General Trochu, whose name had become linked with the surrender of Paris and the humiliating defeat in 1871, would be an easy and popular target.

Auguste Vitu, on the other hand, had been a political journalist, editor of the conservative-Bonapartist *l'Etendard*, which had been founded in 1866 and which had opposed the drift toward the liberal empire. As the counts in the indictment make plain, Vitu represented the conservative Bonapartist belief that the Second Empire had been betrayed, and that the betrayal accounted for all the calamities that had beset France in 1870 *and* in 1871.

---

2. Ibid., pp. 5–6. "Tartuffe in Mangin's helmet" refers to Molière's hypocrite who was willing to betray his oath of fidelity in order to obtain military advancement. Mangin was a well known Parisian pencil-seller, who hawked his merchandise on the streets in an extravagant costume.

The public, little disposed to accept its own part in the defeat, was ready prey for any explanation that absolved it.

Trochu was a particularly vulnerable target, and not merely because he had been a highly placed person associated with defeat and surrender. He had always been reserved, aloof, and seemingly out-of-step with his times— qualities he possessed by birthright, but unlikely to win him either affection or understanding. He had been born on Belle-Ile-en-mer, the island off Quiberon in Brittany, on 12 March 1815. The Trochus were a landed family given to hard work, simplicity, morality, and Catholic piety—qualities to which Trochu would remain faithful throughout life, as well as to the family milieu in which those virtues had been cultivated. In this family of three sons and four daughters, the eldest brother remained at home to manage the farm; Jules, the second son, was sent to Paris to prepare for a military career. In 1845, Jules married Hedwige Maurier, she being from a Catholic Legitimist family of Lyon. To their great chagrin, the marriage proved to be childless.

Trochu's active military service began in Algeria during the July Monarchy. An aide-de-camp to Marshal Bugeaud until Bugeaud's death in 1848, he then occupied a similar post with General Neumayer, who had been appointed to command the National Guard after the February Revolution. An incident at the Satory Camp in 1850, when troops commanded by Neumayer failed to cheer President Bonaparte, cost Neumayer his command and Trochu was put on inactive service. Trochu's excellent military reputation, however, soon compelled Minister of War Saint-Arnaud, to recall and promote him to the rank of lieutenant-colonel. He had reached the rank of colonel by the outbreak of the Crimean War in 1854, and went to the Orient as General Bosquet's divisional chief-of-staff, quickly winning promotion to the rank of brigadier. Offered the position of chief-of-staff for the entire Army of the Orient, he declined, revealing a marked distaste for prominence and positions of command. In the War of 1859, however, he did serve as a brigade commander, and later as a division commander, but took a more congenial position on the general staff in Paris after the war. In that capacity, he served for ten years as inspector-general of infantry.

During that decade he became increasingly controversial. For one thing, he made no secret of his high opinion of Prince Jerome-Napoleon, the emperor's cousin and a member of the imperial family, but whose reliability and loyalty were for good reason doubted at court. Trochu was also welcome in the salons of the Opposition, which made him suspect to some Bonapartists. Yet, Trochu seems to have been confident that he enjoyed the emperor's esteem.

In 1866, following the death of a brother, Trochu adopted his eleven nephews and nieces. When the emperor sent him twenty thousand francs to maintain the orphans, Trochu refused the money, explaining that it would compromise his independence and dignity. Though the refusal was in character, it was easily represented as hostility to the regime. Trochu did ask that his widowed sister-in-law be given a tobacco shop for her support as a substitute for the money.[3]

The publication of Trochu's book, *L'Armée française en 1867*, not only heightened the controversy surrounding him, but contributed to his unwarranted popular image as a radical reformer and as a Republican sympathizer. Strictly speaking, Trochu was nonpolitical. His spirit, his ethics, were legitimist, if not specifically royalist, as would have been understood had he been read more carefully. The emperor, projecting military reforms in 1867, was evidently alone at court in studying the book, which may well account for his faith in Trochu's integrity. While the work was first published anonymously, its authorship was soon revealed. He was not so much the critic of pending military legislation, though he had specific legislation to recommend, as he was the critic of contemporary manners and morals.

He was especially critical of the loss of respect for position and duty—the sense of hierarchical obligation—that he had experienced during his military service. In theory, the army was professional. In fact, he had found it during his career to be an army of mercenaries. Contrary to French military opinion of that day, which held that long-term recruits grew more valuable as they became older and more professional, Trochu argued that they became less valuable. He saw them as chronic drunks, groussers with little dedication to the service or to their duties, or to anything else for that matter.

Their moral deterioration he attributed to the peacetime practice of dividing the army into tiny local garrisons, which invited inactivity and boredom. Thus, he advocated the stationing of an entire army corps in each military district, as was then done in both Prussia and Russia, fully equipped for a campaign and regularly exercised. The best soldiers, he insisted—those with a sense of patriotic duty and professional obligation—were those who managed to retain their loyalty to family ties and to their region of origin despite being retrained through formal military education.

To avoid the evils of long-term service for enlisted men, Trochu by no means advocated the universal military principle of the French Revolution that was then espoused by the Republicans. He would have made the professional army more truly professional and favored retention of the Law of 1832, the military measure that permitted drafting an annual contingent of 100,000 conscripts and allowed exoneration through substitution. He would have kept such recruits for five years of active service followed by four years of reserve duty, the reserves being exercised regularly. Such a system, he

3. Vital Cartier, *Un Méconnu: Le Général Trochu, 1815–1896* pp. 1–33.

believed, could provide an army of at least 500,000 men at any moment without the use of aging enlisted men; but it would be a regular army, not a militia.

As for promotions and awards for both officers and enlisted men, Trochu's professionalism required him to favor merit alone as the basis for advancement, longevity being the enemy of excellence. He also advocated abolishing the rank of marshal, noting that it had been given too often for political reasons or as a mark of favoritism. Even worse, the rank tended to prolong the military control of aging men who could not respond effectively to the rapidly changing conditions of modern war. The conduct of French officers and enlisted men in the Franco-Prussian War of 1870 would only partially confirm Trochu's criticisms of 1867, as he himself ultimately recognized. The absence of true professionalism, as Trochu understood it, *was* revealed in all to many of the general officers, not to speak of the marshals. On the other hand, the "mercenaries" in the enlisted ranks, though grumbling and drunken they may have been, fought bravely and well, and could not be held accountable for the defeat. As for the reserves, Trochu would later note that the Prussian recruits had been conscious of their patriotic duty, in part because military service had become a universal obligation. In contrast, the French conscript had been aware that he had merely drawn a "bad number," meaning that the limited and unfair nature of the French conscription law had contributed to poor morale.[4]

When war seemed imminent in 1870, Trochu was keenly aware that his previous criticism of the military establishment, which reeked of doubt about its future, would not particularly recommend him for a critical command. His sense of duty led him to write Minister of War Marshal Le Boeuf, to offer his services as a division commander, regardless of his seniority. Le Boeuf responded on 15 July by saying that Trochu would be given command of an army numbering 80,000 that would be based in Toulouse in anticipation of Spanish intervention on behalf of Prussia. Trochu, aware that 80,000 men could never be spared from the northern front and that a Spanish invasion was most unlikely, understood he was being shelved by the military chiefs.

After news of the initial reverses along the Rhine reached Paris, Trochu wrote, as the surest way to gain His Majesty's attention, to General Waubert de Genlis, one of the emperor's aides-de-camp, recommending that the surviving forces should be united and withdrawn into the vicinity of Paris to act as a supporting army in the likelihood of a siege. This strategy, which took into account the Prussian numerical advantage, was designed to offset that

4. J. Monteilhet, *Les Institutions militaires de la France, 1814–1932*, pp. 60–61; Jean Brunet-Moret, *Le Général Trochu, 1815–1896*, pp. 278–79; and Pierre de La Gorce, *Histoire du second empire*, 5:332–34.

advantage by drawing the Prussians away from their main supply bases. By using the field army to harass the Prussian supply lines, Trochu reasoned that sufficient Prussian strength would have to be diverted from siege duties to make a total investment of the city impossible, meaning that Paris could be succored from the south. Waubert replied that the strategy had been well-received by the generals conferring at Metz, but that the political risks of abandoning so much territory had produced hesitation.

Trochu, meanwhile, as a critic of an army that had now been driven back, began to enjoy popularity in Paris, and a number of cabinet ministers thought it would be both politic and militarily sound to induce him to accept the position of minister of war. He refused the appointment, adding fuel to the controversy about his reliability, but accepted the command of the new Twelfth Corps then being formed at Châlons. There he met the emperor on 17 August, as Vitu's article in *le Figaro* correctly noted, and reiterated his proposal to have the emperor return to Paris, rally its population, and make the city the nucleus of resistance to the Prussian invasion. Because Napoleon III and Marshal MacMahon agreed with this strategy and were prepared to recall the field armies to cover Paris, the emperor revised Trochu's orders that day: "I nominate you to be Governor of Paris, and commander-in-chief of all forces designated to provide for the defense of the capital. Upon my arrival in Paris, you will receive verification of the decree that invests you with these functions; but from now until then, immediately take all steps necessary to fulfill your mission." [5]

Trochu returned to Paris at once and was received by the empress at one in the morning. The interview opened inauspiciously when the empress, upon reading the emperor's orders, said that she supposed Trochu would now recommend that the Orleans princes should be recalled as a solution to the crisis, a nasty reference to Trochu's alleged royalist sympathies. Neither she nor the new minister of war, Palikao, dared to overrule the emperor's nomination; but the cabinet as a whole telegraphed the emperor a strong recommendation not to return to Paris, insisting that it would be political suicide to return to the capital without a victory. Whatever were the empress's true motives for combatting the strategy outlined by Trochu, she succeeded in preventing its implementation and set the stage for complete disaster in the field. [6] Trochu, in the meantime, set about preparing the city for siege, impeded by the unfortunate hostility of Palikao, who resented the appointment.

The news of Sedan and the capture of the emperor came, and the Pari-

5. Cartier, *Un Méconnu* pp. 260–78; and Michael Howard, *The Franco-Prussian War*, p. 186.

6. See R. L. Williams, *The Mortal Napoleon III*, pp. 192–93; and R. L. Williams, *The French Revolution of 1870–1871*, pp. 78–79.

sian Republicans declared the Empire overthrown. Trochu, already governor of Paris, agreed to accept the presidency of the provisional Government of National Defense, thus arousing the ire of the Bonapartists. His political and military conduct in that office, though entirely consistent with his previous views, soon aroused the fury of the Parisian radicals, who had no doubt they knew more than he about driving the Prussians from the realm. Trochu emerged from the capitulation of 1871, therefore, with enemies on both left and right determined to make him the scapegoat for the defeat.

Trochu was, on the other hand, not universally unpopular. In February, at the time of the elections for the new National Assembly, he refused to be a candidate from Paris, but was returned by ten provincial departments, including his native Morbihan, whose seat he accepted. (Only Thiers won more seats than Trochu.) He meant to resign his seat once peace terms were ratified and reform of the military establishment could be achieved. Thus, when he signed the complaints against *le Figaro* in February 1872, he was still a member of the National Assembly. His decision to go to court was risky in that he had to put his record on display in Paris where the popular press had always been bitterly hostile to him. His action, however, brought into a court of law not merely numerous witnesses of various political persuasions, but also questions about the war and the peace that still preoccupied French society.[7]

Trochu's civil case, a jury trial, was heard before the *Cour d'assises* of the Seine, 27–30 March and 1–2 April 1872. Merveilleux-Duvignaux was the state attorney (Avocat Général). The two defense attorneys were well-known Bonapartists. Vitu chose Michel Grandperret, whom we have already met as public prosecutor in the trial of Pierre Bonaparte. When Ollivier's liberal cabinet had been turned out in August 1870, Grandperret had taken the Ministry of Justice in the conservative Palikao government, only to be retired from public life in the aftermath of Sedan. He had, in other words, more than a financial interest in Vitu's defense. Villemessant was defended by Charles Lachaud, recently Troppmann's defender, the most gifted and celebrated of the Bonapartist lawyers. Trochu, as plaintiff, was represented by Edouard Allou, well known during the Second Empire as a liberal Orleanist, though by no means limiting himself to Orleanist clients. He had been, for instance, Proudhon's attorney; and he accepted both civil and criminal cases. As of 1872, Allou was Thiersist in politics, anti-Republican out of fear of radicalism, and always anti-Bonapartist.[8]

The principals in the case all made brief opening statements. Villemessant acknowledged that he had approved Vitu's articles before publication, explaining that his antagonism was to Trochu the man rather than to Tro-

---

7. Cartier, *Un Méconnu*, p. 140.
8. *Procès*, pp. 3–5; and Georges Le Bail, *Grands avocats politiques XIXe siècle*, p. 104.

chu the soldier. Trochu as the defender of Paris, he said, had been a joke; but Trochu as the man who had sworn to defend a woman [the empress] and had abandoned her—*that* was unforgivable. Vitu claimed that his intent had been neither to libel Trochu nor to manufacture a sensational polemic. He had had a higher purpose: to write history! His language may have been extreme, but considering the subject, was that not "an understandable accident"? He felt certain the testimony from witnesses would demonstrate that he had been a historian, not a pamphleteer. General Trochu, noting that he had made no legal response to the avalanche of attacks and insults that had been his cross since 1870, explained that he had decided to become the civil party in this instance, because the attack had been made on his honor.[9]

The Cast of Witnesses
(For the Defense)

Charles Cousin-Montauban, comte de Palikao, chief figure and Minister of War in the conservative Bonapartist cabinet, 10 August–4 September 1870.

Julien-Théophile-Henri Chevreau, Minister of the Interior in the Palikao cabinet. Bonapartist party leader after 1871.

Pierre Magne, Minister of Finances in the Palikao cabinet.

Henri Busson-Billault, President of the *Conseil d'état* in the Palikao government.

Jules Brame, Minister of Public Instruction and Fine Arts in the Palikao cabinet and a friend of the Empress-Regent.

Eugène Rouher, President of the Senate in 1870 and the dominant conservative during the authoritarian years of the Second Empire.

Joseph-Eugène Schneider, President of the *Corps législatif* 1865–70.

Joachim Piétri, the last imperial Prefect of Police.

Comte de Cossé-Brissac, member of the National Assembly.

Marquis d'Andelarre, member of the National Assembly.

Adolphe Vuitry, former senator and Minister-President of the *Conseil d'état* from 1864 to 1869.

Louis-Adhémar, marquis de Guilloutet, former deputy from Les Landes, who would be reelected as a Bonapartist in 1876.

Théodore de Grave, a journalist.

General Philippe-Xavier Pélissier, younger brother of the late duc de Malakov, who commanded artillery during the defense of Paris in 1870.

General Joseph Lebrun, an aide-de-camp to Napoleon III during the early weeks of the Franco-Prussian War.

(For the Plaintiff)

Marie-Edme de MacMahon, duc de Magenta, the Marshal taken with Napoleon III at Sedan.

General Nicholas-Anne-Théodule Changarnier, Orleanist member of the National Assembly and long an opponent of Louis-Napoleon.

Jean Baze, an official of the National Assembly.

9. *Procès,* p. 11.

Armand, comte de Maillé, a deputy from the Vendée.
General de Lalande, Chief-of-Staff in 1851.
Edmond Lacroix, a retired colonel.
General Gustave-Henri de Place, an aide-de-camp to General Saint-Arnaud in 1851.
General François de Waubert de Genlis, an aide-de-camp to Napoleon III.
Admiral Jean-Pierre-Edmond Jurien de la Gravière, commander of the Mediterranean squadron in 1870.
General Jean-Auguste Berthaut, commander of the controversial battalions of *gardes mobiles* at Châlons.
General Pierre-Isidore Schmitz, Chief-of-Staff for Trochu.
Wachter, a former officer in the National Guard.
Jules-Auguste Lair, a former National Guard officer in Trochu's headquarters.
Charles-Louis Brunet, a former ordnance officer attached to Trochu's headquarters.
General Soumain, former commander of First Corps of the Army of Paris.
General Achille-Charles-Louis de Malroy, a former division commander.
General François-Henri-Ernest, baron de Chabaud-Latour, Chief Engineer during the siege of Paris and an Orleanist deputy in the National Assembly who supported Thiers.
Jules Favre, Republican member of the National Assembly who supported Thiers.
Constant Pollet, a *commissaire de police*.
Etienne Vacherot, a Republican academic who represented Paris in the National Assembly, and who had been mayor of the Fifth Arrondissment during the siege.
Ernest Cresson, a Republican lawyer who had been Prefect of Police briefly in 1870–71.
Frédéric Arnaud (de l'Ariège), former mayor of the Seventh Arrondissement in Paris.

What had been Trochu's attitude toward the *coup d'état* of 1851? [10] Jean Baze, an elderly official from the National Assembly, told the court a long story about the incident at Satory when General Neumayer's troops had failed to cheer the prince-president; but he never got to the point of Allou's question, said he had nothing more to add, and was allowed to step down. [11] Allou drew better results from his next witness, Armand, comte de Maillé, who identified himself as having known Trochu since their school days in 1835.

Armand: He is the most nonpolitical man I have ever known, his actions being dictated by "la loi morale." His private life could not be more respectable, nor his public life more moderate or hardworking. He opposed the

10. Because of the unusual number of witnesses, many of whom testified on more than one issue in the case, I am violating the chronological progress of the trial in order to group the statements by issue, presenting them in chronological sequence. For brevity and clarity, I give here the gist of the questions and the responses rather than the direct quotations in their entirety, unless otherwise indicated.
11. *Procès*, pp. 20–21.

coup d'état, because he was a partisan of propriety; but he did write to Marshal Bugeaud in 1848 urging him to vote for General Cavaignac, fearful of dangers to the country should Prince Bonaparte rise to power. On the other hand, once the *coup d'état* had been ratified by universal suffrage, Trochu served the Second Empire without a second thought. He served it, in fact, with his book in 1867. After Sadowa, he defended the reputation of General Benedek and surprised me by saying that the day would come when he would also have to defend French generals, who would have their turn at being General Benedeks.[12]

Allou obtained from General de Lalande, chief-of-staff in 1851, a statement that it had been well-known at his headquarters that Trochu opposed the preparations for a *coup d'état*. Colonel Edmond Lacroix added that, at the time of the first plebiscite [20 December 1851], voting had not been done secretly in the army. Officers had to sign voting registers placed in their headquarters, and Trochu had made no secret of his no vote. General de Place, at that time an aide-de-camp to the minister of war, testified that Trochu had been put on inactive service and intended to remain on inactive service. But the minister of war had ultimately induced him to return to active service.

Lachaud asked General Lebrun if it were not true that Trochu had enjoyed unusually rapid promotion after 1851. And did this not suggest that he had obtained favor for his services at the time of the *coup d'état?* Certainly not, Lebrun countered, saying that among the military, the rapid promotion had been attributed to Trochu's exceptional talents.[13] In fact, Allou interjected, is it not true that during the Crimean War Trochu was offered the position of major-general, but refused it? General Waubert de Genlis answered yes, though he was technically imprecise. The position offered, and rejected, was that of chief-of-staff. But the point Allou legitimately meant to establish was that Trochu, if promoted rapidly, had been neither improperly ambitious nor opportunistic. As for the incident in 1866 when Trochu rejected the emperor's financial assistance in supporting the children left in Trochu's care, Waubert de Genlis explained his own role as intermediary and the need to explain to the emperor that Trochu felt the obligation to assume the burden himself.[14]

The lengthiest testimony in the trial probed the Bonapartist contention that Trochu had betrayed the imperial couple in August and September of 1870. The comte de Palikao led the parade of witnesses.

Palikao: I appointed Trochu to the command of the Twelfth Corps; and it was understood that, as the senior corps commander in age, he would as-

12. Ibid., p. 21. Benedek was the Austrian general defeated at Sadowa in 1866.
13. Ibid., p. 22.
14. Ibid., pp. 22–23.

The comte de Palikao, "The Seal" ("long live the emperor!").
The sack contains his loot from the Summer Palace in Peking,
a reference to the Anglo-French expedition to China in 1860.
From *La Ménagerie impériale*

sume command of Marshal MacMahon's army in the event that MacMahon were wounded. Forty-eight hours after Trochu left for Châlons to assume his command, we received word of his nomination to be governor of
Paris. I disapproved. There had been no governor of Paris since 1830, and
the empress-regent ought to have consulted the cabinet before approving the
nomination. Under pressure from her, however, I countersigned the order.
Within several hours, General Schmitz brought a message about the return
of the *mobiles* from Châlons. I was astonished! Things were bad enough in
Paris without bringing back reserves from the Belleville district. Schmitz said
it was too late to prevent their return since they were already on the way. I
gave Trochu complete freedom of action, requiring only the observation of
army regulations, which meant sending regular reports to the minister of
war. Yet, I never received one report from General Trochu.

Lachaud: Did Trochu make any commitments to the cabinet?

Palikao: Once a question was raised about a proclamation Trochu had issued in Paris to the effect that he desired to have recourse only to "moral suasion" to maintain order in the city. One of the ministers observed that moral suasion is not always sufficient and asked what Trochu would do in the event of riot. He guaranteed he would suppress an uprising. At a later cabinet meeting, Trochu was told that he was suspected of being hostile to the imperial regime. What would he do, therefore, if the Tuileries or the Chamber should be assaulted? He pledged to die on the steps of either building in question.[15]

Chevreau: I received General Trochu on the night he returned from Châlons with that astounding order bearing the emperor's signature naming Trochu as governor of Paris. As the cabinet met every morning, I told him I would convey the news first thing in the morning. He insisted that the decree should be made public at once because the emperor was only eight hours behind him on the way to Paris. I argued that his appointment required the minister of war's countersignature, and that the empress-regent would have to be informed immediately. Thus, I took Trochu to the Tuileries that very night, where the regent and he had a long, private conversation. He evidently gave her a grim picture of the military situation, but assured her of his complete loyalty. The regent asked me to have General Palikao countersign Trochu's nomination, but I found Palikao very reluctant. He had confidence in Trochu's military capacity in the field, but feared him in a position of political importance. I told him of Trochu's pledge to the empress, repeated to him Admiral Jurien's assurance that Trochu would be a man of his word, until Palikao gave way and countersigned the order. In the published announcement of the appointment, however, we omitted the news of the emperor's imminent return, since by then we had decided to keep him at the front.

Lachaud: Did you see General Trochu on 3 September [the day the news of Sedan reached Paris]?

Chevreau: I took the announcement of the battle and the emperor's captivity to the empress-regent at the Tuileries. She was obviously stricken by the news, but assured me that she would fulfill her duties and gave an order to convene the cabinet. No attempt was made to hide the political implications of the situation from her, for we anticipated that the Opposition would be ready to exploit the grave news. She asked me to take the news to General Trochu. He seemed to be entirely unsurprised, saying that he had been expecting something of the sort; and I know that he had been predicting a military catastrophe. I pointed out to him the empress's difficult situation—

15. Ibid., p. 11.

as sovereign, wife, and mother—and told him that it would do her good if he would call upon her. He said he was weary, had not yet dined, but would go to her after eating. At 10:30 that evening, the empress told me that he had not come.

Lachaud: Did General Trochu see the empress on 4 September?

Chevreau: The cabinet gathered at the Tuileries at 8:15 that morning, and I saw Trochu enter the palace. The empress received him, and the interview lasted about twenty minutes. When she joined the ministers, I said to the empress, "Well, Madame?" She only gave me a look, but it told me that she no longer had any confidence in Trochu's pledges.[16]

Allou asked Pierre Magne for his impression of Trochu's conduct during those critical weeks.

Magne: We ministers had been waiting for some evidence of Trochu's reliability, and on one occasion in a cabinet meeting, when he tried to assure us of the reliability of the National Guard battalions, he said to the empress, "I have only one way to prove my devotion to your welfare and to that of the dynasty: to get myself killed." His remarks were reassuring to us. I had known General Trochu for a long time, I knew that Marshal Bugeaud held him in high esteem, and I was aware of the integrity of his private life. Yet, subsequent events showed that he was inclined to touchiness. From the first it was apparent that there would be a conflict of personality and in authority between Palikao and Trochu. Palikao especially made efforts to ease the difficulties. When the Defense Committee was formed,[17] I myself proposed General Trochu as its chairman; and Marshal Vaillant agreed despite his seniority and rank, though Trochu quite naturally preferred not to bypass Vaillant.

Allou: Were the words, "I am Breton, Catholic, and a soldier," spoken in the presence of witnesses?

Magne: I never heard those words, though I was not present at every cabinet meeting.[18]

Busson-Billault: I believe that Trochu's position was clearly stated on two occasions: Once, after his published hope that public order could be maintained with moral suasion, he assured the cabinet he was prepared to use force if the need should arise. And a few days before 4 September, when we were concerned about the increasingly threatening attitude of the troops stationed around the Chamber, Trochu told us that if rebels invaded either the Chamber or the Tuileries he would defend the buildings with his life. As for the crisis of 4 September, the ministers met that morning, and then went to

16. Ibid., pp. 13–14.

17. A committee of civilians and soldiers, chaired by Vaillant, charged with improving the fortifications of Paris.

18. *Procès*, p. 14.

the Chamber shortly after noon. While the deputies were in their offices trying to examine both the government's and Adolphe Thiers's propositions,
the mob began to break into the building.[19] When matters got totally out of
hand, I left for the Tuileries out of concern for the empress. Jérôme David,
the minister of public works, got there ahead of me, and Chevreau and
Piétri soon arrived. The empress did not want to leave for fear of failing to
do her duty, but we insisted. I then went to my house in the rue de Rivoli,
and while there I heard shouting outside and went to the window. I saw
General Trochu emerge from the Louvre on horseback, preceded by some
of the *mobiles* he had brought back from Châlons, who were waving hats
and flags and shouting V*ive Trochu!* and V*ive la République!* Since he rode
toward the place de la Concorde, I presumed he was on his way to the
Chamber. Instead, he turned right into the rue Castiglione, toward the
place Vendôme and the boulevards. It was about fifteen minutes after the
empress's departure. She left about 3:15 P.M., so it would have been
about 3:30.

Allou: I have noted a discrepancy in this witness's testimony.

Lachaud: We can take it up later.[20] I call Jules Brame to testify as to the
statements General Trochu made to the cabinet.

Brame: The cabinet always had some doubts about Trochu's loyalty.
When the mob began to mill around the Chamber, we felt it necessary to
ask Trochu specifically what he would do in case of insurrection. His first
response was not categorical. The question had to be repeated. He could not
understand how such a question could be put to a French general: he was
ready to be killed on the steps of the Tuileries or of the *Corps législatif.* We
knew, of course, that the *mobiles* had been brought back to Paris without
Palikao's assent.[21]

Lachaud next asked Eugène Rouher if there had been any idea of appointing Trochu as minister of war even before the fall of the Ollivier cabinet [on 9 August].

Rouher: Yes, when the news of the military reverses began to reach Paris,
Trochu's name was mentioned as a possible minister of war; but Eugène
Schneider, after a talk with Trochu, told the regent he was opposed to the
appointment, and in any case he believed Trochu would refuse the nomination. Therefore, the government ultimately turned to Palikao. Later, the
ministers were disturbed when Trochu brought back the *mobiles* to Paris, for
their indiscipline was known, and Palikao feared they would back an insur-

19. To replace the captured Napoleon III, the ministry, aware of the empress-regent's un-
popularity, proposed to revamp the regency by making it a five-man council with Palikao as
lieutenant-general of the council. Thiers wanted the *Corps législatif* to name an executive commission to carry on government and war for the duration of the crisis.

20. Procés, pp. 14–15.

21. Ibid., p. 15.

rection. I know of two occasions when Trochu pledged his loyalty to the empress, but the expression "Breton, Catholic, and soldier" was never spoken in my presence. The empress told me about it later when she was in exile.[22]

Schneider: A group of forty or fifty deputies had called on me at my office to urge the immediate appointment of Trochu as minister of war, some of them naming Palikao as an acceptable alternative. I went to see Trochu to inform him of this support and urged him to make himself available. He declined. I pressed him, citing the national crisis. He reminded me that he had been a critic of the Ministry of War in the past, which had left a residue of personal antagonisms. If he were to accept the portfolio, he would have to be allowed to speak out about his statements of the past. I observed that this might be regarded as an indictment of the regime and found it difficult to comprehend how he could entertain such notions during the national crisis. When we parted, I understood that Trochu would refuse the position; and I reported the discussion to the empress, recommending that it would be unwise to confer the post upon Trochu—though I thought that she ought to consult with him.[23]

Lachaud: What precautions were taken on 3 and 4 September to protect the *Corps législatif?*

Schneider: Our regulations provided for assistance from the Ministry of War, not from the governor of Paris. We appealed for help, therefore, to the Ministry of War and received satisfactory assurances. Deeming it proper to notify the governor's office of the threatening situation, I had my secretary-general [Valette] send word to General Schmitz. We renewed our appeal for aid at 9:00 on the morning of the fourth, but received no reply from either Trochu or Schmitz. When troops ultimately arrived, I did not know who had sent them. Their commanding general [Caussade] warned me he had no real control over his men.[24]

Palikao: On 3 September, Trochu was out in the city as usual, returning to his office only at 8:00 in the evening, so that I was unable to give him any orders; and he made no report on the situation in Paris to me. On 4 September, I remained in the Chamber until the bitter end and was shoved aside when I attempted to speak. From there I went to the Tuileries, finding

22. Ibid., pp. 15–16.
23. Both Pierre de La Gorce and Henri Welschinger believed that Trochu, as a condition for accepting the Ministry of War, made a request that he be allowed to expose the causes of the military insufficiency before the Chambers. His biographer, Cartier, denied that interpretation, noting that Trochu knew perfectly well the impossibility of such a tactic given the national crisis. Trochu wanted a military, not a political, appointment. It *seems likely* that the conservatives around the empress-regent, regarding Trochu as an outsider and uncongenial, also preferred field employment for him. The empress-regent in particular, having never liked the liberal (Ollivier) cabinet, wanted to be surrounded by friends.
24. *Procès*, pp. 16–17.

that a mob had invaded it, and was told that the empress had fled. Therefore, I went home. At that point, General Trochu called upon me to announce that he had just had me replaced as minister of war. He said something to the effect of "What do you think about it?" but I was too distraught by the news of my son's death in battle to make much of an answer. He thanked me and left.

Lachaud: Were you then aware [about 5:00 P.M.] that General Trochu had been to the Hôtel de Ville and was already president of the Government of National Defense?

Palikao: I knew nothing about it and was too preoccupied for him to have been able to give me any explanations. Later, I did conclude that he had come to seek advice in order to clear his conscience. I had known that Jules Favre and Léon Gambetta had been intriguing to get the top military command for Trochu, but I had believed that Trochu was too reliable to accept the position that the left wished to confer upon him. In retrospect, "it seemed to me highly unusual, on 4 September, to have General Trochu as Governor of Paris in the morning and chief of the Government of National Defense by evening."

Auguste Mathieu, Lachaud's assistant at the trial, called the court's attention to earlier testimony given by Kératry before a parliamentary committee. Kératry had said that he had met General Charles Le Flô at the Chamber on 3 September, and that he was there on orders from Trochu. Did Trochu in fact have the authority to order Le Flô to be there? No, Palikao responded, only the minister of war could give such orders. The defense meant to show that Trochu had not only exceeded his orders, but implied that a conspiracy to undermine the Palikao ministry did exist—for General Le Flô would become the new minister of war in the Government of National Defense. Allou, seeking to remove this hint of a conspiracy, then asked Palikao if he had not received a letter from Trochu complaining about their uneasy relationship. Palikao acknowledged the letter, adding that it had concluded with pledges of loyalty.[25]

Piétri: I was aware that the governor of Paris had been receiving members of the radical opposition immediately before 4 September. On the third, the population had become very agitated over the news of Sedan, and we took special precautions that evening to maintain order. There were several incidents. On the boulevard Bonne-Nouvelle, a mob of two or three hundred people attacked a police station. The policemen on duty resisted successfully and managed to arrest two of the leaders. A similar, though more determined assault was launched later in the evening, but also failed. Some *mobiles* were detected among the insurgents, and one of the *mobiles* got a

25. Ibid., pp. 11–12.

cut on his ear. A delegation was chosen from the mob and sent to Trochu's residence to protest against police brutality. Trochu spoke to the delegation: "These brutalities will not be repeated. The people will be armed, and the people will be their own police." He was acclaimed, and the mob disbanded. Meanwhile, shouts demanding dethronement and of *Vive la République!* had been heard on all sides, and I am unaware that Trochu did anything about it. On the evening of 3 September, I dispatched eight hundred policemen to the area of the *Corps législatif*, the focal point of sedition. I do not know who procured the order replacing my reliable police with [unreliable] National Guardsmen, but it must have been one of the radicals.[26] The troops were commanded by General Caussade, if my memory is correct.[27]

The next witnesses for the defense were called to testify to Trochu's defeatism and to his consequent expectation of political upheaval. On 7 August, after the initial military reverses, the comte de Cossé-Brissac said he had heard Trochu remark that his worst expectations were being realized. "I have wanted to preserve myself for the future, but I do not know what my destiny will be. My mind has been on General Dupont and Marshal Marmont." [28] The marquis d'Andelarre then took the stand to say that he had asked the governor of Paris what he thought of Bazaine's chances. "My dear marquis," he had answered, "he is lost." "If MacMahon moves toward Bazaine, we are lost again. There is only one thing to do with MacMahon's army: to retire upon Paris. *There* lies the chance for salvation. If that army does not retire on Paris, all is finished." [29]

Allou, for the plantiff, was now granted permission to call Marshal MacMahon to describe the circumstances that had led him to recommend the appointment of General Trochu to be governor of Paris.

MacMahon: I arrived in Châlons on 17 August 1870. I found the emperor outside his headquarters talking to Prince Napoleon, General Trochu, General Schmitz, and General Berthaut. Prince Napoleon was telling the emperor there was danger of a revolution in Paris, and in his opinion only General Trochu had the prestige to prevent or to control a revolution. This news seemed to surprise the emperor who took me aside to ask my advice in private. I told him that General Trochu was a man of courage and honor, and that he enjoyed my complete confidence.

Allou: In your testimony before the parliamentary commission, did you mean to retract that favorable opinion (that he *is* a man of honor) by saying, as was reported in *le Figaro*, "I believed him to be a man of integrity?"

26. As we shall see, the order in fact had originated with Minister of War Palikao.
27. *Procès*, pp. 17–18.
28. Brilliant officers of the First Empire, who were personally embroiled in the Empire's declining military fortunes and suspected of duplicity.
29. *Procès*, p. 18.

MacMahon: I did not use those words. In recommending Trochu, I simply said that I regarded him to be a man of honor. That was my conviction.

Lachaud: When General Trochu was appointed governor of Paris, was not the return of the *gardes mobiles* to Paris a *sine qua non* condition for his acceptance?

MacMahon: Trochu did, in fact, ask to take the *mobiles* back to Paris, which surprised and displeased the emperor. He consented only on condition that the battalions from Belleville and Montmartre, dangerous districts, be separated from the rest and be sent into garrison in le Nord.

Lachaud: Was there an agreement between Trochu and the emperor that your army would retire upon Paris or march toward Metz?

MacMahon: By then, I had been made subordinate to Bazaine, and I did not know his plans. At the time Trochu left for Paris, however, I did not expect to lead my army toward Metz. The emperor was no longer in command at Châlons. I asked him to express himself precisely about this matter, and he insisted that he had given up his command in the field and would no longer interfere. "I must declare that all the subsequent operations of that army were not of his doing. Only I commanded." [30]

Because MacMahon had denied impugning Trochu's character, Allou immediately called General Changarnier to ask whether he had used the phrase "He is Tartuffe in Mangin's helmet" as quoted in *le Figaro*. The aged Changarnier proved to be a master equivocator, provoking a wrangle between Allou and Lachaud as to the meaning of his testimony, until a juror in some desperation, acknowledging that the general was too well bred to have made the remark in question, asked whether he could have made an appraisal of Trochu that amounted to the same thing! Turning to the jury with a smile, Changarnier said that General Trochu was a gallant man—"a man whom I respect and like very much. Do you want me to repeat a salon remark? I am not an old gossip. May I now be dismissed!" [31]

No one objected, and the court returned to testimony about Trochu's appointment to be governor of Paris.

---

30. Ibid., p. 19. To keep the record straight, it may help to note that when MacMahon had given his earlier testimony before the parliamentary commission, he did assert that the emperor had interpreted the return of the *gardes mobiles* to Paris as Trochu's *sine qua non* condition for accepting the governorship. He further testified that he had been told on 18 August 1870 that the emperor expected to return to Paris on the 19th. MacMahon presumed that the decision had been made on the 17th when Trochu was still in Châlons. As for the army in Châlons, MacMahon had testified that he could not move it until he heard from Bazaine (the new generalissimo); and on the 19th, Bazaine had given him freedom of movement. Admittedly indecisive, MacMahon did not issue instructions to move in the direction of Paris until 22 August, his orders being countermanded that very day by the cabinet in Paris. See *Enquête parlementaire sur les actes du gouvernement de la défense nationale*, (*Dépositions des témoins*) 1:28–31.

31. *Procès*, p. 20.

Lebrun: I did not attend the conference at Châlons on 17 August, though I learned at once what had transpired. Trochu was named to be governor of Paris, and I was very pleased with his appointment, though I regretted the decision to take the *mobiles* back to Paris because they had been undisciplined at Châlons. It was understood that the forces at Châlons would retire upon Paris, not as rapidly as possible, but fighting step by step to delay the enemy advance. The intention was to give Paris as much time as possible to prepare for siege, and to give the city a real chance to defend itself by having a field army operating in the neighborhood.

General Lebrun then asked the president of the court if he might raise several questions about Trochu's role on 4 September, the final day of the Second Empire. He was granted permission.

Lebrun: Most army officers have been disturbed by the established fact that General Trochu did not step foot in the Tuileries on 3 September. I speak for the army here in wanting an explanation.

Allou hastened to assure Lebrun that satisfactory explanations would be forthcoming, and General Trochu nodded his assent. The plaintiff next called Admiral Jurien to the stand.

Jurien de la Gravière: General Trochu told me that, having opposed the views of the previous administration of the Ministry of War, he would have to make clear to the Chamber the previous insufficiency. I believed that no such statement could be made under the circumstances of the military emergency, *and he quite agreed.* Later, when we received word that General Trochu was bringing the emperor back to Paris, we believed it to be unwise for his reputation and position. The empress asked me to use my influence with Trochu to prevent the emperor's return. Trochu held firm to his view that the emperor should leave Châlons as planned, noting that Châlons was a camp, not a fortified post, and could be overrun at any time by an enemy division. The empress countered with a piece of news that as yet had been unavailable to Trochu: a report that Bazaine had won a great battle on the sixteenth. As it turned out, Bazaine had won a victory, but had been unable to pursue his enemy.[32] Given this favorable news, Trochu said there was no longer any reason for the emperor to return. The empress felt strongly that the emperor would run great risk in returning to Paris. What is more, though the nation had no tradition of confidence in women's advice, the empress was quite confident that she could manage the situation herself. *"She was full of joy when it was decided not to let the Emperor return."* Though the empress seemed confident of Trochu's loyalty, he was hampered in his duties as governor of Paris by the great hostility of Chevreau, the minister of the interior.

32. Both sides had claimed victory. See the section on Vionville—Mars-la-Tour in Michael Howard, pp. 144–66.

At last the real reasons for the antagonism to Trochu and his strategy were beginning to seep into the trial. The conservative Bonapartists, having brought down the liberal empire while the emperor was in the field, easily saw the wisdom of keeping him in the field. Meanwhile, the empress-regent, who had seen the drift toward the liberal empire as proof of the emperor's executive incompetence, finally had her ailing husband out to pasture. The decision to overrule Trochu's strategy, backed as it was by Napoleon III and the liberal Prince Napoleon, had been political, but was hardly meant to preserve the emperor's reputation and position. He had already failed in command; she would now pull victory from defeat. Admiral Jurien, who had come to the empress's aid at the time of her flight on 4 September, was too much the gentleman to snipe at her with accusations of incompetence now that she was in exile; but he completed his testimony by reminding the court that he had seen General Trochu regularly after 4 September and had always had absolute confidence that Trochu had wanted to spend every effort to defend Paris and the country against the foreigner.[33] His motives, in other words, had not been political.

Berthaut: I attended the meeting at Châlons on 17 August. I informed the emperor that the camp was not defensible as a position and told him that my battalions of *mobiles* from Paris, though in great part excellent and ready to do their duty under fire, were as yet insufficiently trained and organized as units to give battle. Moreover, arms were still lacking. Only three battalions of the eighteen had *chassepots*. I advised assigning the battalions to fortified places until they were ready for campaigning in open country. The emperor suggested that if these battalions were to be detached from the army of Châlons, it would be best to send them to Paris to defend their own homes.

Allou observed that the article in *le Figaro* had mentioned 12,000 dangerous pretorians led by Trochu. Yet, the emperor himself had given the order to take them to Paris, and many of them were not even armed. Lachaud quite correctly directed the jury's attention to the fact that Berthaut's testimony about the *mobiles* was at some points contradictory to that of Marshal MacMahon's, and an argument between the two attorneys developed over the discrepancies. Finally, Allou called General Schmitz to see if he could resolve the controversy.[34]

Schmitz: Palikao, with whom I had served in China, informed me that Trochu had just been appointed to command the Twelfth Corps and that I was to be his chief-of-staff. I left Paris on 15 August for Châlons and was dismayed by the confusion there when I arrived. The regular troops had the appearance of men who had campaigned for eighteen months. I asked General Berthaut for information about his *mobiles*. "We are not armed," he

33. *Procès*, pp. 23–24.
34. Ibid., pp. 24–25.

replied, "and are here in open country where Prussian cavalry can overrun us." I wrote to Palikao of the seriousness of the situation, telling him that Châlons was an unfortified camp, that it contained seven to eight thousand men on detached service who were troublemakers, that the *mobiles* from Paris were not armed and were discontented, and that, in sum, I advised a retreat from Châlons. I told General Berthaut about my letter, and he agreed with my assessment. Then the emperor arrived. I talked to Prince Napoleon, who was anxious for Trochu's arrival. When he did arrive, we gathered at the emperor's headquarters: Prince Napoleon, Berthaut, Trochu, and I—Marshal MacMahon joining us somewhat later. I spoke first, explaining that the *mobiles* were neither adequately equipped nor trained. It was decided to send them back to Paris. "That is proper," the emperor said. "They are children of Paris; they will defend their homes." I also urged the emperor to appoint Trochu as governor of Paris to take advantage of his popularity; and Prince Napoleon added that he thought the emperor ought to return immediately to Paris, his proper post. At the end of the council, the emperor said he would sign decrees appointing MacMahon to command the army of Châlons and Trochu to be governor of Paris, and he gave Berthaut a verbal order to take the *mobiles* to Paris.

I did not attend the meeting between Trochu and the empress after our return to Paris, but remained in an antechamber. When Trochu emerged, he said that the emperor's name would be removed from the announcement of Trochu's appointment. "The empress wishes it," he told me. We both noted, thereafter, that the cabinet always wanted to omit the emperor's name from public bulletins, and Palikao made his resentment at Trochu's appointment quite clear. As for the meetings Trochu is alleged to have had with certain deputies, the word *meetings* is misleading because it implies something arranged in advance. In truth, the governor's office was virtually a fairground with people, including deputies, continually coming and going in search of news. On 4 September, when General Lebreton informed us of the invasion of the *Corps législatif*, General Trochu ordered me to go to the Tuileries on his behalf to warn the empress. When I got there, the troops were holding firm and the gates were closed. Admiral Jurien told me that fortunately the empress had already departed. When I got back to the governor's office, I found that he, too, had returned, having been unable to reach the Chamber. "It is a revolution," he said. Large, excited groups were milling around the governor's house. He finally said to me, "I am going to have to go [to the Hôtel de Ville] and do a Lamartine."

Allou now questioned Schmitz closely as to the time Trochu departed for the Hôtel de Ville (about 3:30 in the afternoon), what he was wearing (civilian clothes), making the point that he could hardly have left his house in uniform with an escort at 5:00 as Busson-Billault had testified. Before he stepped down, Schmitz asked to make a final statement: "I have always been attached to His Majesty, as I now still am. I would be little worthy of his esteem were I not to declare that all the charges of treason directed against General Trochu are absolutely false. I was close to [Trochu], and had he been anything else [but loyal in his actions], I should not today be his witness. I would be his accuser." [35]

After a brief recess for lunch, Busson-Billault was recalled on the matter of whether Trochu had emerged from his house in uniform to go to the Hôtel de Ville. He not only stuck to his version of that event, but added that a National Guard officer named Wachter had witnessed the scene. Wachter was at once called to testify, but under cross-examination it became clear that Wachter had seen Trochu leave the Tuileries in an attempt to reach the Chamber when he was still in uniform. Allou pressed the issue by calling another National Guard officer, Lair, who had been stationed at Trochu's headquarters. Lair insisted that Trochu had not turned right from the rue de Rivoli into the rue Castiglione, as Busson-Billault had claimed, but had turned left through the porte du Carrousel in the direction of the Chamber. [36] After this, Allou called another officer, Brunet, and asked him to relate what had happened on 4 September.

Brunet: General Trochu called three of us into his office and remarked that we were his friends, not simply his ordnance officers; moreover, we were married men and heads of families. He said the enemy was approaching and a revolution had started. "I am going to make one last effort, which may cost me my life; and I do not want to involve you three without giving you the opportunity to avoid the situation." We were all much touched by his consideration. Soon after, General Lebreton and Monsieur Baze, both officials of the Chamber, came to get the governor. He got on horseback and rode out with them through the porte des Tuileries into the Carrousel, but the crush of the throng soon separated the party. After reaching the pont

---

35. Ibid., pp. 25–27. In his more lengthy testimony before the parliamentary committee, which was not published until 1873, General Schmitz would make even clearer the close association of the decision to appoint Trochu as governor of Paris and the decision to have Napoleon III return to the capital. It was argued that Trochu's appointment would be popular and would assist the emperor to return without unpleasant or dangerous incidents. His departure from the army, moreover, would have allowed MacMahon a clearer hand. Schmitz cited Trochu as saying that he was entirely at the emperor's disposition. "I have had some disagreements with the Emperor's government," Trochu told the emperor, "but I must say that your person has never been a part of my dissent." Schmitz portrayed the emperor as hesitant—that he should consult the cabinet and the regent before making changes, as he had become a constitutional ruler. Prince Napoleon wanted him to act in the emergency and to send the decrees to Paris with Trochu for countersignature. Schmitz was obviously suspicious of the empress-regent's motives in avoiding the use of the emperor's name in announcements. See *Enquête parlementaire sur les actes du gouvernement de la défense nationale*, (*Dépositions des témoins*), 2:276–86.

36. Ibid., pp. 27–28.

de Solferino and talking to Jules Favre, Trochu retraced his steps. The Chamber had already been invaded.

Allou asked if that was the only time Trochu left his residence that day in uniform. Brunet said yes, that was the only time. So, Allou summed up, Trochu returned to his residence and put on civilian dress. He never went into the rue de Rivoli in uniform, much less into the rue Castiglione with his staff and an escort of *mobiles!* [37] Allou had destroyed Busson-Billault's testimony. He now brought forth several witnesses to probe the conflict between Palikao and Trochu and the consequent confusion of authority.

Soumain: Anticipating public disturbances, the minister of war ordered me on 3 September to take measures to assure public order and to protect the Chamber, and then to advise him what measures I had taken. Since I thought that such orders ought to have reached me through the governor of Paris, I felt obliged to send him word of my instructions. [38] My previous orders had come from the Ministry of War, my reports were always sent to the Ministry of War, and I believed this to be an irregularity once the governor of Paris had been appointed. [39]

Malroy: My own orders came from the Ministry of War, which I believed to be irregular; and I knew on 3 September that General Soumain had received a letter from Palikao, not only giving him orders, but instructing him to accept orders only from the Ministry. As far as I could tell, the governor of Paris was being kept isolated by the Ministry of War. General Caussade, who commanded the troops designated to protect the Chamber, also received his orders from the Ministry of War. [40]

Allou: Did General Trochu, as has been alleged, insist on being the president of the Defense Council in 1870?

Chabaud-Latour: On the contrary, it simply seemed that, as governor of Paris, he ought to have been its presiding officer. As for Berthaut's remark that it had not been a "comité de défense" but a "comité de défaillance" [failure], I must say that the siege of Paris did France honor, at least in the eyes of foreigners. We did what was possible; and if MacMahon's army had

37. Ibid., p. 28.
38. These letters have since been published by Cartier, *Un Méconnu,* pp. 407–8.
39. *Procès,* p. 29.
40. Ibid., p. 30. On 13 August 1873, over a year after this trial, General Caussade's nephew released two letters to the parliamentary commission investigating the events of 4 September 1870 in order to help clarify the record. Both were letters from General Soumain to General Caussade; both were dated 4 September. The first directed Caussade to be in position to protect the *Corps législatif* by ten in the morning, noting that the orders originated with the minister of war. "You will take orders from the President [of the *Corps législatif*]," the letter added, "and the minister of war will also be present to give you orders should they be necessary." See *Enquête parlementaire sur les actes du gouvernement de la défense nationale,* (*Dépositions des témoins*), 5:84–85.

retired to operate in the vicinity of Paris, the city would have defended itself successfully.[41]

Jules Favre was now summoned by Allou and asked to account for the contradiction between Trochu's belief that he had met Favre for the first time when they had had their brief encounter at the pont de Solferino on 4 September, and Favre's published statement that he had met Trochu at home *before* 4 September.

Favre: There is a simple explanation. On 20 August, a delegation concerned by the gravity of the military situation called upon Trochu at his residence. I was merely part of that group, and that was my only visit. At the time I believed a large part of the Parisian population would not defend the city should the emperor remain in power.

Allou: Before making his decision to accept the presidency of the Government of National Defense, did not General Trochu insist upon going to see the minister of war [Palikao] about the matter?

Favre: I do not remember precisely whether he made such a condition for acceptance.

Allou: When General Trochu returned from the Ministry of War, ready to accept the presidency of the Government of National Defense, did he not then learn that Henri Rochefort was to be included in the new government? And did he not then raise a question as to whether the new regime meant to defend religion, the family, and private property?

Favre: That is true, but I must add that I recall General Trochu going to the Ministry of War only after he had accepted the presidency.[42]

To refute one more Bonapartist charge, Allou called Constant Pollet, a *commissaire de police*, who had been stationed at Trochu's residence. On 3 September, he said, a delegation of National Guard officers was received in the evening concerning a wounded *mobile*. General Trochu came down into the entry to calm the crowd. He assured them that justice would be done. Lachaud and his assistant were obviously pleased by the remark. But when Allou asked Pollet if Trochu had said, "You will be armed; the people will be able to defend themselves," as Piétri had testified, Pollet said no. He claimed that Trochu had only said the National Guard would be armed. It was Allou's turn to be pleased.[43]

General Berthaut now asked to be recalled to clear up a possible misunderstanding from his previous testimony. At Châlons, he said, when the emperor had decided to send the *mobiles* back to Paris, the possible bad effects of sending back disorderly troops into the capital were pointed out to him.

41. *Procès*, p. 30.
42. Ibid., p. 31.
43. Ibid., p. 32.

Agreeing with the argument, the emperor suggested sorting out the two or three worst battalions and sending them to posts in le Nord; but this was countered with the argument that separating the battalions into two groups might produce even poorer morale in those chosen to return to Paris. Better that they all be kept together. Berthaut also wanted to correct his previous statement about the armament of those battalions. Half of them, he said, had been furnished with *fusils à tabatière* with the intention of supplying them with *chassepots* when they were available. But, six of the battalions at Châlons were not only unarmed, but had no packs. The minister of war had ordered *chassepots* for these troops, but they had not arrived.[44] This testimony reconciled the various versions of what had transpired at Châlons— and entirely in Trochu's favor.

The testimony now shifted to the period of the Government of National Defense, when Trochu had been both governor of Paris and president of the provisional government. Lachaud called Vuitry to the stand, who indicated that he had been in Orleans toward the end of October and into early November 1870. In those weeks when rumors were thick that Bismarck had been demanding harsh terms as the basis for an armistice, Vuitry had heard Thiers (who was passing through Orleans) say he had been unable to convince the members of the Government of National Defense that they must accept the sacrifice in order to avoid harsher terms later on. The defense also called the marquis de Guilloutet, who said Thiers had told him it was regrettable that Bismarck's initial terms had not been accepted. Peace could have been secured by ceding a strip of Alsace and by paying a two-billion-franc indemnity.

Allou: Did not Thiers mention that the radical insurrection of 31 October contributed to our lack of success in negotiations? (He meant to imply by this that the government's negotiating integrity had been compromised by political instability in Paris.)

Guilloutet: I do not recall that situation.[45]

In calling Grave to the stand, the defense called attention to perhaps the most delicate and controversial military action of the Franco-Prussian War, the sortie of 19 January 1871, known as the battle of Buzenval. It had been a dreadful bloodletting with virtually no chance of French success; and since it took place immediately before an armistice was signed with the Prussians, the sortie was widely believed to have been instigated to demonstrate to the Parisians that further resistance was hopeless.

---

44. Ibid., pp. 32–34. The *fusil à tabatière* was a model-1867 converted breechloading rifle used temporarily until it could be replaced by the superior *chassepot*, that went into production in 1866 at the emperor's insistence. See Pierre Lorain and Robert Marquiset, *Armes à feu françaises modèles réglementaires (1858–1918 chargement culasse)*, Cahier #3.

45. Ibid., p. 18.

Grave: I was returning from Versailles about 2 April 1871. There were eight of us in the compartment. One man, who finally identified himself as General Xavier Pélissier, began to talk about the battle of Buzenval with a good deal of anger and expressed himself most vehemently about General Trochu. He had seen Trochu about noon during the height of the battle near Mont-Valérien and had asked him what he meant to do. Trochu had replied that he did not know. Pélissier's criticisms of Trochu amounted to a charge of criminal lack of foresight.[46]

Pélissier was not heard until the following day, by which time he had seen a newspaper account of Grave's testimony. Admitting that the words he used in the compartment might have been animated, Pélissier nevertheless insisted that he could not have said anything damaging to Trochu's character or honor. Perhaps he had noted Trochu's lack of faith in the ultimate success of the defense of Paris, or had noted a frittering away of military resources and a lack of coordination in Trochu's operation. But as for the particular language attributed to him, he denied having used such words.[47]

Allou recalled General Schmitz to inquire further into the responsibility for the Buzenval operation.

Schmitz: Trochu convened a council of war, which was attended by twenty-eight division commanders including Bellemare, Vinoy, Berthaut, and Paturel. General Berthaut proposed the operation against Buzenval. I supported the proposal at once, having long favored such an operation. I did not guarantee a success, but argued that we must employ the National Guard. "These men," I said, "who have been aroused, armed, trained, must be led one last time in the defense of their lives, homes, and families." Immediately after the failure of the sortie, I read in newspapers that the operation had not succeeded because I had allegedly betrayed the operation to the enemy.[48]

Allou: What attempts did the Parisian mayors make to obtain military action before Buzenval, and did they ask for additional efforts even after that battle?

Vacherot: The mayors of Paris had been briefed by General Trochu about two weeks before the battle of Buzenval. We were most favorably impressed by the general's attitude, though he made no attempt to hide from us the seriousness of the situation. After the battle of Buzenval, a second meeting was held with the mayors. General Trochu again described the military situ-

---

46. Ibid., pp. 18–19. In fact, Trochu had opposed such fruitless sorties as that of 19 January, and he forced the Government of National Defense to replace him as military commander in Paris in its aftermath—though he retained the presidency of the government.
47. Ibid., pp. 21–22.
48. Ibid., p. 27.

ation, reporting nothing encouraging. Yet, the mayors were unanimous in their resolve to continue the fight. We wanted a last and supreme effort. General Trochu and Jules Favre (and I think Ernest Picard) did not favor this line, but the majority in the Government of National Defense backed the mayors' proposal. General Trochu then announced that he would refuse to lead such a sortie, because it would produce nothing but useless carnage. One of the mayors (I think it may have been Desmarets) said General Trochu ought to resign. Trochu refused, explaining that it was the obligation of the majority in the government to find another general willing to carry out their military policy. Until such time he would continue to perform his military duties. He would not leave his post, which necessity had imposed upon him, because it was not in his character to escape from the responsibility that had fallen upon him. I shall never forget that scene as long as I live.

Arnaud: Public opinion in Paris required another sortie even after Buzenval. Trochu not only opposed another operation, but vigorously refused to give his resignation when pressed to do so.[49]

Allou then began his formal speech for the plaintiff, which occupied most of Saturday, 30 March. Auguste Vitu, he noted at the outset, had been a Bonapartist current within a *Figaro* that was generally Legitimist. Though ostensibly hired by le *Figaro* for theatrical coverage, he had been allowed to vent his political bitternesses. The two articles in question did not so much condemn Trochu's conduct of the siege of Paris as they condemned his entire career. He was portrayed as a mediocre soldier; as the author of a mediocre book about the army whose ideas had been accepted and which led to military disaster; as an accomplice in the *coup d'état* of 1851; as one who had betrayed the Empire he had helped to forge; as an overthrower of that regime who had made riot and revolution possible; and as a deserter of both his post and of a woman who had placed her confidence in him.

What were the *facts* about that career? Allou recited at length the details of Trochu's distinguished service in Africa under Lamoricière and Bugeaud, his refusal of the post of ordnance officer to the prince-president in 1849, his appointment as aide-de-camp to General Neumayer in 1851, and his no vote in the plebiscite of that year. He had fought in the Crimea as a colonel and as a brigadier general, but had refused appointments implying *political* association with the regime. To those who had complained of Trochu's rapid promotion, Allou answered that promotion, given Trochu's excellent reputation in military circles, could have been even more rapid had he been willing to be a political general. He had refused the gift of 20,000 francs

49. Ibid., p. 33.

from the emperor that Allou characterized not as an act of generosity, but as an indelicate bribe.

As for the controversial book published in 1867, that had been meant to be a warning. Trochu had seen the French living on a dated military reputation. Discipline had weakened, the spirit of sacrifice was evaporating, and in both the Crimea and Italy the French had come within an ace of losing, but victory had concealed that truth from the French, if not from foreign officers who had witnessed the ineptitude of French tactics. The Prussian modernity was in sharp contrast: preparations for cooperation between the regulars and the *landwehr* were under way, topographical and statistical studies were being made, and an army truly national in character and imbued with a reliable sense of duty was being created. Trochu had been a member of the commission that recommended military reforms in 1868; but the Law of 1868, Allou asserted, had emerged largely from the Ministry of War after precious little consultation with the commission. The upshot came in 1870 when Trochu, as the senior division commander, was given command of the Army of the Pyrenees—a ridiculous appointment given his talents and services!

Allou next brought up the matter of Trochu's testament, dated 21 July 1870, and filed with his attorney. Trochu had identified himself in it as a faithful servant of the prince, the state, and the country. As such, he had been critical of errors that might become dangerous. Under the Second Empire, his opposition rather inevitably had been attributed to Orleanism. In fact, his principles, especially his concern for the rights of families, had prevented any sympathy for the Revolution of 1830. In his testament, he cited the rejection of legitimacy in 1830 and thereafter as the principal cause of the national "derailment."

He had seen the approach of war that July with the greatest misgivings, believing that war could be justified only if France could show that her honor had been grievously injured or if her territorial integrity were clearly imperiled. French isolation proved that no such case had been successfully made to other nations. Trochu knew, moreover, that the army was by no means prepared for the conflict, though he acknowledged that a good deal had recently been done to improve the armament and equipment. But the personnel structure was virtually unchanged. The tendency to rely upon improvisation in strategy, upon the traditional *pêle-mêle* in tactics, might produce some immediate successes when pitted against the German order; but the Germans in the long run, sustained by national spirit, would prove to be stubborn, and their order and precision would prevail.

Despite the charges in Vitu's first article, Trochu had had a fine military career; he belonged to no party or faction; he lived a respectable, pious, virtuous private life; he served his country by serving his government. No avowed friend of the Second Empire could have served the regime in a more important way than he had endeavored to do with his book. Clearly, he had been defamed by the article.

In the second article, Trochu had been typed as improperly ambitious. The Empire, Allou said, which initially shunted Trochu aside in 1870, turned to him in its final crisis to profit from his popularity. Yet, he did not take the Ministry of War on 7 August, when it could have been his, for he would take office only under conditions that did not violate his principles. As for the *gardes mobiles*, the so-called *pretorians*, there is simply no evidence that General Trochu made the return of the battalions a *sine qua non* condition for his acceptance of the governorship.

Prince Napoleon was the first to urge the emperor to return to Paris to resume his authority and to propose sending Trochu there at once in the emperor's place as governor of Paris. Trochu accepted the proposal, not because of ambition, but because of his patriotism and sense of duty. Would an ambitious man, Allou asked, have agreed to go to Paris to protect an emperor beaten in the field with a mind to reestablishing that emperor in the Tuileries?

The thrust of Allou's argument, in fact, called attention to a matter that had been (and has been) overlooked; namely, that at the moment of Trochu's appointment as governor, his office would have been critical for only a brief period. It was understood that the emperor would soon be returning to the capital to resume supreme power, at which point the governor would have become his subordinate. When the empress and the Palikao regime blocked the emperor's return, they left Trochu in an unanticipated role and vulnerable to the ire of the conservative cabinet.

The reasons for the emperor's inability to return, Allou emphasized, had been political, not military; and he quoted a letter dated 29 October 1870, that Napoleon III had written to Sir John Burgoyne: [50] "I wanted to bring back our last army to Paris, but political considerations forced us into the most imprudent and least strategic march that ended in disaster at Sedan." In Paris, meanwhile, the emperor's decree nominating Trochu as governor had been altered to remove the emperor's name at the empress's insistence, ostensibly because it had been agreed that the emperor must not return. Trochu, himself already suspect, brought to Paris an "idea repugnant to the empress and the power to command troops around Paris, that was repugnant to the minister of war." Hence, Palikao took upon himself the responsibility for the defensive measures in Paris, enabling him to ignore Trochu.

After a break for lunch, Allou cited those witnesses who had given the lie

50. On the night of 6 September, Burgoyne had transported the empress from Deauville to England on his yacht *Gazelle*.

to the charge that there had been collusion between Trochu and Favre before 4 September. Was it any wonder, given Trochu's treatment at the Tuileries, that he failed to put in an appearance, Allou asked? Instead, he had sent General Schmitz to see the empress on 4 September. Passing through the Carrousel on his way to the Chamber, Trochu saw the flag come down at the Tuileries, meaning that the empress had departed, which Schmitz soon confirmed. At that point, Trochu received an offer through [François-Frédéric] Steenackers to take part in the new government. He consulted his wife before accepting at the Hôtel de Ville, then went immediately to see Palikao to tell him what had transpired. Palikao was very upset, as he testified. In any case, when General Trochu returned to the Hôtel de Ville, he believed he had behaved properly: he was doing his duty, he had served the hierarchy correctly, and his conscience was free.

Allou ended with an appeal in the spirit of Trochu's own patriotism: "Gentlemen, let us join together to found a great national party. Let all the men of order and true liberty unite! [51] No narrow exclusions! No shabby recriminations! It is of no importance from where we come if we all want the same thing! Let the Bonapartists come to serve the country with us, without intrigues, without mysterious carrying-on, without dreams of revenge. Let us put off politics and have a single program: the liberation of our territory and public peace. And let us have confidence. God will yet save France!" [52]

The courtroom rang with applause as General Trochu rose to shake Allou's hand. As soon as quiet was restored, the state attorney, Merveilleux-Duvignaux, took the floor to review the facts exposed in the debates. In conclusion, he asked the jury for a verdict that would state clearly that Trochu had not been guilty of the deeds of which he had been accused. Since, in a civil case, it was the duty of the state to obtain a just verdict, the state attorney's judgment put the defense at a serious disadvantage. The hearing was then adjourned until Monday, 1 April, for the speeches of the defense attorneys.

A large audience was on hand when the judges entered the courtroom at 10:30. Michel Grandperret, speaking in defense of Auguste Vitu, focused first on the battle of Buzenval, quoting other journalists who had referred to the battle as a crime and insisting that Vitu, in his article, had merely reflected general public revulsion over the military action of 19 January. He challenged Trochu to admit that he *had* recognized the need for a bloodletting before capitulation would have been possible. Trochu shook his head negatively.

51. Meaning let us unite not merely against Germany, but against radicalism at home, the reaction to the Commune of 1871.
52. *Procès*, pp. 35–48.

Grandperret attempted a highly emotional line by referring to a speech given by Trochu before the National Assembly about the recent defeat. Trochu had attributed the disaster to defects at home, in France, claiming that "the noble career of arms had become nothing more than a *métier*, that what had defeated the French was *le luxe anglais et la corruption italienne.*" How dare you, Grandperret snarled, tell our glorious dead and their wives, mothers, and sisters, that they fought to make a *métier*. Go ask them what they know about Italian corruption!

Returning to the Buzenval affair, Grandperret read a statement he identified as testimony by Emile, comte de Kératry, before the parliamentary commission to investigate the insurrection of 18 March 1871, the gist of which was that the battle of Buzenval had been ordered to satisfy public opinion and to make capitulation possible.[53]

As for the alleged prejudice of the imperial regime against Trochu, Grandperret denied its existence by reviewing the details of Trochu's rapid promotion. At Châlons, in fact, rather than seeking to hide behind Trochu's popularity, the emperor had chosen Trochu in that desperate hour to be governor of Paris because he sought someone in whom he had absolute confidence. We must recall Marshal MacMahon's words in response to the emperor's question: "Sire, je crois que c'est un honnête homme." Yet, Grandperret added, Trochu went back to Paris with the *mobiles*; and Marshal MacMahon told the parliamentary commission that their return had been a condition for Trochu's acceptance of the governorship (though Grandperret acknowledged that Generals Schmitz and Berthaut had testified otherwise during the trial). MacMahon, he continued, had had no notion of retreating upon Paris, but had intended to go to the aid of Bazaine, a remark that brought the Marshal to his feet.

MacMahon: When I learned from Marshal Bazaine on 19 August that he was retiring into Metz, I believed the retreat from Châlons to cover Paris was the correct thing to do, but was halted by the minister of war. [*Applause*]

Since Allou had skillfully implied that the empress-regent's behavior had been dubious at best, Grandperret replied by reading a letter the exiled empress had written to Anna Murat, duchesse de Mouchy, concerning

---

53. While Grandperret may well have known that this was Kératry's view of the Buzenval operation, I am at a loss to explain the reference to this particular parliamentary commission, before which Kératry was *not* called. He did testify at length before the parliamentary commission that inquired into the acts of the Government of National Defense, but not about the battle of Buzenval. Kératry came from a liberal royalist family prominent during the July Monarchy, served as an officer in the Crimea and in Mexico, resigning from the army in 1865. He made a name for himself in sensational articles on the Mexican fiasco and was elected as a deputy from Finistère in 1869. After 4 September, he was named prefect of police, but resigned in October, left Paris by balloon, and was given command of the French forces in Brittany by Gambetta. Thiers appointed him to several prefectures in 1871–72.

Trochu's claim that the regent had stricken the emperor's name from the proclamation of Trochu as governor of Paris; Eugénie denied in the bitter letter that she had been motivated by any personal ambition or any desire to betray her husband. It had been necessary, she claimed, to delete from that proclamation the phrase "the general precedes the emperor by only a few hours," since it had been decided not to allow the emperor to return to Paris.

Technically that was true, though it hardly accounted for the decision not to allow the emperor to return. On the other hand, the letter contained a sentence far more revealing than the empress, and evidently Grandperret, recognized: *"You who know how much more dear the emperor has become to me since our misfortunes* [italics mine], you who know how much I admire his self-sacrifice, his courage, his unshakable calm in the face of the vilest charges, do you believe that I chose such a moment to repudiate him!"

Concerning what transpired between Trochu and Favre on the Solferino bridge on 4 September, Grandperret indicated that he again based his argument on Kératry's testimony: Trochu, in fact, had known Favre before that particular encounter, and Trochu thereafter had returned to the Louvre to await the invitation to join the new regime that he expected would be formed at the Hôtel de Ville. When Trochu first entered the Hôtel de Ville, Grandperret continued, he laid down three conditions for his participation in the new government: the government must affirm its faith in God, the family, and in private property. Once he found that those principles were acceptable, he demanded the presidency of the government as the price for his participation. Only then did he go to see Palikao to explain what had happened.[54]

Grandperret obviously meant to prove that the Second Empire fell as the result of a conspiracy of which Trochu was a part. In retrospect, it seems risky to have found such a defense upon bits and pieces of Kératry's deposition; for a reading of that deposition in its entirety makes it indisputably clear that Kératry believed that those who decided to establish the Government of National Defense on 4 September did so "to give Napoleon III no opportunity to sign a shameful treaty on behalf of France, and to prevent radicals from establishing the Commune in the Hôtel de Ville." He saw no prior understanding between Trochu and the opposition nor any conspiracy.[55] What is more, Jules Favre's testimony before that very commission had revealed that those who established the Government of National Defense had anticipated offering the presidency to Thiers. And Thiers turned them down on 4 September—further evidence of no prior understanding

---

54. *Procès*, pp. 48–55.
55. *Enquête parlementaire sur les actes du gouvernement de la défense nationale*, (*Dépositions des témoins*), 1:649–51.

The Great Libel Case in Paris—General Trochu in Court (courtesy of The New York Public Library, Astor, Lenox and Tilden Foundations)

with Trochu.[56] So irritated was Trochu at Grandperret's summation that he asked the court's permission to respond immediately and was given the floor.

Trochu: Vitu's intention was to show that I, as Saint-Arnaud's aide-de-camp, had collaborated in the *coup d'état* of 1851, and that I ultimately conspired to destroy the regime I had helped to found. He also meant to show that the "crime of Buzenval" had been designed by the Government of National Defense to lead the Parisian population to capitulate. The Maître Grandperret seems surprised that I, having been jeered, insulted, and libeled both during the siege and after, should have been astonished by insults and defamation in *le Figaro* to a point of abandoning my usual reserve. I did so in this instance, because I thought the articles damaged two men whom I have held in high regard throughout my career and whose esteem has honored me, namely, MacMahon and Changarnier. I discussed with Mac-Mahon the discrepancy between his statement "I believe that he is a reliable man," and his statement, given to the parliamentary commission, "I believed him to be a reliable man." Marshal MacMahon assured me that he had meant no change in his opinion. [Only the time had changed, hence the change in tense.] I also wrote to General Changarnier about the article and received assurance from him that his high opinion of me had never altered. On the other hand, neither MacMahon nor Changarnier thought it to be their duty to protest to *le Figaro*, so that I felt I must sign the complaint.

Le Figaro, Trochu continued, would have it that the *mobiles* were nothing more than a collection of revolutionaries dedicated to becoming pretorian guards in an uprising. In fact, the *gardes mobiles* of Paris comprised eighteen battalions. Six of them were employed to defend the southern forts and in special perimeter defensive operations, invariably conducting themselves well. The remaining twelve battalions were billeted in Saint-Denis. At the outset, they were very active in preparing the defenses of that area. As time went on, the main problem in Saint-Denis, as in Paris itself, was drunkenness—by far a greater problem for the government than either indiscipline or sedition. On those days of popular sedition, 31 October and 22 January among others, the *gardes mobiles* were not among the battalions that sided with the insurgents. During the battle of Buzenval, several battalions of *mobiles* were included in our right wing and conducted themselves very properly.

I have seen in this courtroom, Trochu went on, evidence of the very suspicions of treason that we experienced in Paris duing the siege [and he implied that the defense was relying on such suspicions to win its case]. Suspicion has fallen on the likes of General Schmitz, a man I tried to decorate

56. Ibid., 1:333.

with the Cross of Grand Officer [in the Legion of Honor], but who refused it. At the end of the siege, I tried to promote Schmitz to the rank of division general. He refused that too, saying he was personally devoted to the emperor, and he wanted his military efforts in the defense of Paris to be nothing but a demonstration of that attachment. No personal rewards! This trial had degenerated into a political test. Both French Empires required wars to maintain themselves, and both required scapegoats to account for military disaster: Dupont for Baylen, Grouchy for Waterloo. Now another one is required.

Trochu continued to describe his career and his attitudes at some length to demonstrate that he had never been a man of opposition, but rather a man of conviction. Having fought the military system, he had found himself duty-bound to try to save it. When the emperor proposed to make him governor of Paris, he had responded that, if he could be of use to the Empire and to the country, he was prepared to leave immediately for Paris. Once there, he had found himself typed as an Orleanist, "evidently because they found me too bourgeois to be a Legitimist." After a brief discussion of the battle of Buzenval, in which he essentially supported General Berthaut's testimony, Trochu sat down to the prolonged applause of the gallery.

The state attorney then addressed the jury for the second time: the question before us is not whether General Trochu made mistakes nor whether he was incompetent in the administration of our national affairs. The question is whether he has been telling the truth. Indeed, it would not be fair to make him assume sole responsibility for the administration of the Government of National Defense. Other members of that regime remain untouched; while he, the loyal and independent servant, is persecuted. After hearing the general, I am convinced that his cause is even more just than it seemed to be on the opening day of this trial.[57]

The defense, if increasingly battered, had one more opportunity in Charles Lachaud's speech for Villemessant. "Some expiations are inevitable," Lachaud remarked in opening the final day of the trial. "God wishes it to be so. When those expiations are slow in coming, they who must submit to them, caught by a blind fatality, act to hasten the moment of their accounting. General Trochu has accounts to settle with history that history has been tardy in summing up. He has, consequently, desired to hasten the settlement. May he be satisfied!"

Lachaud took the state attorney to task for prejudices derived from reading the wrong newspapers. He challenged Trochu's claim that they were in the midst of a political trial. Villemessant, after all, had never been a Bonapartist; and he, Lachaud, while treasuring the memory of the imperial couples'

57. *Procès*, pp. 57–61.

graciousness, owed nothing to any regime and could be called a political independent.[58] He insisted, therefore, that the jury focus its attention upon three major issues raised in the trial. (1) Did General Trochu, either at the time of the *coup d'état* of 1851 or later, manifest an attitude that made him legitimately regarded as an opponent of that *coup?* (2) In regard to the empress and the *Corps législatif,* did General Trochu remain steadfast to the oaths of allegiance he had taken? (3) Was the battle of Buzenval really undertaken for the defense of Paris or as a result of a wretched calculation on the part of the Government of National Defense?

In reviewing Trochu's admittedly fine military career, Lachaud endeavored to show that, though Trochu may have disapproved of the *coup,* he adhered to the regime by becoming General Saint-Arnaud's aide-de-camp and by accepting the promotions and honors that rewarded his excellent service. Yet, on 17 August, at Châlons, he had made the return of the *gardes mobiles* to Paris a condition *sine qua non* for his acceptance of the governorship according to the testimony of Marshal MacMahon; and it would be an offense to the entire country to deny the testimony of such a man! As for the meeting between the regent and Trochu, Lachaud claimed that Trochu had completely misunderstood the meaning of her question about recalling the Orleans princes. It had been her offer to put aside politics during the emergency in the national interest, the offer of a courageous and noble soul. Contrast this with such pledges as, "I shall get myself killed for the *Corps législatif* and for the empress," and "Count on me, trust me, I am a soldier, a Catholic, and a Breton." Lachaud admitted that no one had heard those last words, but the empress had reported them—she whose behavior was so exemplary during that terrible crisis.

I note, Lachaud continued, that both Trochu and Jules Favre have gone to great pains to indicate that they did not know each other in order to disprove the charges of a plot to overthrow the regime. Yet, Charles Floquet said in his testimony before the parliamentary commission that the two men had shaken hands in his presence.[59] General Trochu has told us that he had to do his duty to the nation in the crisis, and that what happened on 4 September was not a revolution but a collapse. But where were the nation's rep-

---

58. While Lachaud was "independent" in that he had never received official appointment during the Second Empire, he had run for the *Corps législatif* in 1869 (unsuccessfully) with official blessing; and he was an ardent Bonapartist after 1870.

59. In fact, Floquet's testimony had not necessarily implied that Trochu and Favre were acquainted. He said that on 4 September he had gone to the *Corps législatif* and had found some Republicans trying to draw up a list of new government members in an outer room. When they started for the Hôtel de Ville, he joined them. They met a general on horseback struggling to move in the direction of the Chamber, and Floquet was told it was Trochu, whom he did not know. Favre extended his hand, they talked, and the general then rode off in the direction of the Carrousel. See *Enquête parlementaire sur l'insurrection du 18 mars,* (*Dépositions des témoins*), 2:279.

resentatives? Were they at the Hôtel de Ville with triumphant demagogy? Was there no *Corps législatif?* Was it not *there* that France was represented? Was it not true that the illustrious M. Thiers had received genuine authority from the *Corps législatif?* The empire may have vanished, but France and her representatives remained. I say that you had the choice between what remained of legality and insurrection, and that you chose insurrection. That is what must be recorded by history. Are we to be condemned for having censured such a choice!

In recalling the intense suffering and misery during the siege of Paris, I note the fact that the Government of National Defense failed to make peace after 31 October when softer terms were available. I ask the jury not to believe that the resistance was sublime and heroic. The defense was "an episode where the grotesque competed with the lugubrious, where ineptitude reached such limits as to be nearly criminal." [Trochu, obviously angered, kept shaking his head negatively.]

Trochu, Lachaud went on, who ought to have been defending Paris, actually had no confidence that the city could be defended. The whole business was a massive deception of the population, culminating in Buzenval. The government's duty was to exercise its authority according to reliable information rather than to have allowed itself to be driven by the blind and insane multitude. The government should have fallen rather than consenting to the butchery of Buzenval. I read to you the words of [the marquis] de la Rochethulon before the parliamentary commission where he states that the battle of Buzenval was launched without any great hope of success by the military leaders, but because the government needed to reduce public pressure. One member of the government proposed that National Guard troops be used in the assault since it would help calm public opinion if ten thousand of them were killed. [60]

Trochu, now infuriated, interrupted Lachaud to protest that such testimony as Rochethulon's had been entirely false. Be that as it may, Lachaud had touched truthfully upon the near-paralysis of the Government of National Defense in the face of radical agitation; and many of its military decisions had been just as political in motivation as had been those of the Palikao regime. Lachaud's speech, if inaccurate on critical points, amounted to a skillful play upon the feelings of national humiliation. In concluding, he asked the jury to render the same verdict that history must ultimately render, no matter how unpleasant it might be to strike down a man like General Trochu. "Let it not be said that in this poor, beaten-down country, where so little remains, that even justice itself has become enervated!" [61]

60. Lachaud did quote Rochetulon correctly. Ibid., 1:399.
61. *Procès*, pp. 62–68.

President Legendre: The debate having concluded, I am required by law to give the jury a résumé of the arguments. In this particular case, however, I think that it would be useful for me to comment on some points of law as well as upon the facts. In this civil case, following General Trochu's complaint, Villemessant and Vitu have been charged with two crimes: defamation and outrages [public injuries] to a functionary during the exercise of his duties. Precedence requires that the publisher of the journal in which the cited articles appeared be held to be the principal person responsible, the writer of the articles being regarded as his accomplice. Defamation is understood to mean any allegation or accusation that damages the honor or the reputation of the person about whom the allegation is made. Any insulting [*outrageante*] expression, term of contempt or abuse, that does not include the imputation of any fact, is a punishable insult or outrage.

The law differentiates between private and public persons in matters of libel, Legendre continued. A private person libeled is protected by the law, whether or not the accusations made are true. But in the instance of a person libeled in the course of his public functions, the authors of the libel are allowed to try to prove the validity of their charges; and they are protected by the law in the event they can prove their charges. This is based upon a law of 1819, that was intended to protect the public and to serve as a warning to those in public office that they could be denounced with impunity if the denouncer be in complete command of the facts. Public officials are not immune from the truth. This law of 1819 was repassed by the National Assembly in April of 1871.

As for the defendants in this case, Legendre explained, both are veterans of journalistic battles. One of them has been repeatedly fined and warned for offenses against the public or private lives of citizens. In this instance, they have demanded the right to prove their defamatory charges. [He then gave a brief résumé of the allegations against Trochu and Trochu's response to the charges.] Finally, I must remind the jury that the state attorney, as the public representative, has asked the jury to consider the case strictly in legal terms, because it is all too easy to consider this case as a matter of political prejudice. Your problem, therefore, is not to decide whether Trochu's actions, words, or conduct merit criticism or praise, but strictly to discover whether the defendants have been able to prove the validity of the defamatory charges in their articles.[62]

The president completed his summation and legal instruction to the jury shortly before one o'clock on 2 April, and the jurors retired to deliberate. At three o'clock, they were ready to present their verdict. Trochu was not present in the courtroom when the court resumed its sitting. Warning the

62. Ibid., pp. 68–69.

audience against any demonstration out of respect for justice, the president asked the chairman of the jury for the verdict: "On all matters relative to defamation, *not guilty*. On all matters relative to outrage, *guilty*." While it might seem strange that the jury had refused to condemn on the defamation issue, they were technically correct in that Trochu was not a private citizen, but a public figure invested with public authority. Therefore, the case properly focused on outrages to him in that capacity. Had he been a private citizen, he would easily have won on the defamation issue.

The court then retired for a half hour to consider the sentences. Upon the judges' return, Villemessant and Vitu were each sentenced to one month of imprisonment and fines of three thousand francs. The issues of *le Figaro* containing the offensive articles were to be suppressed. Notice of the sentences was to be inserted in both the *Gazette des Tribunaux* and in *le Droit* at the defendants' expense, and the defendants were made liable for the court costs. The trial closed without demonstration or noise, the audience filing out slowly, groups discussing the outcome in the corridors for more than an hour.[63]

Vindicated in a court of law, and by a jury of Parisians, General Trochu prepared for obscurity, though only fifty-seven. He resigned his seat in the National Assembly on 1 July 1872, and his military retirement became effective the following year. He took up residence in Tours where he died in 1896. Probably he recognized that the rectitude of his cause would avail him little in a country so needful of partisan explanations for the defeat and violence of 1870–71. La Gorce, the greatest historian of the Second Empire, knew of the trial and was never unfair to Trochu, but most subsequent historical accounts have been stained with a hostility born of political partisanship. Even men favorable to Trochu were favorable on partisan grounds. "Judicial eloquence," Thiers wrote to Edouard Allou in congratulating him on his speech in the trial, "has produced nothing finer, but I do not say enough by saying judicial eloquence. Yours was political eloquence, and of the best." [64]

This brief civil case, so evidently a political trial, did more than vindicate Trochu's honor. It heard testimony about the defeat of 1870 from many witnesses who had never been called before the parliamentary commission that investigated the Government of National Defense.[65] And that testimony, sharpened and refined by the cross-examination of distinguished attorneys, exposed the political motives of the conservative Bonapartists in reaching their military strategy, and focused the responsibility for the *magnitude* of

63. Ibid., p. 71.
64. Le Bail, p. 106.
65. Of the thirty-seven witnesses cited in this chapter, twenty-two did not give testimony before a parliamentary commission.

the defeat precisely where it belonged. The trial, moreover, provided evidence of the empress-regent's desire to supplant Napoleon III.

Beyond the political opportunism that found in Trochu a convenient scapegoat, we should recognize the likelihood that his intense professionalism contributed to making him an alien and inscrutable figure. In September of 1870, he refused additional salary for his presidential function, saying that his military salary sufficed. At the time of the armistice in 1871, he proposed to the minister of war that he, Trochu, along with his staff officers, should be placed at the head of the list of prisoners of war under the armistice terms and not be given preferential treatment by the incoming French regime. Several months later, learning that Thiers wished to honor the valiant defence of Paris by promoting him, Trochu wrote Thiers that he would accept neither higher rank in the Legion of Honor nor the marshalate that could be his, because of the political implications of such promotion.[66] This keen sense of honor was as little appreciated in his own time as it would be in ours. What went into retirement in 1873 was a profound professionalism rooted in legitimacy.

66. Cartier, *Un Méconnu*, p. 422; and Brunet-Moret, *Le Général Trochu*, pp. 279–80.

Epilogue

BOVE all else, these legal cases have been presented to exemplify the French courtroom as a political arena in the nineteenth century. Opponents of established regimes regularly made political gain from both criminal and civil cases, confusing judicial issues for the juries and contributing to the manufacture of those political myths still affecting historical interpretations. For many attorneys, notably defense attorneys, the legal career was a political career, one that avoided the hazards of conventional political life so long as the attorney refrained from seeking elective office.

Once such a use, or abuse, of the legal system became frequent, neither politicians nor the public could take even the most prosaic case at face value. Its issues could become distorted, not simply by interested parties, but through an atmosphere of resolute skepticism that subtly modified the evidence for both jurist and historian. Thus did skepticism, which ought to generate meditative inquiry, in fact breed gullibility. The conventional antagonism to the Second Empire, evident in France to this very day, owes much to the skill of legal polemicists, both inside the courtroom and out, who cared more for political advantage than for justice.

Bibliography

PRIMARY SOURCES

Allou, Roger, ed. *Discours et plaidoyers d'Edouard Allou.* 2 vols. Paris: Durand et Pedone-Lauriel, 1884. The Trochu case is found in vol. 1, pp. 411–526.

Attentat du Mois d'Août 1840 (Cour des Pairs). Paris: Imprimerie Royale, 1840.

1) Attentat du 6 Août 1840: Rapport fait à la Cour par M. Persil, l'un des commissaires chargés de l'instruction du proces déféré à la Cour des Pairs par ordonnance royale du 9 août 1840.

2) *Interrogatoires des inculpés.*

Barbey d'Aurevilly, Jules. *Polemiques d'hier.* Paris: Albert Savine, 1889. Articles written between 1865 and 1869, the final one dated 4 November 1869, "Les Assassins contre les rhéteurs, Troppmann contre Jules Simon."

Berryer, Pierre-Antoine. *Les Oeuvres conplètes.* 9 vols. Paris: Didier, 1872–78. The last four volumes contain his courtroom speeches, the trial of 1840 being in the second.

Bertrand, Dr. Amédée. *Etude médico-légale au sujet de Troppmann.* Paris: Published by the author, 1869. A nineteen-page brochure written before the Troppmann trial, the introduction being dated 27 December 1869.

Bonaparte, Louis-Napoleon. *Oeuvres de Napoleon III.* 5 vols. Paris: Henri Plon, 1869.

———. *The Political and Historical Works of Louis Napoleon Bonaparte, President of the French Republic, with an Original Memoir of His Life, brought down to the Promulgation of the Constitution of 1852.* 2 vols. London: Illustrated London Library, 1852. Contains an account of the trial of 1840.

Bourg, Edme-Théodore (called Saint-Edme), *Procès du prince Napoléon-Louis et de ses coaccusés devant la Cour des Pairs.* Paris: A. Levavasseur. 1840. A reliable account of the trial that contains brief biographies of the major conspirators.

Chaix-d'Est-Ange, Gustave-Louis. *Discours et plaidoyers.* 2 vols. Paris: F. Didot, 1862; 3 vols. Paris: Durand et Pedone-Lauriel, 1877. The Orsini case is covered in vol. 1, pp. 403–70, of the first edition; vol. 2, pp. 479–540 in the second.

[Claude, Antoine-François]. *Mémoires de Monsieur Claude, chef de la police de Sûreté sous de second empire.* Paris: Jules Rouff, 1881–82. This is the original ten-volume unabridged edition of this spurious work.

Constant, l'abbé Alphonse-Louis. *La Clef des grands mystères.* Paris: G. Baillière, 1861. Constant used the name Lévi Eliphas. In this volume, he reports about Verger seeking help with black magic.

Dossiers in the Archives de la Préfecture de Police:
  1) Boitelle, Symphorien-Casimir-Joseph, E a/22 6
  2) Jud-Poinsot, 33064
  3) Lagrange, Michel, B a/1.138
  4) Macé, Marie-Placide-Gustave, E a/89 and B a/1165
  5) Piétri, Joachim-Marie, E a/22 7
  6) Piétri, Pierre-Marie, E a/22 5

Enquête parlementaire sur les actes du gouvernment de la défense nationale. 18 vols. Versailles: Cerf, 1872–75.

Enquête parlementaire sur l'insurrection du 18 mars. 3 vols. Versailles: Cerf, 1872.

Favre, Mme. Jules, ed. *Plaidoyers politiques et judiciaires de Jules Favre.* 2 vols. Paris: E. Plon, 1882. His speech for Orsini is in vol. 1, pp. 580–87. These volumes do not include Favre's parliamentary speeches, which were published by Mme. Favre in four volumes in 1881.

Fermé, Albert. *Les Grands procès politiques: Boulogne d'après les documents authentiques.* Paris: A. Le Chevalier, 1869. Fermé, a lawyer, gives a reliable transcript of the trial and publishes a number of documents preliminary to the trial.

Fouquier, Armand. *Causes célèbres de tous les peuples.* 8 vols. Paris: Lebrun, 1858–67. Contains a reliable account of the Verger case in vol. 1.

Gazette des Tribunaux, Journal de jurisprudence et des débats judiciaires:
  1) Boulogne conspiracy, année 15 (May–October 1840), issues 8 August–7 October;
  2) Sibour assassination, année 32 (January–June 1857), issues 4 January–31 January;
  3) Orsini attempt, année 33 (January–June 1858), issues 16 January–14 March;
  4) Murder of Victor Poinsot, année 35 (July–December 1860), issues 7 December–30 December; and année 36 (January–June 1861), issues 10 January–23 February; and année 36 (July–December 1861), issues 16 October–28 November;
  5) Troppmann murders, année 44 (July–December 1869), issues 20 September–31 December, and année 45 (January–June 1870), issues 1 January–20 January.

Ghisalberti, Alberto M., ed. *Lettere di Felice Orsini.* Rome: Vittoriano, 1936.

La Semaine Religieuse, revue du culte et des bonnes oeuvres. 7 no. 167(25 January 1857), and no. 169(8 February 1857) contain articles on Verger.

Lemarchand, M.–G. *Procès du prince Pierre-Napoléon Bonaparte devant la Haute Cour de Justice.* Tours: Mazereau, 1870; and Paris: Lacroix, Verboeckoven, 1870. Lemarchand was an official stenographer for the Senate who transcribed this trial.

Marchal, Charles [Charles de Bussy]. *Les Conspirateurs en Angleterre (1848–1858).* Paris: Lebigre-Duquesne, 1858. A Catholic exposé containing an account of the trial of Dr. Simon Bernard in London, 12–17 April 1858.

Maritain, Paul. *Jules Favre, mélanges politiques, judiciaires et littéraires.* Paris: A. Rousseau, 1882.

Montijo, Eugénie de. *Lettres familières de l'impératrice Eugénie.* 2 vols. Paris: Le Devan, 1935.

Nauroy, Charles. *Le Curieux.* 2 vols. in one. Paris: 6 rue de Seine, 1883–88. These are bound pamphlets which were published biweekly. Also see his *Les Secrets des Bonaparte,* Paris: Emile Boullion, 1889, which reproduces genuine documents along with dubious gossip.

Papiers secrets et correspondance du second empire. Paris: Auguste Ghio, 1873.

Parent du Chatelet, Martial. *Réponse à quelques malveillants et calomniateurs.* Paris: Dubuisson, 1857. An apology for his role in the Verger case.

Procès du Général Trochu contre MM. Vitu et de Villemessant du Figaro. Paris: Journal la Petite Presse, 1872.

Sangnier, Félix. *Plaidoyers de Charles Lachaud.* 2 vols. Paris: Charpentier, 1885. The Trochu case is covered in vol. 1, the Troppmann case in vol. 2.

[Sibour, Marie-Dominique-Auguste]. *Mandements, lettres et instructions pastorales de Monseigneur Sibour.* 2 vols. Paris: Le Clère, 1853–57.

Trochu, Louis-Jules. *L'Armée française en 1867.* Paris: Amyot, 1867. The book ran through many editions.

Turgenev, Ivan S. *Devant la guillotine.* Paris: E. Flammarion, 1892. This translation from the Russian was published nine years after Turgenev's death and describes the Troppmann execution.

Verger, Jean-Louis. *Réflexions impartiales d'un auditeur aux débats de la cour d'assises de Seine-et-Marne, séant à Melun le 15 novembre 1856.* Paris: Cosse et Dumaine, 1856. Verger's version of the Lamy case.

Vervorst, Chanoine Firmin. *Autographe de Louis Verger, rectifiant quelques assertions et justifiant le clergé.* Paris: Les principaux librairies, 1857. While he published a few of Verger's letters, the primary intent was to criticize the recruitment and retention of clergy who early showed signs of moral disqualification—as Verger did. Vervorst had no patience with Verger's sophistry.

MEMOIRS AND CONTEMPORARY HISTORIES

Alton-Shée, Edmond de Lignères, comte d'. *Mes mémoires.* 2 vols., Paris: Lacroix-Verboeckhoven, 1869. Reached the age to assume his peerage in 1836, and by 1848 was a democratic opponent of the July Monarchy. Devoted himself to business during the Second Empire.

Baroche, Céleste [Mme. Jules]. *Second Empire, notes et souvenirs de seize années, 1855–1871.* Paris: G. Crès, 1921. The wife of the conservative Bonapartist minister.

Beaumont-Vassy, Edouard-Ferdinand, vicomte de. *Mémoires secrets du dix-neuvième siècle.* Paris: F. Sartorius, 1874. Covers the first half of the century. He is inaccurate about Miss Howard.

Canler, Louis. *Mémoires de Canler, ancien chef du service du sûreté.* Paris: J. Hetzel, 1862. He held the post from 3 March 1849 until the Orsini attempt in 1858.

Castellane, Esprit-Victor de. *Journal du maréchal de Castellane, 1804–1862.* 5 vols. Paris: Plon-Nourrit, 1895–97. At the time of the Orsini affair, Castellane commanded the Lyon military region.

Castille, Charles-Hippolyte. *Histoire de la seconde république française.* 4 vols. Paris: Victor Lecou, 1854–56; A novelist, publicist, and historian, Castille became a Bonapartist and was probably financed by Napoleon III.

Claveau, Anatole. *Souvenirs politiques et parlementaires d'un témoin.* 2 vols. Paris: Plon-Nourrit, 1913–14. Claveau was a *secretaire-rédacteur* for the *Corps législatif* and for the National Assembly, 1865–73.

Cresson, Ernest. *Cent jours du siège à la préfecture de police.* Paris: Plon-Nourrit, 1901. Prefect of Police from 2 November 1870 to 11 February 1871.

Darimon, Alfred. *Histoire de douze ans, 1857–1869.* Paris: E. Dentu, 1883.

———. *A Travers une revolution.* Paris: E. Dentu, 1884.

Darimon, Alfred. *Histoire d'un parti.* 5 vols. Paris: E. Dentu, 1885–89. Darimon was a Republican journalist and deputy.

Delord, Taxile. *Histoire du second empire.* 6 vols. Paris: Germer Baillière, 1869–75. A leading Republican journalist.

Des Glajeux, A.-Bérard. *Souvenirs d'un président d'assises.* 2 vols. Paris: Plon-Nourrit, 1892–93.

Du Camp, Maxime. *Paris: Ses organes, ses fonctions et sa vie dans la second moitié du xixè siècle.* 6 vols. Paris: Hachette, 1875.

Faurie, General. *Souvenirs.* Rodez: Georges Subervie, 1937. He interviewed Trochu in the 1890s, but learned little that was new.

Fleury, Maurice, comte, ed. *Memoirs of the Empress Eugénie.* 2 vols. New York: D. Appleton, 1920.

Flourens, Gustave. *Paris livré.* Paris: Lacroix, Verboeckhoven, 1871.

Greville, Charles C. F. *The Greville Memoirs* (pt. 3), A Journal of the Reign of Queen Victoria from 1852 to 1860. 2 vols. London: Longmans, Green, 1887. Important for the period after the Orsini attempt.

Grison, Georges. *Souvenirs de la place de la Roquette.* Paris: E. Dentu, 1883. Mostly about cases in the 1870s.

Guettée, René-François-Wladimir. *Souvenirs d'un prêtre romain devenue prêtre orthodoxe.* Paris: Fischbacher, 1889. He devotes a chapter to the Verger case.

Hamel, Ernest. *Histoire illustrée du second empire.* 3 vols. Paris: Degorce-Cadot, and Librairie de L'Echo de la Sorbonne, 1873–74. Anti-Bonapartist popular history.

Haussmann, Georges Eugène, baron. *Mémoires.* 3 vols. Paris: Victor-Havard, 1890–93. The second volume covers the préfecture of the Seine from 1853 to 1870.

Hübner, Alexander von, ed. *Neuf ans de souvenirs d'un ambassadeur d'Autriche à Paris, 1851–1859; comte Joseph de Hübner.* 2 vols. Paris: Plon, 1904.

Janzé, Mme. Alix (Choiseul-Gouffier) de. *Berryer, souvenirs intimes,* Paris: Plon, 1881. Brief, eulogistic, but intelligent.

Kératry, Emile, comte de. *Le 4 septembre.* Paris: Lacroix-Verboeckhoven, 1872. Was briefly prefect of police before Cresson in 1870. The heart of this book is his testimony before the parliamentary commission that investigated the Government of National Defense.

Kossuth, Count Louis. *Souvenirs et écrits de mon exil. Période de la guerre d'Italie.* Paris: Plon, 1880. Reveals the attempts of Napoleon III, Prince Napoleon, and Pierre Piétri to relate the Hungarian national movement to Italian affairs in 1858–59.

Lefébure, Constant. *Souvenirs d'un ancien directeur des prisons de Paris.* Paris: H. Louvet, 1894. Very brief and of limited value.

Limet, Charles. *Un Vétéran du barreau parisien, quatre-vingts ans de souvenirs, 1827–1907.* Paris: Lemerre, 1908. One of the liberals of 1848 and a friend of Emile Ollivier.

Macé, Gustave. *La Police parisienne: Le Service de la Sûreté.* Paris: Charpentier, 1884. M. Claude's successor.

Maupas, Charlemagne-Emile de. *Mémoires sur le second empire.* 2 vols. Paris: E. Dentu, 1884–85. A conservative Bonapartist who was briefly head of the police.

Ménière. *Mémoires anecdotiques sur les salons du second empire.* Paris: Plon-Nourrit, 1903.

Metternich, Pauline von. *Souvenirs d'enfance et de jeunesse.* Paris: Plon-Nourrit, 1924. This contains the story of Lachaud and Troppmann's alleged accomplices.

Moreau, l'abbé Georges. *Souvenirs de la Petite et de la Grande Roquette.* 5th ed. Paris: J. Rouff, 1884. Some of the information came from l'abbé Abraham-Sébastien Crozes, but Moreau also read Du Camp, Grison, and the bogus M. Claude.

Ollivier, Emile. *L'Empire libéral, études, récits, souvenirs.* 18 vols. Paris: Garnier frères, 1895–1918. Vol. 12 deals with the Ministry of 2 January.

————. *Journal, 1846–1869.* 2 vols. Paris: René Julliard, 1961.

Orsi, Count Giuseppe. *Recollections of the Last Half-Century.* London: Longmans, 1881. One of the Boulogne conspirators. He says nothing about Miss Howard.

Paléologue, Maurice. *The Tragic Empress: Conversations of the Empress Eugénie, 1901–19,* New York and London: Harper and Bros., 1928. Dated memories, but they do her honor.

Parquin, Denis Charles. *Souvenirs du capitaine Parquin, 1803–1814.* Paris: Boussod-Valadon, 1892. A participant in both the Strassburg and Boulogne attempts. These souvenirs were written during his detention at Doullens.

Regnault, Elias. *L'Histoire de huit ans, 1840–1848.* 3 vols. 2d ed., Paris: Pagnerre, 1860. He was interested in the financial resources behind the Boulogne expedition.

Rochefort, Henri. *Les Aventures de ma vie.* 5 vols. Paris: Paul Dupont, 1896.

Rocquain, Félix. *Notes et fragments d'histoire.* Paris: Plon, 1906. An official of the Archives Nationales who provided some of the information used by comte Kératry.

Sanson, Henri. *Sept générations d'exécuteurs. 1688–1847.* 6 vols. Paris: Dupray de La Mahérie, 1862–63. The Sansons were among the most famous of the dynasties of headsmen.

Sardou, Victorien. *Les Papiers de Victorien Sardou.* Paris: A. Michel, 1934. The playwright and librettist who attended the Troppmann execution, but left no record of it here.

Senior, Nassau William. *Conversations with Distinguished Persons During the Second Empire from 1860–1863.* 2 vols. London: Hurst & Blackett, 1880.

Simon, *La Peine de mort,* Paris: Lacroix, Verboeckhoven, 1869.

Trochu, Louis-Jules. *Oeuvres posthumes.* 2 vols. Tours: A. Mame, 1896. The first volume, on the siege of Paris, was compiled between 1878 and 1890. The second volume, entitled *La Société, l'état, l'armée,* was written between 1874 and 1890.

————. *Pour la vérité et pour la justice: Pétition à l'assemblée nationale.* Paris: J. Hetzel, 1873. His commentary on the reports published by the parliamentary committee that investigated the Government of National Defense.

Vermorel, Auguste-Jean-Marie. *La Police contemporaine.* Paris; Lebigre-Duquesne, 1864.

Vidocq, Eugène-François. *Les Mémoires de Vidocq.* Paris: Editions Baudelaire, 1967. Vidocq was an interesting writer, but the *Mémoires* are spurious; and he greatly disapproved of them when they were originally published.

Viel Castel, Horace de Salviac, Count de. *Memoirs: A Chronicle of the Principal Events, Political and Social, during the Reign of Napoleon III from 1851 to 1864.* 2 vols. London: Remington, 1888.

Vingt ans de police, souvenirs et anecdotes d'un ancien officier de paix. Paris: E. Dentu, 1881.

Wolff, Albert. *Mémoires d'un Parisien.* 3 vols. Paris: V. Havard, 1884–88. A witty journalist with a good deal of insight.

Zola, Emile. *La République en marche.* 2 vols. Paris: Fasquelle, 1956.

SECONDARY SOURCES

Allou, Roger and Charles Chenu. *Grands avocats du siècle.* Paris: A. Pedone, 1894. Contains sketches of Edouard Allou, Berryer, Lachaud, and Chaix d'Est-Ange.

Auzies, Célestin. *De la surveillance de la haute police.* Paris: E. Thorin, 1869. An essay on jurisprudence, notably touching on the laws of 8 December 1851, 12 July 1852, and 13 May 1863.

Balthazard, Doctor. "Le meutre de Victor Noir." *Revue médicale française* 14 (1933):119–121.

Barrault, André. "Louis Verger (1826–1857), assassin de Mgr. Sibour." *Bulletin de la Société d'histoire et d'art du diocèse de Meaux* 13(1962):170–72.

Bastid, Paul. "L'Affaire Victor Noir." *Revue politique et parlementaire* 72, no. 811(1970):57–63.

Baumgarten, Raymond. "La mort de Mgr. Sibour." *La Vie judiciaire,* no. 633(26–31 May 1958):8–9.

Benoît-Lévy, Edmond. *Jules Favre.* Paris: Picard-Bernheim, 1884. Superficial and very dated.

Bouchardon, Pierre. *L'Assassinat de l'archevêque.* Paris: Arthème Fayard, 1926. While he notes the haste of the *instruction,* he does not take sides as to whether the verdict was proper.

———. *Troppmann.* Paris: Albin Michel, 1932. A fictionalized treatment of the case, but he has used the *Gazette des Tribunaux.* No nonsense about Prussian spies.

Brunet-Moret, Jean. *Le Général Trochu 1815–1896.* Paris: Haussmann, 1955. The trial of 1872 is barely mentioned, and inaccurately at that.

Buisson, Henry. *La Police: Son histoire.* Vichy: Wallon, 1949. Authoritative survey by a professor at the École Nationale de Police.

Cahuet, Albéric. *Napoléon délivré: Le Coup de théâtre de 1840,* Paris: E. Paul, 1914.

———. *Retours de Saint-Hélène (1821–1840).* Paris: Fasquelle, 1932.

Cartier, Vital. *Un Méconnu: Le Général Trochu 1814–1896.* Paris: Perrin, 1914. Sympathetic biography which includes fifty pages of documents.

Chacornac, Paul. *Elphas Lévi: Rénovateur de l'occultisme en France (1810–1875),* Paris: Chacornac freres, 1926. Biography of Alphonse Constant.

Corley, T. A. B. *Democratic Despot: A Life of Napoleon III.* London: Barrie & Rockliff, 1961.

Corti, comte E. E. "Correspondance du roi Louis et de Louis-Napoléon interceptée par la police de Metternich, 1833–1840, (première partie) Louis-Napoléon et son projet de mariage avec la princesse Mathilde," *Revue des études napoléoniennes,* 26(January–June 1926):156–76. (Deuxième partie) "Les Complots de Louis-Napoléon et l'état d'âme de son père," ibid., 233–50.

Cristiani, le chanoine L. "L'assassinat de Mgr. Sibour." *l'Ami du clergé* 67, no. 49(5 December 1957): 735–37.

Cudet, François. *Histoire des corps de troupe qui ont été spécialement chargés de service de la ville de Paris depuis son origine jusqu'à nos jours.* Paris: Léon Pillet, 1887.

Dansette, Adrien. *L'Attentat d'Orsini.* Paris: Editions Mondiales, 1964. He understands that Napoleon III used Orsini to bring his own youthful dreams to fruition.

———. "L'échauffourée de Boulogne." *Revue des deux mondes,* pt. 1 (15 April 1958): 609–27; pt. 2 (15 May 1958): 275–86.

————. *Louis-Napoléon à la conquête du pouvoir.* Paris: Hachette, 1961.

————. *Religious History of Modern France.* 2 vols. Freiburg: Herder, 1961.

Delair, Paul. *Silhouettes du palais.* Paris: E. Dentu, 1891. Contains a brief sketch of Edouard Allou.

Desjoyeaux, Claude-Noël. *La Fusion monarchique, 1848–1873.* Paris: Plon-Nourrit, 1913. Information on Berryer's politics.

Du Plessis, comte Joachim. *Berryer.* Paris: La Bonne Presse, 1946. Selections from his speeches arranged topically.

Dupuy, Aimée. *1870–1871, la guerre, la commune et la presse.* Paris: Armand Colin, 1959.

Esmein, Jean-Paul-Hippolyte-Emmanuel-Adhémar. "France: Law and Institutions." *Encyclopedia Britannica,* 11th ed. 10 (1910):906–29. Good authoritative survey.

Eugénie de Grèce. *Pierre-Napoléon Bonaparte, 1815–1881.* Paris: Hachette, 1963. The author is the daughter of Prince George of Greece and Marie Bonaparte, thus the great-granddaughter of Prince Pierre.

Fleury & Sonolet. *Le Société du second empire.* 4 vols. Paris: A. Michel, 1911.

Garçon, Maurice. *Histoires curieuses.* Paris: A. Fayard, 1959. Chapter 9 is entitled "La Vraie histoire de Jud," and is virtually identical with Garçon's article "Le Mystérieux crime de Jud," *Miroir de l'histoire,* no. 121(January 1960): 47–55. While Garçon had access to reliable sources, he seems to have used "M. Claude" uncritically.

Gével, Claude. *Deux carbonari: Orsini et Napoléon III.* Paris: Emile-Paul frères, 1934. No bibliography, no footnotes, and a great deal of speculation.

Gramont, Elisabeth de, duchesse de Clermont-Tonnerre. *Le Comte d'Orsay et Lady Blessington.* Paris: Hachette, 1955. Brief sketch of people who were significant in the people they knew and entertained.

Grant, Elliott M. "L'Affaire Poinsot-Jud, Mérimée et Zola." *Les Cahiers naturalistes* 9, no. 23(1963):313–15. Zola used the murder of Poinsot in preparing his *la Bête humaine,* helping to perpetuate the rumor that the murder was a crime of vengeance. Grant did not know the facts in the case at all.

Griffiths, Major Arthur. *Mysteries of Police and Crime.* 2 vols. London: Cassell, 1899. Brief sketches of Jud and Troppmann reveal that he based himself on "M. Claude."

Guériot, Paul. *Napoléon III.* 2 vols. Paris: Payot, 1933–34.

Guest, Ivor. *Napoleon III in England.* London: British Technical and General Press, 1952. Useful for the Boulogne affair.

Hales, E. E. Y. *Pio Nono: A Study of European Politics and Religion in the Nineteenth Century.* London: Eyre & Spottiswoode, 1954.

Hearder, H. "Napoleon III's Threat to Break Off Diplomatic Relations with England during the Crisis over the Orsini Attempt in 1858." *English Historical Review* 72, no. 284(July 1957):474–81. Based upon his doctoral dissertation on Malmesbury (London, 1951).

Hessling, Peter. *Trois monstres.* Paris: Gallimard, 1958. Popularized account of Troppmann case generously borrowed from Bouchardon.

Howard, Michael. *The Franco-Prussian War.* New York: Macmillan, 1962.

Jacomet, Pierre. *Avocats républicains du second empire: Jules Favre—Léon Gambetta.* Paris: Denoël et Steele, 1933.

————. *Berryer au prétoire.* Paris: Plon, 1938. He thinks that Berryer's performance in 1840 was one of his greatest.

Jerrold, Blanchard. *The Life of Napoleon III.* 4 vols. London: Longmans, Green,

1874–82. Material on the period before the Second Empire is more reliable than that on the reign.

Jesse, F. Tennyson. *Murder and its Motives.* London: George G. Harrap, 2d ed., 1952. Chapter 6 on Orsini.

Kershaw, Alister. *A History of the Guillotine.* London: John Calder, 1958.

———. *Murder in France.* London: Constable, 1955. He has a chapter on Verger in which he makes some peculiar observations about the French.

Kurtz, Harold. *The Empress Eugénie, 1826–1920,* London: Hamish Hamilton, 1964. He has a higher opinion of the empress than most writers have had.

La Gorce, Pierre de. *Histoire du second empire.* 7 vols. Paris: Plon-Nourrit, 1894–1905.

Lagrange, François. *Vie de Mgr. Dupanloup, évêque d'Orléans,* 3 vols. Paris: Poussielgue frères, 1883–84.

Lano, Pierre de. *Le Secret d'un empire: La Cour de Napoléon III.* Paris: V. Havard, 1892. Lano liked Napoleon III, but not the entourage.

Le Bail, Georges. *Grands avocats politiques XIXè siècle.* Paris: Berger-Levrault, 1934. Sketches of Allou, Berryer, and Favre.

Lebey, André. *Les Trois coups d'état de Louis-Napoléon Bonaparte.* Vol. 1, *Strasbourg et Boulogne.* Paris: Perrin, 1906. A valuable study.

Le Clère, Marcel. *Histoire de la police.* Paris: Presses Universitaires de France, 1947. A brief survey. He has read and swallowed "M. Claude," and the section on the Second Empire is deeply prejudiced.

Lecomte, Maurice. *Le Prince des Dandys: Le Comte d'Orsay, 1801–1852.* Paris: Lemerre, 1928.

Lorain, Pierre & Marquiset, Robert. *Armes à feu françaises modèles réglementaires (1858–1918 chargement culasse).* Paris: Collection J. Boudriot, 1969.

Madden, Richard Robert. *The Literary Life and Correspondence of the Countess of Blessington.* 2 vols. New York: Harper, 1856–60. Pure eulogy.

Marchand, Louis. *Les Idées de Berryer.* Paris: Nouvelle Librairie Nationale, 1917. An important book, not about Berryer's legal cases but about his political and social views.

Martin, Sir Theodore. *Life of the Prince Consort.* 4 vols. London: Smith, Elder, 1875–80.

Maurain, Jean. *La Politique ecclésiastique du second empire de 1852 à 1869.* Paris: Félix Alcan, 1930.

Maurois, Simone André. *Miss Howard and the Emperor.* New York: Alfred A. Knopf, 1957.

Maury, André. "L'Assassinat de Victor Noir." *Miroir de l'histoire,* no. 91(July 1957): 93–98. A popular account, but remarkably fair and accurate.

Mélot, Paul. "L'Assassinat de Mgr. Sibour, archevêque de Paris." *Miroir de l'histoire,* no. 93(September 1957): 353–56. This contains some serious inaccuracies of which Berrault was properly critical.

Mermet, Pierre. "L'Assassinat de Mgr. Sibour, archevêque de Paris." *L'Information historique* 19, no. 5(1957): 197–99. Does not touch any of the serious issues in the case, but his facts are accurate.

Monteilhet, J. *Les Institutions militaires de la France, 1814–1932.* Paris: Félix Alcan, 1932.

Morny, Charles-Auguste. *Un Ambassade en Russie, 1856.* Paris: Ollendorff, 1892.

Mouneyrat, Edmond. *La Préfecture de police.* Paris: Bonvalot-Jouve, 1906. A thesis in law (Paris) giving a historical and technical explanation of the prerogatives and the jurisdiction of the Préfecture de Police.

Packe, Michael St. John. *Orsini: The Story of a Conspirator*, Boston: Little, Brown, 1957. Despite the fact that the book is based on some primary sources, it is not entirely reliable. Well-written, but many inaccuracies.

Payne, Howard C. *The Police State of Louis Napoleon Bonaparte, 1851–1860*. Seattle: University of Washington Press, 1966. Authoritative.

Perreux, Gabriel. *Les Conspirations de Louis-Napoléon Bonaparte: Strasbourg, Boulogne*. Paris: Hachette, 1926. Brief and contributing nothing new.

Pinkney, David H. "The Myth of the French Revolution of 1830," David H. Pinkney and Theodore Rapp, eds. *A Festschrift for Frederick B. Artz*. Durham: Duke University Press, 1964.

Platel, Félix. *Portraits d'Ignotus*. Paris: n.p., 1878.

Poujoulat, Jean-Joseph-François. *Vie de Mgr. Sibour, archevêque de Paris*. Paris: E. Repos, 1857.

Reclus, Maurice. *Jules Favre, 1809–1880*. Paris: Hachette, 1912. Originally a thesis (Toulouse) based upon primary sources. Good bibliography.

Reichart, Robert. "Anti-Bonapartist Elections to the Académie Française During the Second Empire." *Journal of Modern History* 35, no. 1(1963): 33–45.

Rendu, Ambroise. *Deux grands avocats: M. Allou et M. Rousse*. Paris: Durand et Pedone-Lauriel, 1885.

Robert, Henri. *Lachaud*. Paris: Delamotte fils, 1889; reprinted as *Les Grands procès de l'histoire* in 1924.

Rousselet, Marcel. *Les souverains devant la justice, de Louis XVI à Napoléon III*. Paris: A. Michel, 1946. A chapter on 1840.

Scott, Sir Harold. *The Concise Encyclopedia of Crime and Criminals*. New York: Hawthorne Books, 1961.

Semelaigne, Dr. René. *Les Pionniers de la psychiatrie française avant et aprés Pinel*. 2 vols. Paris: Baillière et fils, 1930–32. The second volume has a section on Dr. Tardieu.

Simpson, F. A. *The Rise of Louis Napoleon*. London: Longmans, Green, 1909.

———. *Louis Napoleon and the Recovery of France, 1848–1856*. London: Longmans, Green, 1923. A third edition was published in 1951. Contains an excellent bibliography.

Spencer, Philip, *Politics of Belief in Nineteenth Century France*, London: Faber & Faber, 1954.

Stead, Phillip John. *The Police of Paris*. London: Staples, 1957. His brief history of the police forces is reliable, though the historical milieu is often dubious.

Tchnernoff, J., *Le Parti républicain au coup d'état et sous le second empire*, Paris: Pedone, 1906.

Thompson, J. M., *Louis-Napoleon and the Second Empire*, Oxford: Blackwell, 1954.

Tuckwell, Reverend William. *A. W. Kinglake: A Biographical and Literary Study*. London: G. Bell, 1902. Brief and eulogistic. Antagonistic to Napoleon III, as was Kinglake himself.

Vizetelly, Ernest Alfred. *Court Life of the Second French Empire*, New York: Charles Scribner's Sons, 1907.

Weill, Georges, *Le Parti républicain de 1814 à 1870*, Paris: Félix Alcan, 1900.

Wellesley, F. A., *Secrets of the Second Empire*, New York: Harper & Bros., 1929.

Williams, Roger L. *Henri Rochefort: Prince of the Gutter Press* New York: Scribner's, 1966. Republished as *Le Prince des polémistes: Henri Rochefort.* Paris: Editions de Trévise, 1970.

———. *The French Revolution of 1870–1871,* New York: W. W. Norton, 1969.

———. *The Mortal Napoleon III,* Princeton: Princeton University Press, 1972.

Wright, Vincent. "La Loi de sûreté générale de 1858." *Revue d'histoire moderne et contemporaine* 16(July–September 1969): 414–30.

Zeldin, Theodore, *Emile Ollivier and the Liberal Empire of Napoleon III,* Oxford: Clarendon Press, 1963.

Zévaès, Alexandre [Alexandre Bourson]. *L'Affaire Pierre Bonaparte (le meurtre de Victor Noir).* Paris: Hachette, 1929. For the Republican version of events.

Index